Send More Shrouds

Send More Shrouds

The V1 Attack on the Guards' Chapel, 1944

Jan Gore

Pen & Sword
MILITARY

First published in Great Britain in 2017 by
PEN & SWORD MILITARY
An imprint of
Pen & Sword Books Ltd
47 Church Street
Barnsley
South Yorkshire
S70 2AS

ISBN 978-1-47385-147-4

A CIP catalogue record for this book is available from the British Library.

Typeset by Concept, Huddersfield, West Yorkshire, HD4 5JL.
Printed and bound in England by TJ International Ltd. Padstow PL28 8RW

Pen & Sword Books Ltd incorporates the imprints of Pen & Sword Archaeology,
Atlas, Aviation, Battleground, Discovery, Family History, History, Maritime,
Military, Naval, Politics, Railways, Select, Social History, Transport, True Crime,
and Claymore Press, Frontline Books, Leo Cooper, Praetorian Press,
Remember When, Seaforth Publishing and Wharncliffe.

For a complete list of Pen & Sword titles please contact
PEN & SWORD BOOKS LIMITED
47 Church Street, Barnsley, South Yorkshire, S70 2AS, England
E-mail: enquiries@pen-and-sword.co.uk
Website: www.pen-and-sword.co.uk

Contents

List of Plates

The Bishop of London's sermon.
The congregation and bishop.
Keith Lewis.
The band laying a wreath for the musicians.
Families after the service.

Acknowledgements

I should like to thank all those connected to the Guards' Chapel who have helped and encouraged me with my research, and who have given me information that has helped me along the way. Especial thanks to padres Kevin Bell and Bill Beaver: Kevin, for inviting me to become involved in the memorial service in 2014, and Bill, for encouraging me to write more for the programme, for facilitating access to records not in the public domain and assuring me my work would make a book. He then organised an introduction to a publisher; I am forever in his debt. I should also like to thank Joan Mallett of the Guild of St Helena who had worked with Jamie Glover-Wilson of Pen & Sword on publishing projects and was able to effect an introduction for me, via Bill.

My thanks go to the Guards' Chapel Committee for all they did to make the service in 2014 such a moving one, and for all their help since then. I am especially grateful to Lesley Manchester, at that time secretary to the Senior Chaplain, for her unfailing help and good humour throughout our work together. She was pleasant and approachable, and able to remove obstacles when required while keeping an eye on the fine detail. It was thanks to her persistence that I was able to access a lot of material previously unavailable. I am also very grateful to Colonel Simon Vandeleur, regimental adjutant, Coldstream Guards; Colonel Conway Seymour, archivist, and Major Grant Baker, regimental adjutant, Grenadier Guards; Colonel Tom Bonas, regimental adjutant, Welsh Guards; Lieutenant-Colonel Andrew Foster, regimental adjutant and Lance Sergeant Leighton Platt of the Scots Guards; and Colonel Timothy Purdon, OBE, regimental adjutant of the Irish Guards. Alan Cooper has been extremely helpful, approaching me after the service to give me some useful material and later being willing to respond to queries at very short notice; he has shared his expertise about Major Windram and the band of the Coldstream Guards. I also owe a considerable debt of gratitude to Keith Lewis, the last known survivor of the incident, for being willing to share his memories with me and for giving me permission to quote from his account of that terrible day in June 1944.

My thanks also to the Royal Voluntary Service (previously the WRVS) for giving me access to material not in the public domain; thank you to Matthew McMurray, archivist, and Mrs Alice Cleland, CBE.

Thank you also to Pen & Sword for your patience and encouragement, especially Jamie Glover-Wilson, Rupert Harding and Susan Last.

I am especially grateful to everyone who shared information with me. To Shane Duffy, of New Zealand, for telling me more about Olive Crooke, and to Tracey Leigh for her material on Kango hammers, and to her father Robert Leigh for information about Gordon Beningfield's stained glass.

Above all, I'd like to thank the relatives for all their help and support, and especially: Gareth Watson, nephew of Derek Weaver, for his memoir of his uncle; John Anslow for help and information about his uncle, Sidney Newbould; John Holden, for allowing me to quote from the David Gurney letter, and for information about his uncle Harold Dods. The Sheridan family for all their help and support. Tony Titcombe, for memories of his father; Narelle Morrow for information about her father, Chaplain Gordon Gladstone Wood; Michael Curtis and family for information about Hettie Ruthin Neilson and her son; Zena Carter for emails and photographs of Phyllis Roper; Barry Gibson for material about his father Dennis. Tom Gidley-Kitchin and his sister Penelope for information about their father, grandmother and aunt; Jenny Jackson Jones for information on Agnes Moscrop and help and support. John Coles for information about Dennis Hooper, and Tom Crozier for material about Annie Ellen Irving and family. Martine Fratoni for information about her uncle, Martin Bacchiolelli; Clarissa Mitchell for her help with the Mitchell family; Lindsey Nieuwhof for details about Alfred Bowyer. Barry Jameson, whose grandmother Phyllis died in the incident; Anne Smith, granddaughter of Alan and Edith Coleman; and Susan Willmott for telling me more about Diana Milton-Willmott. Robert Fairgrieve, for information about his aunt, Ida Thomson; Joanna Freeman for material about Gwen Gray Horton; Janet Wyatt for information about Mabel Maultby; and especially Katharina Miller for information on her grandfather Nathaniel Turton. Also Lucy Whitrow, daughter of the Reverend Ralph Whitrow, for sharing details of her father's life and correspondence. I am so grateful to all of you for your help, and I apologise in advance if I have inadvertently omitted anyone.

I should also like to thank my friends, especially Julia Wright, Michelle Bailey, Ann Brueckner White, Pat Perry and Pamela Moriarty, for their support. Thanks also to Marcia Hughes and friends at the Landmark.

Finally, my special thanks to my son, Alan, for all his help, from trips to Brookwood Military Cemetery some years ago to accompanying me to the Chapel service and the Officers' Mess. His sense of humour and excellent technical support are much appreciated.

Every effort has been made to trace copyright holders and I should like to thank all those who have kindly granted permission to use quoted material. Any errors or omissions that persist are my responsibility alone.

Preface

How it all began: 'My friends went to the Guards' Chapel and they never came back'

This book tells the story of what has become known as 'the Guards' Chapel incident', the single worst V1 incident of the Second World War; it places it in its context and talks in detail about the incident and the rescue effort. It provides biographies of all those who died, and attempts to trace some of the injured. It also looks at the postwar rebuilding of the Chapel and the commemorative service that was held in 2014. Although this is a detailed story about a specific event, it also stands as an analysis of a typical incident during the summer of 1944.

Let me explain how I became involved. It all began with my mother Enid, so let me tell you a little of her story.

In June 1944, Enid Sykes was 20. She had left her home in Yorkshire to attend university, the first of her family to do so; she was small, dark-haired and shy, but remarkably determined. She was a gifted linguist, and was studying French, Latin and Spanish at King's College, London. However, as King's had been evacuated to Bristol in 1940, she began her studies in the West Country rather than London. In November 1942 she met a fellow student, Alan Mitchell, at a dance; this was the start of a relationship that would last fifty-two years, until her death in 1994.

Alan graduated in 1943 and went to work as a government scientist near Bournemouth. The arts section of King's College moved back to London, to its original site at the Aldwych, during the summer; Enid was one of the students who helped the college with the move. She had to find somewhere to live, and moved to rented accommodation ('digs', as she called it) at the YWCA in Earls Court, at 28 Penywern Road. It's a tall building (now a hotel), part of a white stucco terrace behind Earls Court Tube station, and it would be an easy journey by Tube from there to King's on the Strand. Gradually she got to know the other residents; three of them, in particular, became friends, and she would talk of how they used to go for walks together. They used to explore the splendid Gothic Brompton Cemetery, off the Old Brompton Road and just a few minutes' walk away. It was one of the most impressive green spaces nearby, and they went there often.

On the morning of 18 June 1944, Enid's three friends decided to go to morning service at the Guards' Chapel on Birdcage Walk. The music there was especially fine. Perhaps they asked Enid to accompany them. However, she was studying hard for her final examinations and was indifferent to both music and religion; she had French and Latin to revise. She was passionate to succeed, and wanted a career in teaching. Did they agree to meet later?

They never came back.

Enid rarely spoke of what had happened. All she would say was: 'One Sunday my friends went to the Guards' Chapel. They never came back'. She would not give their names. She was a very private person, a quiet woman with a deceptively strong will, so I did not dare pursue it.

Afterwards I wished I had asked her more about her life, and especially about her time as a student. Too many might-have-beens. But that sentence stayed with me.

I believe the death of her friends had a profound effect on my mother. She would never say any more about the incident or its aftermath, and she never gave any details about the friends she lost. Once, when I was talking about a close friend, she asked 'But why do you care so much about your friends?' I was bewildered and distressed by her question, but perhaps a quotation about wartime life I found recently provides an explanation:

> You didn't get involved with people, because people were dying, and you couldn't cope with it … So although you had friendships, they were surface friendships. They could be deep, but you didn't allow yourself to think too much about what was happening.
>
> (Frank Wilcox, contributor to *Lost Resort: Memories of Wartime Bournemouth*)

So what had happened that June morning? Only a week after the Normandy landings, the German military began to use a new weapon against England. It was the V1 rocket, an early form of cruise missile, designed for terror bombing against London. It was a type of pilotless plane with a simple autopilot to regulate altitude and airspeed; the first flying bombs were ground-launched from occupied France. They were designed to fly for a maximum range of about 150 miles; at a pre-set point, the engine would cut out, sending the V1 into a steep dive until it exploded on impact. The first flying bombs arrived in the UK on 13 June. By Friday 16 June they were arriving in increasing numbers.

It was not until Sunday 18 June that any rockets landed in Westminster. Not long after 11 o'clock, a V1 rocket hit the Guards' Chapel in London and exploded; the roof and most of the walls collapsed, burying many of the congregation, who had been attending morning service, in rubble up to 10 feet deep. Over 120 people were killed, and well over 100 injured. The rescue efforts went on for several days and nights. It was the worst V1 incident of the war, although the news embargo at the time meant that it was some weeks before the general public found out the full details.

My mother's words had always stayed with me, but once she and my father were both dead, I initially saw no way I could find out more about the story. Time passed. I took up a new library job a few minutes' walk from the Guards' Chapel. One day I walked over there in my lunch hour and went in. I looked at the gilded portico, the only remaining element of the original chapel, and thought about that day in 1944 when the V1 had landed. There were two books of remembrance: one for the military dead, and one for the victims of the Guards' Chapel bomb. I looked at the victims' page, open at the letter M. To my surprise, one of them shared my maiden name: Janet Mitchell. So now I was also curious to find out about her and all those who had died with her.

Every librarian loves a research challenge, and this was mine. I went back to the Chapel, and was given a short, unassuming A4 list of victims, with names, ages, ranks and place of burial, if known. My initial idea was to update the list (I could see there were a lot of gaps) and discover the last resting places of the non-military dead. But first I had to discover the names of Mum's friends.

To begin with I thought they were fellow students from King's, but a visit to the King's College Archives revealed no casualty records that matched. I had to rethink my strategy; if they weren't students from the same university, then was there a location link? I logged on to the Commonwealth War Graves Commission (CWGC) site, and looked through the records for Second World War civilian war dead for Westminster, then narrowed it by date. The records give names, ages, details of parents/spouse, date and location of death. It took a long time, but eventually I found them: Beatrice Isabel Gardner, Margaret Ellen Norris and Marjorie Souter, all of 28 Penywern Road, Kensington, who had died at the Guards' Chapel. Marjorie had attended the service with her younger sister, who was also in London on war work; Jessie was badly injured, as was another girl from the YWCA, Barbara Howard. Both were taken to St Thomas' Hospital; Jessie remained in hospital for at least another month.

By the next anniversary of the Guards' Chapel incident, I had put together an updated list of those who had died, using the CWGC records and family history tools such as Ancestry and Find My Past. I brought a copy of it to the Chapel on the anniversary. By the following June the A4 list had grown, and I decided biographies would be useful.

It was becoming a minor obsession. I read extensively about the Home Front in the Second World War and wartime life. I started trying to find out more about each victim; by now I wanted to say more about their families and background, if possible. While I did not want to identify living relatives, in accordance with family history protocol, I wanted to give at least some idea of how the V1 incident had affected the victims' family and friends. Lives had been cut short, parents had lost their children, siblings had died together and young children had been orphaned. I wanted to be able to tell their stories and commemorate their lives.

I visited the Imperial War Museum, where I discovered a harrowing first-hand account by a nurse at St George's Hospital; she described how three of her friends had gone to the Guards' Chapel service. She herself was on duty, but by late morning became aware that the wards were filling with wounded servicemen. She had heard the impact of the V1. One of her friends was able to walk from the Chapel, one was seriously injured and the third had been taken to hospital, but there was no further information. Eventually the Matron of St George's asked her and a friend to make enquiries about the missing nurse. They ended up being directed to the mortuary at Glasgow Terrace, where they were asked to identify a body. Initially they were unable to make a definite identification, but as they turned to go, they heard the slight noise of an ornament falling to the floor. It was the moon and stars brooch that their friend had always worn in her hair.

I continued to search for information. My son and I visited Brookwood Military Cemetery, where we found two lines of well-kept gravestones dedicated to the Guards' Chapel dead. Several other casualties also lie there, including one of the Free French and an Australian padre. I found various references in books and websites. Elisabeth Sheppard-Jones, the writer, was a friend of Pauline Gye and went with her to the Chapel; Pauline was killed outright, and Elisabeth never walked again. In her book, *I Walk on Wheels*, she told the story of the incident. Peggy Graves, wife of the writer Charles Graves, was a good friend of Dick Brewster Thornton and his wife Rosemary; in *Married to Charles* she described the terrible wait for news on and after the 18th. I also found two websites that agreed to host my biographies; one was Diane Flanagan's Irish Guards World War Two site, and another was a local history project in South Wales (they had led me to the last resting place of Bryn Davies, which had eluded me for years). Every year I would find more material had become available, either on the web in general or on sites such as Ancestry. People started to contact me with information about their relatives, or to volunteer material about their ancestors. More recently, I was allowed to see the service records of the Guardsmen who died, and to discover a little more about where they served.

It has been a long search, and I am sure there is still more to discover. It has been a privilege to be able to tell the stories of all those who came by chance, by allegiance or by profession to the Guards' Chapel that day in 1944. I shall always be grateful to all those who have helped me along the way, and I hope that I have done their stories justice here. This book is for them, and their relatives and friends.

Chapter 1

'An Intensive Blue Flash'

The Guards' Chapel, 18 June 1944

Between 1939 and 1944 the Guards' Chapel at Wellington Barracks was damaged several times. On the night of Friday 20 September 1940, less than two weeks after the start of the Blitz, a 1,500-pound high-explosive bomb exploded 25 yards from the east end of the Chapel. All the windows were blown out, with the exception of the Rose window over the West Gallery. All the pieces that could be saved were collected in numbered bags and sent to the firm of Lowndes and Drury for reconstruction. This cost £1,700, and was paid for by a voluntary levy on one day's pay by members of the Brigade. The Chapel was clearly much valued by the Guards, and was viewed as a family church; it was the location of choice for Guardsmen's weddings, their children were baptised there and often funerals and memorial services were also held there. It was an integral part of the Guards' lives.

During the following week in September, a shower of incendiary bombs landed on the Chapel roof. Despite the best efforts of the Chapel orderly and the fire party, a large fire took hold; the whole roof was destroyed, leaving only the brick vaulting undamaged. The building had to be closed while a new roof was built, and for the next three months services moved to Christ Church, Westminster (which suffered a similar fate in April the following year, when it was destroyed by bombs and incendiaries). Temporary repairs to the roof were carried out by Harry Stuart Goodhart-Rendel (1887–1959); he was a former officer in the Grenadier Guards, a musician and at one time President of the RIBA, and was known for his church projects (he later designed the Household Brigade memorial cloister in 1956). The roof was replaced with one made of concrete, presumably because this would be far less at risk from incendiaries than the original wooden beams had been; the decision was to have unforeseen consequences when the Chapel was bombed in 1944. Despite a further incendiary attack in November, the Chapel reopened for worship just before Christmas 1940. It sustained further superficial damage over the next four years, but remained structurally intact.

On Easter Sunday 1944, the Chaplain-General, the Reverend C.D. Symons CB MC DD KHC, mounted the pulpit to preach, and even as his eyes wandered slowly over the upturned faces of the Guardsmen, many noticed the sad, almost pitiful shadowing of his face. His voice shook a little as he spoke to them of 'our loved chapel'. After the parade service, he confided in a friend his impression of a strange, unfamiliar sadness and doom overshadowing the sacred precincts. 'Was it some premonition of what was soon to come?'

By the summer of 1944, the war was beginning to enter a new phase. Although Londoners had vivid memories of the 1940/41 Blitz, and there had been a further 'Little Blitz' earlier in the year, there had been very few 'incidents' (as bombing raids came to be described) since mid-April. The 'Little Blitz' had caused considerable concern among the civilian population; although people had been able to adapt over time to the sustained attacks of the Blitz four years before, they found the renewed attacks hard to tolerate. They were therefore hoping that there would be a lull in raids on London and the south-east. However, the government and the military were aware that the Germans were preparing to use a new weapon against London: the V1 flying bomb, a pilotless plane that could be launched by day or night. (The V1 weapon is discussed in more detail in the next chapter.)

Although the preparations for D-Day were in theory secret, in practice they were on such a large scale that it would have been very difficult for anyone in southern England not to draw their own conclusions about where the build-up of troops was heading. The tide of war was turning, and D-Day marked the start of the Second Front. Despite the day's delay in the landings, and the initial heavy casualties, the Allied forces made landfall all along the Normandy beaches and were able to make considerable inroads, driving the German forces back from the coast. Only two months later, Paris would be liberated.

For some considerable time, the Germans had been preparing two secret weapons, one of which was the V1, which could be launched against London and the south-east. They had organised launching sites along the French coast and were modifying them so that the weapons could be launched at short notice; this work was matched by the repeated and continuing efforts of the Allies to counter-attack and destroy the launch facilities. It is ironic that the success of the Allied landings in France meant that Hitler decided he had nothing to lose; it was time to use his secret weapon.

Churchill had been making thinly veiled statements about the new weapon for some months, and Parliament and the military were already aware that flying bombs were a possibility. However, nobody was certain quite how serious such attacks might be. How many flying bombs could be launched in 24 hours? How accurate were they? And how many casualties might there be?

Less than two weeks after D-Day, London began to discover what the new weapons were like.

David Gurney, a 23-year-old lieutenant in the Scots Guards, described his experiences:

The first flying bombs (what to call them? buzz-bombs, pilotless planes or robot planes) came over London on Tuesday night, the 13th June, but no one knew what they were and we thought it was an ordinary raid. On Thursday night we had our first experience of flying bombs, and very frightening it was too. I wrote at the time 'Soon after the alert sounded, distant gunfire was heard and then coming nearer. The noise of planes' engines getting closer and closer (pursued by guns) and then apparently just skimming the roofs. Grinding of the engine clearly heard. I hid under the bedclothes.

The skimming of roof tops is a common characteristic of attack by these planes. Their engines (compared to the noise of a cheap out-board motor) have the capacity of making everyone feel that the plane is passing over his particular roof. People as widely spaced as in these barracks and in Curzon Street thought these planes passed over their roofs.

At lunchtime on Friday 16 June, Herbert Morrison made a statement in the House of Commons, saying pilotless aircraft were now being used. At 1.00pm the new attacks were mentioned on the BBC News. Many people were at work, so they missed the radio item; however, the evening papers led with the story on their front page, using headlines such as 'London under attack by pilotless aircraft'. The civilian population had now been made officially aware of the new threat, but were yet to discover how best to protect themselves. Meanwhile, the rockets continued to come over southern England, with London their intended target.

Sunday 18 June was bright and fairly warm, with temperatures in the mid to high sixties (degrees Fahrenheit). It was such a pleasant day that some of the Guards officers chose to spend the morning at their boathouse at Maidenhead. The Brigade of Guards Club was somewhere that members could relax after the rigours of ceremonial duties or society functions, and it was very popular during the summer months. A number of officers who might otherwise have attended the service chose to go on the river instead; this proved to be a wise decision.

Services at the Guards' Chapel were always popular, and there is a suggestion that public admission was by ticket only for this particular one. It was a special service for both active and retired Guardsmen and their guests, according to the author H.E. Bates. Officially, the morning service was to commemorate the anniversary of the defeat of Napoleon at the Battle of Waterloo on 18 June 1815; 'Waterloo Day' was a date of special significance for the Guards. However, there was another significant event, perhaps not officially acknowledged, but nevertheless of vital importance to many who attended that day: Guardsmen, their families and friends all wished to offer thanks for the success of the D-Day landings that had begun only twelve days before. The tide of the war in Europe was turning. So the service was one of thanksgiving, both for a historic victory in Belgium almost 130 years before, and for the Normandy landings that had begun the liberation of Europe.

The service was not only for the military and those Guardsmen on church parade. Other groups also attended regularly. Nurses from various London hospitals had seats reserved for them and would attend when off duty. On this occasion a group of nurses attended from St George's Hospital, Hyde Park Corner; it was a short walk from there along Constitution Hill to Birdcage Walk. Beryl Clark and her friends Mary and Anne called for their colleague Patricia Clewett at the dining-room door of the hospital, but she had to go on duty and could not join them. Peggy Arnold from Westminster Hospital attended the service in uniform; she had come from the nearby nurses' home in Page Street. Edna Shooter, a nurse from King's College Hospital, Denmark Hill, went with her friend, Mabel Maultby, of the British Red Cross Society.

It has also been suggested that the Chapel was a place to go to see and be seen, a place where the elite went to worship. Although the congregation that day included the son-in-law of Stanley Baldwin and the brother-in-law of Harold Macmillan, along with a number of the 'great and the good', including lords and ladies, old Etonians, political figures and other well-known people, in many respects it was a microcosm of society. The superb music provided another incentive to attend; concerts were especially appreciated at this time, and the lunchtime concerts by Myra Hess at the National Gallery had proved invaluable in raising public morale in wartime. The bands were well-known to the public and frequently performed in open-air concerts, as well as in concert halls; they were also regularly heard on the radio. Major Windram and the Coldstream Guards Band were universally popular and the combination of military pageantry, skilled musicians and a spectacular setting had considerable appeal. Where better to celebrate the success of the Normandy landings, along with other Guards families and friends?

The first V1s to fall in Westminster had landed earlier that morning. David Gurney continued:

> On Sunday 18th June, I was Picquet Officer [Guards term for Duty Officer] and as such I had to supervise the PAD [Picquet Aid Detachment] working including roof spotters. I went on to the roof to see if I could see flying bombs. Such was our disdain for the creatures that I wrote the previous day 'there seems no reason for thinking they are unusually lethal, in fact probably less so than normal bomb attacks from

planes'. It is now known that the blast effects are enormous but the penetrative and general effects are not so large.

Soon after getting on the roof, a plane fell in the direction of Victoria Street and we had an excellent view of the column of dust which rises as soon as the bomb falls. In this case a fire broke out afterwards and we saw the smoke of this.

Because of the increasing number of V1s coming over and the frequent alerts, some people had had a very bad night on Saturday, with little sleep, and so chose not to attend the service. David Gurney noted that Tommy Coke (a major in the Scots Guards and later 5th Earl of Leicester) had taken Ivan Cobbold to the Chapel and there left him as he, Tommy, had had a bad night and did not feel like a service indoors. Nevertheless, well over 250 people made their way there that fateful morning.

It would be easy to assume that the majority of attendees were Londoners, but this was by no means the case. They came from areas as varied as Yorkshire, Lancashire, Northumberland, Devon, Scotland, Wales and Northern Ireland. The congregation consisted of officers, Guardsmen, Allies, friends and family. It included an American colonel, an Australian padre, two Canadian soldiers and two Free French troops, as well as a soldier serving with the US Army in London and another serving with a US bomber squadron in Norfolk. One of the women had been a hospital pharmacist in the First World War, serving in France; she had just returned, aged 73, from New Zealand because she wanted to help the war effort.

Elisabeth Sheppard-Jones was a 24-year-old officer in the ATS (Auxiliary Territorial Service), based at the Clerks Training Centre, Golders Green; this was a unit in Spaniard's Close, Hampstead. That morning, she met her childhood friend, Pauline Gye, outside the Tube station in the Strand. They had grown up together in Penarth, near Cardiff, and remained close friends now that both were working in London. Pauline was working in a hospital, and was also an Air Raid Warden, but was off duty that day. They had no set plans, beyond wanting to spend time together, but: 'As it was early and it was Sunday, a good way of starting a long day would be at divine service at the Guards' Chapel, Wellington Barracks – not far to walk, and a place loved by us both, and visited by us in other, pre-war days'. The siren sounded while they were discussing where to lunch afterwards. They sat on a bench and watched the Guards drilling on the square.

David Gurney's account went on:

At 10.40 hours I went 'on parade' with Capt Leslie Wall [who died in the incident, along with his wife] to inspect the Church of England church party for the Military Chapel morning service. When we got to the door of the Chapel – I had marched the men there – I asked for leave to 'fall out' as the alert was still on and I felt that I should be available for immediate duty if anything happened. John Quilter, the assistant adjutant, had told me that as he was in barracks I could go to Church; but I felt this was an excuse for getting out [of] attending a ritual for which I have little or no reason attending.

At the same time, a guardsman came up to Leslie to say he was an atheist and therefore might he be excused from attending the service. Leslie referred him to the Drill Sergeant [Nathaniel Turton, who also died that day] who let him dismiss after some argument. Yet another (. . .) reason for atheism.

I walked back to the Officers' Mess from the Chapel and passed the Commanding Officer Lord Edward Hay, Harold Dods, Dickie Thornton and James Duberly on their way to worship.

This was the last time he would see them; all four perished in the Chapel.

Many families with relatives who were serving Guardsmen would come to the Chapel to pray for their safe-keeping. Mothers and wives would attend morning service so that they could remember sons, husbands and brothers serving abroad; by praying for their safe return in the Chapel dedicated to the Guards, they felt closer to them.

Hettie Ruthin Neilson had spent the previous day at Northwood with her daughter's family. They had wanted her to stay, but she was determined to leave that Saturday, because she wanted to attend morning service at the Guards' Chapel the following day; her flat in Murray House, Vandon Street, was just around the corner from it. Her son Captain Andrew Shennan Neilson was serving in the Scots Guards and was attached to the 2nd Battalion of the Coldstream Guards; he was in Italy and had been wounded on 23 May. She attended the Chapel regularly, because she always felt close to him there; she planned to have lunch with her other daughter in Beaconsfield after the service, but had telephoned to say that she might be late.

At the YWCA near Earl's Court, a group of young women were having breakfast. Ellen Norris and her cousin Beatrice Gardner were discussing their plans for the day; they were planning to attend morning service at the Guards' Chapel, as was Barbara Howard. Marjorie Souter, another resident, was going with them; her younger sister Jessie, who was also down from Scotland on war work and lodging not far away in Cranley Gardens, was going to join them. They asked Enid Sykes, a quietly-spoken university student, if she wanted to join them; she was revising hard for her final examinations at King's and declined. She went back to her room, and they left for the Chapel.

Agnes Moscrop and Ida Thomson were in London, attending a telegraphers' Morse Training Course at Cornwall House. Agnes was working for the Post Office and had come down from Newcastle for the course. She was tall, aged 19, and had striking deep auburn hair. Ida was a year younger and had been born in New York (where her father had been working as a plasterer on the Empire State Building before they moved back to Edinburgh). They were new to London and were staying in digs there; it is believed that they chose to attend the service together because they had a day off from training and wanted to experience some of London's pageantry.

Vera Mitchell had come to London to see two of her three children. Her younger son, Ian, was serving in the navy in the north of Scotland. Her daughter, Janet, had been working as a hospital nurse in London for some time, and had been granted 24 hours' leave. They planned to attend the service in the Guards' Chapel so that they could see Janet's brother, Mike (Vera's elder son), in his new role as a lieutenant with the Guards. He had joined the Coldstream Guards in 1941, just before his 20th birthday, and was badly injured by a mine during an attack on the Mareth Line in March 1943; his leg had to be amputated below the knee. By early 1944 he was learning how to cope with an artificial limb, and was ready to return to duty; the Guards had been able to find him a role that would accommodate his disability. On 18 March 1944, three months to the day before the incident, he was appointed their assistant regimental adjutant. Vera's husband, Alexander, was planning to drive up from Gloucestershire and join them, but his car broke down.

Phyllis and Mary Jameson were going to the Chapel to pray for the safety of Captain John Jameson, who was in the 3rd Battalion of the Grenadier Guards and was fighting in Italy. (He and Mary had married in 1942; he was Phyllis's only son.)

Dorothy Gidley-Kitchin attended with her daughter (also Dorothy, but known by her second name, Rosemary); they came to pray for their son and brother, Greville, who was camped in Charing in Kent with his battalion and all their Churchill tanks. He was preparing to go across to France with the 4th Battalion of the Guards Armoured Division. Rosemary had joined the ATS on 12 May 1944, less than six weeks earlier. Kath Hunt, an ATS colleague of Rosemary's, came with them.

The Thorn family also attended Chapel together. Elizabeth, aged 84, was staying at the Pembridge Gardens Hotel. Her son, Terence, was a major serving abroad in the Royal Engineers, but was home on leave that weekend. His wife Cornelia, originally from New York, was a section officer in the WAAF at Abbey Lodge, but was able to join her husband and mother-in-law. One of Elizabeth's friends, Violet Wilson, also staying at the hotel, accompanied them.

Adelaide Wilson and Isabelle Dewar-Durie were in their early seventies and had been friends for some years; they normally attended Chapel together, and today was no exception.

Phyllis Margaret Roper was planning to meet her old friend Elsie Goodson at the Chapel; it was a friendship of long standing. Back in 1927, when Phyllis travelled to the United States, she stayed with Elsie and her husband in California for part of the time. More recently, Phyllis had named Elsie as one of her executors. However, that morning Elsie was late; Phyllis went in without her, and by the time Elsie arrived the Chapel doors had been closed.

Major James Causley Windram, senior director of music of the Household Division, was to lead the band at the service. In theory, this was to be his last official appearance (as, sadly, it proved to be in reality) because he was awaiting a medical interview on the following Monday; because of this, his wife Olive attended the service with him. He had been in poor health for some years, with a range of complaints including arthritis and angina. Doubts had been expressed about his fitness to serve overseas with the band; he had been excused marching with them that same week because of his arthritis. There was also the possibility of a job offer from the BBC, were he to be obliged to leave the Guards.

One Guardsman had hoped to spend the day with his family. Coldstream Guardsman Tony Titcombe had been taken prisoner at Tobruk in June 1942, and had been sent to Italy as a prisoner of war. In September 1943 he managed to escape to southern Italy, by then in Allied hands, after a thirty-day walk to freedom. He returned home for Christmas 1943. In June 1944, he requested leave to celebrate both his sixth wedding anniversary on 20 June and his son's fifth birthday that month, but was turned down.

Keith Lewis, an 18-year-old Grenadier Guardsman, walked over to the Chapel with his friend Guardsman West. He noticed that it was a beautiful day. Both were happy because they had been detailed to the choir, rather than detailed for compulsory church parade; this meant they could find their own way to the Chapel. Guardsman West was talking about a V1 that had landed not far from the barracks earlier that morning; this would have been the bomb that hit Carey Mansions, Rutherford Street, at 8.50am. (Ten people died and sixty-two were injured.) He suggested they should go and see the bomb site 'to see what damage a ton of explosive could cause'.

David Gurney continued to patrol the area. 'The "all clear" sounded at about 10.55 so I made my routine tour of barracks and returned to the Mess at 11.05.'

Meanwhile, Elisabeth Sheppard-Jones and her friend Pauline went into the Chapel. They took seats near the back. Elisabeth later remembered seeing a young Canadian officer (probably Captain John Gall, aged 25, of the Canadian Grenadier Guards), an elderly colonel with his wife and daughters and a section of ATS girls.

The service began promptly at 11.00am. The musicians of the Coldstream Band were to play, and the bishop of Maidstone (Dr Leslie Owen) was to be the guest speaker; he took a seat in the sanctuary to await his turn to preach, while the band sat up in the gallery. The new chaplain to the Brigade of Guards, Reverend Ralph Whitrow, was officiating.

Lord Edward Hay read the first lesson, in his capacity as commanding officer, Westminster Garrison, a post he had held since its formation in November 1943. Part way through the lesson, the telephone in the vestry began to ring, and the chapel keeper (William Silver, a former Grenadier Guardsman) and his orderly for the day, Guardsman John Brobbel (1908–1981) of the Coldstream Guards, hurried from the Chapel to silence it.

Soon afterwards, a distant buzzing could be heard. It was an approaching V1. Lord Hay did not falter, even when the noise became a roar overhead. He had just finished the lesson and was walking back to his seat when the engine cut out. The congregation were about to sing the *Te Deum*.

Keith Lewis described what happened next:

It was during the reading of the lesson that it all happened. The Commanding Officer, Lord Edward Hay, was about halfway through the text when we heard the by now familiar 'motor-cycle-engine' sound of a V1. It became quite loud but I was sure it would continue on its way to some other unfortunate part of London, as all the others had done so far.

Suddenly, the engine noise stopped. What happened then was all within a nano of time, although I still see and hear it in sequence thus: a large semi-circular area at the top half of the south wall collapsed; there was an intensive blue flash; I saw the Commanding Officer still standing but backwards at an angle of around 45 degrees. I remember noticing the ash-grey colour of his face (and later, I concluded that he was already dead at this moment); there was a very loud explosion (again later, I likened it to the loudness of a bang of an AA gun outside in St James' Park); then some giant was hammering me all over my back.

David Gurney had witnessed the scene from the steps of the Officers' Mess, some distance away:

At [11.05], the Old Guard ... marched back from Buckingham Palace ... and began to dismount on the square. At 11.10 the noise of a buzz bomb was heard approaching and I went on to the front steps to watch. The Captain and Subaltern of the Guard (Robin Barnes-Gorell and Nigel Mitchison) were walking towards the Mess and the Ensign (Peter Daubeny) was dismissing the men. There were about sixty men on the square some 150 yards away from the Chapel. At 11.11 the bomb crashed through the roof of the Chapel and exploded inside. I saw the bomb falling and noticed its square cut wings. I threw myself on the ground and my glasses flew off. A considerable explosion occurred but not one man on the square was touched (some of them lay down).

Elisabeth Sheppard-Jones described her experience:

Then there was a noise so loud it was as if all the waters and the winds in the world had come together in a mighty conflict, and the Guards' Chapel collapsed upon us in a bellow of bricks and mortar.

There was not time for panic ... One moment I was singing the *Te Deum*, and the next I lay in dust and blackness, aware of one thing only – that I had to go on breathing.

Chapter 2

Doodlebug Summer

The V1 Campaign

The V1 that hit the Guards' Chapel was only the third to land in Westminster since the start of the campaign, although between 13 and 18 June 1944 about 500 had already been launched against southern England. The general public were mostly unprepared for the new weapon, although government scientists, intelligence officers and the military had been aware for some considerable time that the Germans were developing something very different from their previous range of bombs. At this point in the campaign there wasn't even a consensus about how to refer to the V1.

The name V1 comes from the German *'Vergeltungswaffe* 1', meaning 'revenge or retaliation weapon No. 1', and it remains the standard way to describe them. In incident reports they were originally referred to as PACs, an abbreviation of Pilotless Aircraft, until the end of 18 June; the V1 is referred to as a PAC in the Guards' Chapel incident reports from that day. The following day it was renamed a 'flying bomb'. Both the general public and the news media also used more colloquial terms; it was known as a 'buzz bomb', because of the noise, a 'robot bomb', alluding to the fact it was pilotless and sent on a pre-programmed course, or a 'doodlebug', a semi-affectionate term designed to minimise the terror and focus on the noise. The Germans called them 'hell hounds' or 'fire dragons'. They were an early pulse-jet powered form of cruise missile.

Norman Longmate's book *The Doodlebugs: the story of the flying bombs* is one of the most definitive works on this aspect of the war, as is *Most Secret War* by Professor R.V. Jones; both books provide far more information and analysis for the interested reader or researcher than I have space to provide here, and I owe them a great debt of gratitude. Professor Jones describes the political and scientific background to the campaign and gives a first-hand account of the race to find and destroy the launching sites; he makes it clear how intense the struggle was for both the Germans and the Allies, from his perspective as a key government scientist working in the intelligence community. In contrast, Norman Longmate takes a social historian's view and gives a considered account of both the development of the weapon and the way the campaign was experienced by the civilian population at the time.

Longmate described the V1s as 'ungainly monsters'. From below, they looked like a black cross as they sped through the air. But it was the noise that set them apart from other weapons. It began as a distant hum, then grew to a loud, deafening rattle; this was described variously as the sound of a Model T Ford going uphill, a two-stroke motorcycle, or a stick being drawn against a corrugated iron fence. This would then either gradually diminish, as the V1 went on its way, or, more ominously, abruptly stop. The wait was terrible and seemed interminable – as if the world held its breath; witnesses described it as a 'deafening silence'. In reality the explosion would normally follow in about twelve seconds. This would perhaps give just enough time to take cover under a table (if indoors or at work) or in a doorway or behind a wall (if in the open), but not enough time to find a public shelter. In addition, you, the potential victim, needed to be fully aware of what was happening so that you could take swift evasive action; the Guards' Chapel V1 was still a relative novelty, five days after the V1 campaign began, and in any case, the brutal truth is that there was nowhere to take cover. Nobody was prepared for what happened that morning.

The V1 was a very effective weapon; it was comparatively cheap to manufacture as it was made mainly of thin sheet steel and plywood. It could cause considerable casualties and damage to buildings without the risks implicit in a traditional bombing campaign, especially once the V1 modified sites were used. In contrast to the demands of a conventional bombing attack, there was no need for supplies of fighters, bombers or pilots for the initial sortie, and no need for repairs or extra personnel. Attacks did not need to take place under cover of darkness or in favourable weather conditions; being able to send rockets at any hour of the day or night gave a propaganda victory to the Germans, and had a significant effect on civilian morale. There was no longer any near-certainty that raids would be at night and preceded by an air raid warning so that shelter could be sought.

The details of the V1's firing sequence were as follows. At a modified site in northern France, the bomb was manhandled on to a modified four-wheeled trailer and put into position for firing. It then went to the checkout platform, where the wings were added and the warhead in the nose was armed; after that it moved on to the waiting platform for the final examination. It then went to the square non-magnetic building, where the gyroscopic controls were set. Finally, it was fuelled and wheeled to the foot of the ramp (150ft long and 16ft high) where it rested on twin guide rails, with its tail separately supported on a sledge. Beneath the rails was a tube containing a piston that fitted into a metal housing beneath the bomb. The catapult was powered by burning hydrogen peroxide. As the pressure built up, the trolley was held back by a bolt, until this fractured and the trolley leapt forward, hurling the bomb into the air; the engine provided enough thrust to keep it airborne.

The V1 was made up of four sections: the main fuselage, a propulsion unit and two wings. (The Imperial War Museum, London, has a V1 on display in its entrance hall.) It was just over 25ft long, including its engine; this equated roughly to the length of a wartime double-decker bus. Its wing span was 17½ft. Its overall weight was approximately 2 tons, of which 1 ton was Amatol (a highly explosive mixture of TNT and ammonium nitrate). In front was a master compass to keep the aircraft on course. The fuel tank held 130 gallons. The course was pre-set beforehand; two motors could adjust the rudder at the tail or the elevators on the wings to correct any error. The height was controlled by an aneroid barometer, and the distance by a milometer, pre-set to a certain number of revolutions and operated by a small propeller. It started off at about 340mph, then sped up as the fuel burned, reaching about 400mph; it would cross the coast at about 2,400ft. It had a maximum range of about 150 miles, later increased to 250 miles to enable it to be launched from Holland instead of northern France.

When the pre-set distance was reached, a circuit was closed which caused two detonators to be fired. These lowered two flaps, which put the machine into a dive. As it tipped downward, the fuel supply to the engine was cut off and the noise would cease; this was the point when the light at the tail also cut out. About 12 seconds later, the V1 would explode.

The V1s killed more than 6,000 civilians in southern England during the main ten-week campaign, with almost 18,000 suffering life-changing injuries and over a million buildings wrecked or damaged. Once the initial launch sites were over-run during the Allied advance into Europe, other launch methods would be used, and V1s would continue to plague East Anglia, the Midlands and the North until March 1945.

The first veiled allusion to a possible new weapon came very soon after the start of the war, on 19 September 1939, when Hitler spoke in Danzig about a weapon that 'cannot be used against us'. The UK Intelligence Services were keen to discover what it might be; Dr R.V. Jones (a young British physicist and scientific military intelligence expert) was tasked with finding out. He concluded at the time (November 1939) that Hitler was talking of his air force, but suggested the reference might allude to gliding bombs, aerial torpedoes or pilotless aircraft.

Work on designing a pilotless aircraft did not begin till 1942. By June that year, the outline for a self-powered flying bomb was settled and became a firm project: it would need short wings to facilitate handling, but that would lead to a high stalling speed, which meant a need to launch it by catapult. Several companies were involved. Work on the design continued throughout 1942, and it was hoped it would be ready for action by the end of 1943. The weapon was to be launched by being catapulted from a ramp, powered by an 'Argus duct' that would develop 670lb thrust; it would then fly at about 400mph, at a height of between 700 and 6,500ft.

On 15 May 1942, a Spitfire reconnaissance pilot photographed the area around Peenemünde, a German research station and Luftwaffe test site at the edge of the Baltic Sea that had been opened in 1937. The prints were sent to RAF Medmenham, Central Interpretation Unit, which specialised in photographic intelligence. Constance Babington-Smith, a young WAAF officer, remembered noticing the name Peenemünde. There was evidence of some 'extraordinary circular embankments' and heavy construction work; however, no one thought this of special significance, so the photos were filed away and no further action was taken at that time.

In February 1943 the War Office asked the interpretation staff at Medmenham to look for 'long-range projectors capable of firing on this country from the French coast'. When two captured German generals, held as prisoners of war, were heard talking in their cell about huge rockets that had reached the testing stage and were likely to be in use soon, it was time to look for evidence to support this. On 19 April 1943 the Air Ministry warned Medmenham to be on the lookout for a long-range gun, remotely controlled rocket aircraft and 'some sort of tube out of which a rocket could be squirted'. Duncan Sandys, Churchill's son-in-law, was asked to undertake a special investigation. He then commissioned further surveys of Peenemünde.

In June 1943, one of Constance Babington Smith's fellow interpreters, André Kenny, made the first identification of two V2 long-range rockets lying horizontally on road vehicles at Peenemünde. At the same time, Constance Babington Smith was briefed to look out for 'anything queer'. Examining a photograph taken on 23 June she spotted 'four little tail-less aeroplanes taking the air' which 'looked queer enough to satisfy anybody'. What she had seen, it turned out, were four Me 163 liquid rocket fighters. But V2 long-range rockets were identified from photographs of Peenemünde for the first time that month.

On 28 June the Cabinet Defence Committee (Operations) received the Sandys report. They agreed to check out northern France for evidence of any suspicious works, and to attack Peenemünde. There was a belated acknowledgement that there might be two secret weapons being developed: a rocket (V2) and a flying bomb (V1).

The flying bomb was formally known as the Fi.103. There were plans to produce 50,000 a month from June 1943, but then things went wrong. The A.4 was the rocket. Hitler wanted both projects to go ahead. After a series of devastating raids on Hamburg (Operation Gomorrah) on 24 July 1943, his desire for revenge became even stronger.

In the early morning of 18 August 1943, the Allies carried out a massive attack on Peenemünde (Operation Hydra); this marked the start of the strategic bombing campaign against the V weapon programme. Work on the rocket was set back by two months, but the flying bomb work was scarcely affected.

From August 1943, the German military were working on three different plans: producing the missiles, training the crews to fire them and building the launching sites. There were a number of changes in design. Higher specification models were ordered, but could not be made ready till February 1944. There were also problems producing the control gear and diving mechanism because of air attacks on the Gerhard Fieseler Werke at Kassel, where these were being produced. It was hoped that trials would be complete by early February. Training the troops who were to fire the missiles was far easier than producing the missiles themselves; the troops became Flak Regiment 155(W), with Colonel Max Wachtel as their commanding officer. This became part of Army Corps LXV from 15 December 1943; they were based at St Germain, near Paris. By 23 September 1943, 40,000 labourers and artisans were assigned to build the launch sites; ninety-six were planned along the 140 miles of French coastline between Calais and the Seine, along with two storage bunkers. Fifty-eight of the first sixty-four sites were planned to be ready by the end of November 1943.

Meanwhile, information about the German plans began to leak out. On 12 August a document arrived at MI6 which talked of two separate weapons: a rocket projectile known as A.4 and a pilotless aircraft officially known as Phi.7. On 10 September the chiefs of staff agreed that Duncan Sandys should concentrate on studying evidence relating to the long-range rocket, while the Air Ministry should collect information about the flying bomb.

On 21 September 1943, Churchill made his first guarded reference to the threat in the House of Commons. He talked of the German leaders' 'mysterious allusions to new methods and new weapons which will presently be tried against us'. Although he acknowledged that this could be rumour-mongering, 'there is probably more in it than that'.

Dr R.V. Jones stated in a chief of staff paper on 25 September: 'It is probable that the German Air Force has been developing a pilotless aircraft for long-range bombardment in competition with the rocket and it is very possible that the aircraft will arrive first'.

By using signals intercept, British intelligence was able to decipher the results of every test-fire of the flying bombs. The speed was around 400mph, the height 1,000–6,000ft, and the flying bombs' accuracy was increasing. Locating and (ideally) destroying the launch sites was becoming a matter of urgency. On 28 October 1943 Duncan Sandys ordered the whole area of north-west France within a 150-mile range of London to be re-photographed.

In early November, the first 'ski site' was spotted; it was so called because the layout of the storage chamber buildings looked rather like a ski on its side, long and narrow but curved gently at one end. All these sites had 'a long platform pointing towards London'. By 8 November the team at RAF Medmenham had identified nineteen sites under construction, and by 10 November they had found twenty-six. By 22 November the total had reached ninety-five. Further work on photographic identification made British intelligence realise 'the most imminent cross-Channel threat ... was going to be a flying bomb'. On 28 November an RAF Mosquito, piloted by Squadron Leader John Merifield, flew over Peenemünde and returned with a new set of photographs. As Flight Officer Constance Babington Smith studied them through her stereoscope, she identified a sort of ramp holding a tiny cruci-form shape on rails. It was a flying bomb being prepared for launch.

The evidence from Medmenham meant that elimination of the launch sites was now a priority, under the codename Operation Crossbow, and on 16 December Wing Commander Leonard Cheshire led a night attack against one of the 'ski sites' near Abbeville. Unfortunately, although generally on target, the raid was not accurate enough to destroy the site. Two days before, the deputy chief of air staff had told the prime minister that if present rates of construction were maintained, work on twenty sites would be completed by January 1944 and the rest by the following month. The launching points were in the Pas de Calais and Somme/Seine area, and they were oriented on London. Intelligence reports suggested that rockets were already arriving at sites to be assembled. Agents' reports suggested that each site included a square building which contained no metal; the experts concluded that what-ever the building contained needed to be free from magnetism, which implied some form of sensitive compass steering. (The assembly routine seemed to be to have the rocket tube already assembled, add the wings in a small building near the ski-slope, then launch the rocket via the ramp.)

Operation Crossbow was intended to have two objectives: to attack plants where the V1s were manufactured, in order to eliminate the source of supply, and to damage the launching sites in France, so that the V1s could not be made operational. Air Chief Marshal Sir Trafford Leigh-Mallory, head of the recently set up Allied Expeditionary Air Force, was ordered to attack the targets, along with heavy bombers of the US Eighth Air Force, whenever the weather ruled out attacks on Germany. This meant that the US had to be notified officially about what was happening. They were swift to take action.

On 12 January 1944 General Marshall, chief of staff of the US Army, ordered the American Army Air Forces to give top priority to working out the most effective method of attacking the launching sites. On 25 January General 'Hap' Arnold, commanding general of Army Air Forces, ordered Brigadier General Grandison Gardner to get the job done in days, not weeks. Practice techniques were tested in the US; the most successful proved to be a minimum altitude attack by fighter aircraft to pinpoint very heavy bombs on the most vulnerable point of each site. General Gardner and his team flew to England to demonstrate the new method of knocking out the ski sites.

Attacks had begun on 5 December 1943, when three of sixty-four sites were raided, but the results were disappointing at first. Sites could generally only be damaged by a direct hit. They were also heavily defended, and the aircraft were vulnerable because of the weight of their bombs. Initially Typhoons and Spitfires were sent, but the raids were both dangerous and risky. Medium and heavy bombers began to be used. However, German ground fire proved lethal to large numbers of Allied aircraft. There was also another issue: possible harm to civilians. The Germans often positioned sites in orchards or back gardens in remote villages, even on a village street. Night bombing proved less dangerous than daylight raids, but without visual clues it could be inaccurate; pinpoint accuracy was required to damage the key areas of the launching sites. Gradually, though, the Allied attacks took their toll; so many sites required repairs that in January 1944 more than half of the first hundred sites were abandoned.

Launch sites continued to be hit heavily, even as the build-up to D-Day continued. The US Eighth Air Force carried out many sorties; UK Bomber Command made somewhat fewer because of the numerous other demands on their resources. However, the Germans rapidly increased the defences of their sites. As a result, 154 Allied aircraft were lost, and 771 aircrew were reported dead or missing. By the end of May 1944, eighty-two of ninety-six ski sites were believed to have been neutralised. Between 5 December 1943 and 12 June 1944, almost 32,000 tons of bombs were dropped, the majority of which (23,000 tons) landed on the ninety-six ski sites. Thanks to the Allied efforts, neither the large sites nor the supply sites ever came into action.

Throughout this period there were still restrictions on what could be reported about the secret weapon. On 22 February, in the House of Commons, Churchill mentioned 'attack on this country either by pilotless aircraft, or possibly rockets, or both, on a considerable scale.' In January, Herbert Morrison had met selected newspaper editors to warn them about the weapon. The following month he wrote to the regional commissioners of the five civil defence regions most at risk to warn them 'the main threat is now from pilotless aircraft'.

Two months later, on 26 April, the regional commissioners were told that police, wardens and members of the Royal Observer Corps in areas likely to be affected should now receive appropriate instructions to prevent publication of any reports that would reveal to the enemy where the missiles had fallen. These instructions were sent out to posts in most of southern England, and included a description of the pilotless aircraft. It was thought to resemble a small monoplane, with a 20ft wingspan and a maximum speed of 400mph; it would probably cruise at about 6,000ft.

The Home Guard took the news very seriously, but there was a lot of unjustified optimism as time passed and no attack materialised. Even the Air Ministry hoped that by the end of April the remaining twenty ski sites would be knocked out and the threat would disappear.

Suddenly, at the end of April 1944, one of the interpreters at Medmenham spotted a new development near a village called Belhamelin, on the Cherbourg peninsula: a long concrete platform with studs, and further away a heavily camouflaged square building. This was a much simpler type of launching site. They were hard to spot initially, but twelve were identified within days. By 16 May nineteen had been found. However, these were largely ignored by the Allied forces; only one was attacked, and no further raids were instigated.

Another part of the puzzle was solved when on 11 May a mystery plane crashed in Sweden. This was reported by the press as a 'radio bomber'; it was in fact a flying bomb, powered by a pulse-jet engine. British experts were able to gain access to a sample of its fuel; they analysed the bomb's design and confirmed that it could carry a sufficient payload to be capable of effective attacks on England. An intensive examination of the evidence also solved the questions about the flying bomb's guidance system. The bomb was prepared for launching in an ordinary building, then its compass for the guidance system was pre-set in a non-magnetic building. This, then, was the explanation for the square building seen on so many of the photographs.

By the start of June, the number of modified sites was steadily increasing, with most of them oriented towards London. The Germans had changed the assembly methods for the sites, with rails for the launch area and prefabricated panels for the square building being brought in from elsewhere for faster assembly. Over sixty unbombed modified sites had been found by RAF Medmenham by early June. Just before D-Day, Wing Commander Kendall told a Crossbow meeting in London about the new methods. The clear implication was that the modified sites in France could be made ready for use within 48 hours; it might also be possible to make operational some of the ski sites that had seemed to be abandoned. The significance of the new methods was perhaps not fully appreciated. With the preparations for D-Day increasing in intensity, it could be argued that attacks on the ski sites were perceived to be a diversion of effort. Neutralising these sites had not in fact averted the danger.

It is remarkably poignant to read about the months leading up to June 1944: the Allied efforts to destroy or disable launching sites and weapons as soon as these were discovered, pitted against the continuing German efforts to bring their V1 project to fruition. The sense of urgency was palpable, as was the race against time on both sides. The Allied plans for the Normandy landings were being finalised during the same period; it was perhaps inevitable that these should take precedence, politically and operationally, over continuing attempts to disable the launching sites. Vast numbers of troops were being marshalled in great secrecy; nevertheless most people in southern England would have been aware that something momentous was about to happen and that this could mark a new and potentially decisive stage in the war. There is also the irony that it was the success of the Normandy landings that in essence made the start of the German V1 attacks unavoidable; the Germans had to go ahead with the much-delayed V1 launch in an attempt to destroy British civilian morale. Hitler had little to lose and potentially everything to gain. The V1s were to live up to their name: revenge weapons.

Originally the German V1 attack was to start on 15 February, but nothing happened. On 17 March Colonel Wachtel was told that even by 15 April the total stock of flying bombs would only be 3,000. Should these be used as part of a heavy bombardment, or be sent over as a continuous but lighter rain? Eventually a compromise was reached as production targets had not been met. The attack was to be coupled with the beginning of the proposed invasion. On 16 May the final orders were given by Hitler; the bombardment against London was to begin in the middle of June.

On 20 May, Colonel Wachtel began withdrawing his men from the ski sites and moving them to the still intact modified sites. The new modified sites were reduced to the two key elements: concrete foundations for the launching ramp and the 'square building' where the aircraft would have its compass set. In future the missiles were to be delivered ready fuelled and then dispersed among the trees for camouflage. However, the Allied saturation bombing of the ski sites continued; ninety-three sites suffered at least some damage, and only eleven escaped completely.

The Allied invasion, originally scheduled for 5 June, took place a day later. One of its unexpected consequences for the Germans was that the bombing raids associated with it wrought havoc with the French railway system, so many of the catapults for the V1s failed to arrive and the vital ingredient of permanganate of potash (needed to produce the explosive mixture) was in short supply. The start of the V1 operation, originally scheduled for 12 June, was postponed again just before midnight that day. However, it was only put back by a few hours; it was rescheduled to start on 13 June after 3.30am.

The weather on 13 June 1944 was cold, with the threat of rain later, and the sky was overcast. Soon after midnight the Germans fired about thirty heavy shells, mainly at Folkestone, where they caused considerable damage to property, but also inland towards Maidstone; the intention was to divert attention from the imminent arrival of the V1s. Just before 4.00am there was an air raid warning over most of Kent; it was followed by an all clear, and then almost immediately by another warning. At 4.08am 2 Observer Corps on

Romney Marsh, Dymchurch, spotted 'a strange shape, the size of a small fighter, surrounded by a red glare from the rear of the fuselage and emitting a noise like "a Model T Ford going up a hill"'. They identified it instantly from the description given to them in April, and phoned Maidstone Observer Corps, using the agreed code words: 'Diver! Diver! Diver! On four, north-west one oh one'. Maidstone reacted instantly, and repeated the Diver call across the Operations Room. This was relayed to No. 11 Fighter Group at Uxbridge, and the report was passed on to Air Defence of Great Britain headquarters at Stanmore. The missile continued to be tracked via the various Observer Corps as it travelled over southern England.

The first flying bomb to land on British soil exploded at 4.13am on Tuesday 13 June at Swanscombe, near Gravesend, just to the north of the A2; it left a shallow crater and damaged a large area of crops and a house. The second landed at 4.20am in Sussex, near Cuckfield; a cottage nearby had all its windows blown out, and all 18 acres of a nearby field were 'mown' by the blast. The fourth bomb landed at 5.06am at Platt, near Sevenoaks; it caused slight damage to property but no casualties.

Only one of the four, the third V1, reached London. It exploded at 4.25am on the bridge over Grove Road, Bow; this carried the main line between Chelmsford and the LNER terminus at Liverpool Street. All four lines over the bridge and the road beneath it were blocked. A number of nearby houses were damaged, and there were casualties, some fatal. The final figures were six people killed, thirty seriously injured and 200 made homeless. Although it was soon apparent that this was likely to be a pilotless aircraft, the authorities had to make sure by checking the wreckage and the effect of the blast. The local view was that it might be a German plane that had been shot down, because it dropped so suddenly. However, it was soon confirmed that this was a PAC. Specialists collected the wreckage and began to examine the evidence. There was no reference to the raid in Tuesday's papers, but thousands of commuters were aware there had been a major incident because their trains stopped short at Stratford or were diverted to Fenchurch Street. Mainline services were also affected. However, two of the lines had reopened by the end of Tuesday 14 June, and the other two by 8.00pm that Friday.

The general official reaction was one of relief. The Germans' first attack had been far smaller and less significant than had been feared. Various reports and accounts of the incidents contained unreliable information. The report to the Cabinet from the chief of air staff on the evening of 13 June was especially misleading, talking of up to twenty-seven pilotless aircraft arriving in three waves. Herbert Morrison suggested the damage done was no greater than a parachute mine and rather less than a 2,000lb bomb. It was agreed that no information should be published in the press about the attacks at present, and any future information would say only that a raid had occurred in southern England.

Unfortunately the Air Ministry then issued a communiqué, which appeared in the *Evening Standard* and *The Times*. It mentioned that a raider had been brought down in East London, and even referred to the damage to the railway line. This meant that the Germans knew that at least one of their V1s had reached London.

The attacks on 13 June could be deemed a failure; of the ten bombs launched, five had crashed immediately, and one came down in the sea. The Germans spent the next few days ensuring as many sites as possible were fully equipped; fifty-three were made operational within two days. Colonel Wachtel sent out new orders on Thursday 15 June, telling his commanders to 'Open fire on target 42 [London] with an all-catapult salvo' at 11.18pm, with a range of 130 miles, followed by sustained fire till 4.50am the next day.

The bombardment started promptly. By noon on 16 June, 244 missiles had been launched. Forty-five crashed on take-off, destroying nine launching sites in the process. Some of the remaining 199 went off course or simply disappeared, but seventy-three reached Greater London. Eleven of those were shot down over the capital; Flight Lieutenant Musgrave of 605 Squadron, flying a Mosquito, was the first pilot to shoot down a V1.

For many people, this was the first they knew of the flying bomb campaign. While the engine noise was deemed distinctive, a number of witnesses thought the missiles were planes with their lights on, or burning aircraft; onlookers were delighted to see what they thought were enemy aircraft being shot down in flames. Many of the missiles came up the Thames Estuary and a number of attempts were made to hit them as they roared overhead. The air raid warnings kept sounding, and a warning was still in force when people were going to work in London the next morning.

Later on Friday 16 June, Herbert Morrison made a statement in the House of Commons, saying pilotless aircraft were now being used. There was to be no information given about where the air raids had taken place beyond 'southern England'; this was to avoid helping the enemy by revealing exact details of the attacks. He then went to give Churchill and the War Cabinet a more detailed account. He told them the attack had been much heavier than on 12 June; first reports suggested about fifty killed and 400 injured, but those numbers would probably rise. He urged that everything possible be done to minimise the attacks by dealing with the launch sites.

Air Marshal Sir Douglas Evill, vice-chief of air staff, was surprisingly optimistic: he spoke of 150 aircraft, fifty of which had fallen in the Greater London area, from about forty sites. They flew at a height of 1,000–4,000ft, so within range of light anti-aircraft fire or balloons. Allegedly eleven had been shot down by fighters, twelve by anti-aircraft guns. There was, however, a concern about bringing flying bombs down over populated areas; for this reason, the guns in the capital were soon to be withdrawn and moved further south.

At 12.15pm on 16 June, Admiral Thompson, chief press censor, issued a 'Private and Confidential Memorandum' to the press, which formally laid down the stricter censorship rules. No information was to be given about aircraft shot down 'whether pilotless or piloted', so that the Germans would be unaware where the V1s were landing. Obituary notices for those killed by enemy action were rationed to not more than three from the same district in any one issue. (This is why obituaries for those who died in the Guards' Chapel were couched in vague terms: 'recently, in southern England' or 'in June, by enemy action' provided as much detail as could be allowed. This makes research a little challenging for the contemporary researcher, as well as for the Germans in 1944.)

At 1.00pm, the new attacks were mentioned on the BBC one o'clock news; however, their importance was played down. Most people were at work so missed the information. However, the evening papers led with the story. The *Evening Standard*'s front-page headline for 16 June was 'Morrison announces new German "air weapon"; pilotless planes now raid Britain'. Londoners travelling home would have seen the billboards and realised a new type of weapon had arrived, even before they tuned in to the evening news bulletin.

In the afternoon there was a staff conference with the prime minister, which agreed the following plan: to take all possible steps to neutralise the launching sites, subject to other requirements in the Battle of France, to avoid sounding an air raid warning for just one aircraft, to engage with pilotless aircraft, to redistribute gun, searchlight and balloon defences to counter the attacks and to consider using armed cables on balloons.

That weekend was not only the first, but also the worst for the new weapons. The Ministry of Home Security issued new guidance: if a V1 was seen or heard, people should take cover. If the V1's engine stopped and the light in the tail went out, an explosion was likely to follow shortly, within 5 to 15 seconds, so people should take refuge from the blast and 'use the most solid protection immediately available'. By 6.00am on Saturday 17 June, fourteen London boroughs had been hit, with eighteen people killed and nearly 250 injured; there was considerable damage to property. Later that day a V1 landed on a shopping centre near Clapham Junction. St Mary Abbot's Hospital, in Kensington, received a direct hit and had to be closed, with the loss of 832 beds.

Until the morning of Sunday, 18 June, no bombs had landed in the City of Westminster. Early that day a V1 landed on Hungerford Bridge, damaging the railway track but causing no casualties. At about 8.50am, a second V1 exploded at Carey Mansions in Rutherford Street; ten people were killed and a further sixty-two were seriously injured.

The third bomb, about the 500th to be fired, was responsible for the worst V1 incident of the war. This was the V1 that destroyed the Guards' Chapel and caused widespread damage to property in the surrounding area. Many people witnessed the last few seconds before the explosion. The V1 'appeared to hover over the high black shape of Queen Anne's Mansions' in Queen Anne's Gate, then used as naval offices.

The bomb was heard but not seen by Dr R.V. Jones, who was in the SIS (MI6) HQ at 54 Broadway, not far from Wellington Barracks:

> I [was] in the office. Shortly after 11 o'clock I was on the telephone to Bimbo Norman at Bletchley when we heard the unforgettable noise of a flying bomb ... Then the engine cut out. I remarked to him that this was going to be pretty near, and that we were getting under our desks. There was a deafening explosion, and I can remember Norman's voice saying 'Are you alright? Are you alright?' and I assured him that we were. I then went out of the office to see what had happened.
>
> I ... found that the bomb had fallen about 150 yards away on the Guards Chapel ... There was nothing for me to do, for the Guards had everything under control, and were already carrying out the dead. But that sight ... brought home to me the difference between 1 ton of explosive in actuality and the 1 ton that we had predicted in the abstract six months before.

The bomb exploded at 11.11am, just after Lord Hay had read the first lesson. He was walking back to his seat, the congregation had risen to sing the *Te Deum*, and in the gallery above them the musicians of the Coldstream Guards band were starting to play. There was a vivid blue flash, and then the concrete roof crashed down and the walls crumbled, burying the congregation in up to 10ft of rubble. Only the portico and altar areas remained intact. (The aftermath of the explosion and the rescue effort that followed are covered in greater detail in Chapter Three.)

The King's Guard had just finished drilling in the square. The Guardsmen threw themselves to the ground and thus avoided injury from the blast. They were first on the scene and began to work to clear the debris, prising up the blocks of concrete and carrying out those who were freed.

The chief warden of Westminster had been at the Rutherford Street incident, a few minutes' walk away, and was quick to arrive at the Chapel. He assessed the situation as 'a rescue job from first to last'; he telephoned the deputy Heavy Rescue officer at control, described the scene to him and suggested Heavy and Light Rescue parties, mobile cranes and ambulances. These were on site in a matter of minutes, and the painstaking rescue effort began. It would continue without a break for a further two days and nights; the last victims were not removed until late on the night of Tuesday 21 June.

The Women's Voluntary Services set up an incident inquiry point in Wellington Barracks. They handled enquiries from relatives and friends about those who were thought to have attended the service, provided refreshments and helped coordinate information about the civilian dead. (The military kept their own records.)

The death toll was heavy, with a mixture of military and civilian casualties. Initially 119 people were described as having died at the scene, but several more died in hospital later that day, including Major Windram, the director of music. Musician Jock Hart died of his injuries on 13 April 1945, more than nine months later. This brought the number of those who died to 124, including a woman buried in Westminster Cemetery who remains unidentified to this day; in total, sixty-five military and fifty-nine civilians were killed. Another 102 people were seriously injured, many of them removed unconscious from the rubble, and taken to hospital; some had life-changing injuries. Elisabeth Sheppard-Jones would never walk again; her spine had been irrevocably damaged by the same block of concrete that killed her childhood friend, Pauline Gye. At least thirty-nine people were treated for their injuries at a first aid post; however, there is no record of those who were injured but did not seek treatment, or those who were able to walk away from the incident but were suffering from shock.

The Guards' Chapel attack was the most serious V1 incident to date, and the heavy casualty rate meant government strategy had to be revised. Once again London and southern England were in the front line. On Monday 19 June, the Civil Defence Committee decided that the policy of shooting down pilotless aircraft over London with anti-aircraft guns should be stopped; the risk of causing additional casualties was too great. The guns were relocated closer to the coast and formed part of a multi-layered defence. The following day a barrage balloon centre and 'diver' defence headquarters were established at Biggin Hill, Kent. The committee also decided that, partly for reasons of morale, pilotless aircraft should in future be referred to as 'flying bombs'; the former term implied some kind of mechanical monster, while the latter was more accurate and less alarming. The general public may well have disagreed with this viewpoint, but for Whitehall, semantic accuracy was to prevail.

The casualty figures laid before the committee were disturbing. Already 499 people had been killed by V1s, and this figure was likely to rise as more bodies were recovered. A total of 2,051 had been seriously injured (in other words, had been admitted to hospital), another 2,028 had been slightly injured and a further 633 had suffered wounds of unknown severity. This made a grand total of more than 5,000 killed or injured since Tuesday 13 June, less than a week before. 137,000 buildings had been damaged and needed repairs. All this had been done by 647 V1s that had so far made landfall, not all of which had reached London. The committee decided to discourage large gatherings and ensure that all schools had adequate shelters; they also debated what would happen if a flying bomb pierced the Tube tunnels under the Thames.

Later that day Churchill and his military advisers endorsed the earlier decisions. By then the casualties had risen to 526 dead and 5,856 total casualties. They decided there should be no official evacuation of schools, and the Underground should continue to run during raids. They were also concerned about the threat to industry caused by the time lost taking shelter when V1s were coming over. Eventually many factories would devise their own early warning systems, whereby work only stopped if there was deemed to be imminent danger.

By 29 June, a fortnight after the first major raids had begun, 1,679 people had been killed. This was likely to be an underestimate because of the nature of the incidents. A further 5,000 had been seriously injured, with almost the same number slightly injured; and more than 270,000 houses had been damaged. By the end of June, 20,000 additional Morrison shelters had been issued and another 4,000 a week were being distributed; they provided a two-metre long indoor cage, and were designed to be slept in at night and used as a table, with a steel top and wire mesh sides. They were intended to protect the occupants from masonry and debris if the house was hit by a bomb. (They were an indoor alternative to the Anderson shelter, the corrugated iron building that had to be half-buried in soil in the garden.) The Morrison shelters were normally placed in a downstairs room; for example, my grandparents in Acton placed theirs in the scullery, next to the kitchen.

On Monday 3 July, the evacuation of London began; the official voluntary scheme opened on 5 July, and by 17 July 170,000 people had left. By 3 August, 225,000 mothers and children had left London. This figure would eventually reach 1,450,000. Londoners took to spending their nights in the Underground once more, as they had done during the Blitz. Over 73,000 people were sleeping in the Tube at the height of the attacks, although this figure dropped as the summer progressed.

Churchill eventually realised that his censorship policy was no longer sustainable. On 6 July he made a statement in the House, which was reported in the *Evening Standard*. He said that until 6.00am that day 2,754 flying bombs had been launched, and 2,752 people had been killed: 'almost exactly one person per bomb'. He made it clear that London had borne the brunt of these attacks. It was not until Monday 10 July that the blanket ban on identifying locations of incidents was lifted, and for the first time the public learned via the newspapers of the destruction of the Guards' Chapel three weeks before.

It had previously been referred to only as 'a church in southern England'. Even those Guards serving abroad were not formally notified of the tragedy until early July.

Although the Guards' Chapel incident was the largest and perhaps most often cited of that 'doodlebug summer', there were a number of other serious incidents. On 30 June, a V1 exploded in the roadway at the Aldwych, 60ft from Bush House and only 40ft from the Air Ministry headquarters in Adastral House, at the corner of Kingsway. It was lunchtime, just after 2.00pm, and a fine day. People were going about their daily business: queueing at the nearby post office or bank, taking their lunch breaks, travelling along the Strand by bus, sunbathing on the roof of Adastral House or looking out of their office windows to see what was making that ominous sound ... 46 people died, 399 were seriously injured and another 200 were able to go home after treatment: a total of almost 650 casualties from just one V1.

The Guards' Chapel incident was noteworthy for its large number of military casualties, but six days later on 24 June, at 6.00am, forty-six soldiers serving with the 6th (Guards) Tank Brigade workshop REME were killed outright when a flying bomb fell on a repair workshop for tanks at Newlands, Charing, Kent. Opinions vary; some say it was shot down by a fighter-bomber, others that the bomber tipped the wing of the V1 so that it fell to the ground and exploded. A further eighty men were wounded, six of whom later died of their wounds. They had been waiting to embark for Normandy, and were due to be sent there the following week. The victims were buried in a mass grave in Lenham; it was an active service burial and took place at night for security reasons, with the grave dug by their fellow Guardsmen. This was the worst V1 incident in Kent, according to H.E. Bates, writer in residence to the Air Ministry, but later better known as an author.

A lesser-known tragedy occurred on 3 July, when a V1 exploded at Sloane Court East at 7.47am. A US Army company was stationed there: the 130th Chemical Processing Company. The commanding officer had spotted the V1 coming over and had called to his men to take cover; they were mustering in the street for transport at the time. Nevertheless, at least sixty-five (possibly seventy-four) American servicemen (at least sixty-two of whom were from the 130th Chemical Processing Company) and nine civilians lost their lives, with at least fifty people seriously injured; this was the worst V1 incident affecting American troops. Members of SHAEF (Supreme Headquarters Allied Expeditionary Forces) were stationed at Sloane Court and also suffered casualties; two American servicemen were killed and a further nineteen were wounded. In addition, two Canadian batmen were killed, with two officers injured. Because of wartime censorship, little was reported at the time, so this attack is frequently omitted from accounts.

On 28 July there were two serious incidents with heavy civilian casualties. One was in Lewisham; the V1 exploded in Lewisham High Street, in front of the clock tower, when it hit the roof of an air raid shelter outside Marks & Spencer. This was at 9.41am, when the bustling street market was full of shoppers. The siren had not been sounded, because it was policy not to do so for a single flying bomb, so nobody had the chance to take cover. The market stalls outside Marks & Spencer, Woolworths and Sainsbury's took the full force of the blast; shops on both sides of the road were damaged. Two passing buses were blown to pieces and the nearby post office was badly damaged. The final official casualty count was fifty-one dead, with 124 seriously injured and 189 treated at first aid posts. (Some accounts suggest the death toll was fifty-nine.) This was the worst single V1 incident in south London.

The second incident that day was at 1.30pm in Kensington at the junction of Earls Court Road and Kensington High Street. All the cafes were packed, and people were out shopping in their lunch hours. Forty-five people were killed, fifty-four seriously injured and 116 slightly injured. The two V1s had killed a total of ninety-six or more people, seriously injured another 178 (all of whom would have required hospital treatment) and wounded another 305, making a grand total of nearly 580 casualties from two explosions. Nor would these have been the only casualties that day. Churchill's much-quoted figure about each V1 killing 'only' one person could at times prove a woeful underestimate.

The final major incident of that doodlebug summer was on 23 August 1944 at New Southgate, where a V1 glided down and exploded right in the heart of the Standard Telephones and Cables site just before 8.00am. The roof spotter just had time to shout over the factory speakers: 'Lie down! For God's sake, lie down!' and this saved many lives. Two of the buildings took the main force of the blast and one caught fire. Twenty-one people died on the spot and a further twelve died later; about 200 were seriously injured.

The incidents described above were some of the most noteworthy in terms of casualties; they also demonstrated the range of possible incidents. However, most families in London and the south-east would have their own V1 story. While my mother would never speak about her friends from the YWCA who had died, she was less reluctant to tell me about her own near miss. In late August 1944, two months after the Guards' Chapel incident and the loss of her friends, my mother was visiting my father at his parents' home in Churchfield Road, Acton. They were in the upstairs sitting-room when they heard a V1 approaching; the engine cut out. With great presence of mind, my father leapt up, pulled the settee away from the wall and dragged my mother behind it to protect her from broken glass. The windows were blown in, and the V1 exploded on the other side of the level crossing by Acton Park; four people were killed. I was told this story as a child, and whenever we visited my grandparents and I looked out of their sitting-room window I would be reminded of it. It was just one story, one experience out of many, but it still had the power to make me shiver fifteen years later.

The V1 campaign would intensify until late August and early September 1944, when the German launching sites in northern France and Holland were overrun by the advancing Allied forces. The Germans evacuated their flying bomb sites on 23 August 1944, and by 16 September all the French sites had been captured. Until then the V1s had a devastating effect on London. The widespread damage and devastation placed a great strain on the civilian population; raids came at any hour of the day and night, unpredictably, unlike previous attacks. By late June as many as 50–100 V1s were reaching London every day, with little if any gap between one warning and the next. The noise could be heard from a long way off, as far as 30 miles away, and the V1s rarely came singly; they 'seemed to fly on an invisible track, as straight as a train' and often came over on parallel trajectories a mile or so apart. Those living through that summer described feeling as if they were being stalked by death; it might come at any time, at home or at work, and they felt powerless to avoid it. The fact that there was nobody inside the weapon to pilot it just added to the eeriness, as did the noise; while in the past some people had eventually become nonchalant about manned raids, very few could tolerate the protracted suspense of a V1 attack. First the siren, then the drone of the V1, and finally the silence, when you waited to know if it was overhead. The fact that you could see them coming seemed to make it worse, and the sheer number made the attacks feel relentless. As Norman Longmate said: 'Death came in many ways and many guises that summer, to people of all ages and backgrounds'.

The V1 could cause huge damage to both people and property. Where it struck, houses and other buildings would be totally demolished. In residential areas, terraced houses were crammed together and they would collapse like a pack of playing cards – sometimes up to twenty houses at a time. Brick walls were reduced to dust. Further away from the explosion, the external elements of the houses would be ripped out by the blast; walls, doors and windows would vanish, so that the inside of the house was open to view. Further out still, all the windows would be blown out and roofing slates blown off. Every time a doodlebug landed, hundreds of houses were damaged; some were no longer fit for habitation, while others needed significant repairs to make them weatherproof. Tens of thousands of Londoners had to move out, or tolerate the cold and damp in roofless, windowless houses, until repairs could be carried out. By early August an estimated 800,000 houses in London had been damaged, some more than once.

The effects of the explosion were not always predictable. The surface explosion caused a blast wave that rippled out from the epicentre; this left a vacuum, which caused a second rush of air, giving a pushing and pulling effect. Victims could essentially die of suffocation while appearing otherwise physically intact; their lungs had been paralysed by the blast. They might be killed by the explosion itself, or irremediably crushed by flying debris or the falling masonry that followed the initial explosion. There was also the risk of injuries from flying glass, especially during the earlier part of the campaign when people were as yet unaware of the danger (for example at the Aldwych). Some victims were blinded by glass shards, while others lost limbs. The blast area of a V1 could be as large as 400–600 yards from the explosion. Anyone unlucky enough to be near the point of impact would be blown apart. Others would be trapped beneath collapsed buildings and have to be dug out by the heavy rescue service.

As the summer went on, the type of injuries began to change. At the beginning people were caught by surprise out on the street or at work, or were curious about the new weapons; they might stop to look up when they heard the strange noise overhead, or gaze out of the window to see what was happening. Injuries from flying glass were very common. Later on, people realised that they needed to take shelter swiftly; those at home without a Morrison or Anderson shelter would hurry to take cover under the stairs, for example, as this was thought to be the safest place. This minimised the risk from flying glass, but led to more crush injuries when people became buried in the ruins of their collapsed homes.

From mid-July, the UK defences were reorganised, with a first line of gun defences established on the south coast. The gun batteries on Romney Marsh between Hythe and Rye became more and more accurate. By 23 August the percentage of 'kills' had risen to 60 per cent; in the last week it rose to 74 per cent. The anti-aircraft guns fired shells with newly-developed proximity fuses, meaning the shell had only to get within 30ft of a V1 to destroy it. They were followed by fighter patrols closer to London; these were intended to shoot down the V1s as they came over, or as strategy developed, to endeavour to tip the wings of the rockets so that they plunged to the ground, far from London. There were far more fighters: Spitfires, Tempests and, from the end of July, Meteors. There was a further wave of gun positions nearer London, followed by barrage balloons to the south of London, which were intended to stop many of the remaining V1s getting through. About 45 per cent of V1s were destroyed before they reached London; 25 per cent were destroyed by fighters, 17 per cent by anti-aircraft guns and 5 per cent by barrage balloons. Only 29 per cent of V1s penetrated as far as the London area. The Allied strategy became increasingly sophisticated as the summer progressed and fighters became more skilled at tipping V1s out of the sky.

Once the German bombing sites in northern France and Holland were overrun, the second phase of V1 attacks began. This lasted from 16 September

1944 to 15 January 1945 and was organised from bases in occupied Holland and Germany; at this point 'Doodlebug Alley' moved eastwards from Kent and Sussex to Essex. The V1s were launched from Heinkel He 111 aircraft flying over the North Sea. There were fewer bombs and often the targeting was inaccurate. On 24 December they launched an attack on Manchester, but few V1s reached the area. In all 608 V1s were launched, of which about 10 per cent reached the target areas of London and Manchester. The V2 attacks (the former A.4 rocket projectile mentioned earlier in this chapter), which began on 8 September when a rocket hit Staveley Road, Chiswick, continued until 27 March 1945. In the third phase, from 3–29 March 1945, 124 V1s were ground-launched from sites in the Netherlands. Only thirteen reached their target, London.

During the V1 campaign, over 10,400 V1s were launched. Approximately 9,251 of these were fired against London during an eighty-day campaign; V1s were also aimed at Southampton and Portsmouth. A number of the flying bombs went off course or landed in the Channel, or were shot down over water; about 25 per cent of them failed to cross the Channel. 7,488 flying bombs crossed the south coast of England; 3,957 were shot down, but 2,419 reached the capital. No borough escaped attack; Croydon received the most V1s, with 142, with Wandsworth and Lewisham close behind at 122 and 114 respectively. South and south-east London boroughs received a disproportionate number: Camberwell, Woolwich, Greenwich, Lambeth, Beckenham and Orpington each received over fifty. Westminster had only twenty-nine, and the V1 that hit Acton (described earlier) was one of only seven to land in the borough.

It is perhaps easy to imagine that London bore the brunt of the attacks; after all, this was Hitler's intention. However, the areas described as 'Doodlebug Alley' were also at risk. Kent paid a heavy price for being the area of England closest to the launch sites; in total, a thousand V1s were shot down over the sea, with a further 1,444 crashing on land. 448 communities were damaged, some more than once. During the first week of the campaign, 101 doodlebugs were shot down over Kent; after that, an average of twenty incidents occurred each day. Although it was far less densely populated than central London, as a rural area, 156 people were killed and a total of 1,716 were injured.

Sussex was hit by 880 V1s (again, many would have been shot down by coastal defences or by fighters and gunners), and Surrey by 295. The east coast of the UK also suffered V1 attacks in smaller numbers, from Yorkshire (7) through Norfolk (13) to Suffolk (93) and Essex (412). Lancashire, Cheshire and Derbyshire had a few doodlebugs each; from the North to the Midlands and beyond, east of a line running south from Derbyshire to Hampshire, no county escaped attack altogether.

In all, 6,184 people were killed, with 17,981 seriously injured; some of the injured bore the scars for the rest of their lives, and many of their injuries were life-changing. Norman Longmate paid tribute in describing the human cost: 'For some families the effects of the flying-bombs can never be wiped out. Their loved ones lie ... beneath headstones on which only the words "By enemy action" and the date reveal how they died.'

Chapter 3

The Aftermath

The Guards' Chapel Rescue Effort and What Followed

Sunday, 18 June 1944

- 11.11am – a V1 hit the Guards' Chapel during morning service.
- 11.20am – the rescue effort was in progress. Incident Inquiry Point set up by WVS.
- 12.30pm – first estimate of the gravity of the incident: 400–500 casualties, some trapped.
- 2.00pm – eight ambulances in attendance.
- Revised casualty total: 94 known to be killed: 53 military, 41 civilian. Of those trapped, 104 had been released and about 50 remained trapped. The rescue work continued all night.

Monday, 19 June

- 8.30am – Incident Inquiry Point resumed work.
- 9.30am – casualties estimated to be 53 military dead and 41 civilians, a total of 94. Some 50 military personnel had been seriously injured, along with 10 civilians, a total of 60. That made a grand total of 154 casualties, but rescue work was still in progress.
- The services on the spot included six Heavy Rescue parties removing the rubble, five Light Rescue parties carrying out the casualties, two ambulances to take the injured to hospital, and two mobile cranes to assist with the heavy lifting and clearing.
- First newspaper report of the incident; full details would not appear until 9 July.
- 4.35pm – the next progress update was issued: 'Casualties to present 46 civilian dead, 53 military dead. Injured 53 including civilian and military. Rescue work proceeding.' Another Heavy Rescue party was ordered from St Marylebone to take over the evening shift.
- Another casualty estimate at the end of the evening: 53 military dead, 47 civilians dead, 81 persons injured (does not include hospital dead).
- The rescue work continued all night, apart from a V1 alert at 1.00am.

Tuesday, 20 June

- Mid-morning – latest total: 106 dead, 53 wounded. There were two Light Rescue parties, four Heavy Rescue parties and two mobile cranes on the spot. Work was proceeding satisfactorily. Half an hour later there was a request for an ambulance; someone had been recovered alive after almost 48 hours. This was probably the last casualty to be recovered alive.
- More bodies were found until late on Tuesday evening.
- Death notices began to appear in local and national papers: 'recently, by enemy action'.

Wednesday, 21 June

- First funeral held for Guards' Chapel victim, at Golders Green.
- By late afternoon, the work was drawing to a close. There were still two Heavy Rescue parties and one Light Rescue party on site.
- 11.35pm – three and a half days after the explosion, the incident was declared closed. The total of those who died was thought to be 119, with 64 people injured (the latter number later corrected to 81).

Thursday, 22 June

- More funerals at Golders Green Crematorium.

Friday, 23 June

- 2.30pm services held at Brookwood Military Cemetery for 12 Guardsmen and Private Phyllis Potter; 2 Canadian servicemen buried in the Canadian section of the cemetery; Reverend Wood was buried in the Australian military section; Martin Bacchiolelli in the French section.
- Many other funerals that day.

Saturday, 24 June

- Further funerals.

Monday, 26 June

- Memorial services and further funerals.

Tuesday, 27 June–Thursday, 29 June

- Funerals arranged by Westminster City Council held at Westminster City Cemetery.

Friday, 30 June

- Memorial services for George Kemp-Welch and Ivan Cobbold.

*   *   *

Sunday morning, 18 June 1944

At 11.11am on Sunday 18 June 1944, the third V1 to reach Westminster hit the Guards' Chapel during morning service. William Sansom described the scene:

> The bomb roared down over the high black shape of Queen Anne's Mansions, and then fell almost vertically, onto the roof of the gun-grey chapel. The roof and heavy concrete girders collapsed instantly and fell down inside on the congregation.

The direct hit completely destroyed the roof, most of its supporting walls and pillars and the portico of the Chapel's western door. Tons of rubble fell onto the congregation; the debris included the remnants of over 2,000 small memorial plaques, dedicated to the service of Guardsmen since 1660.

Some 123 soldiers and civilians were killed that day (one other would die the following April from his injuries) and 141 others were seriously injured. 102 people were sent to hospital and a further 39 received treatment at first aid posts. There is no record of those who received less serious injuries or walked away, but were later found to be suffering from shock. The high death toll included the officiating chaplain, the deputy assistant chaplain general, the Reverend Ralph Whitrow (who had only assumed duty a month before), several senior British Army officers and a US Army colonel. The congregation included ATS girls, soldiers and civilians. Fortunately it was smaller than usual; an ATS company attached to the barracks had been excused church parade that morning because of sleepless nights. According to the *Daily Mirror* of 10 July 1944, some 200 ATS girls had been due to attend a parade, but it was cancelled at the last moment.

Ironically, the Coldstream Guards Band were not supposed to be playing in the Chapel that Sunday. They were originally on the rota to do the Guard Mount, but had swapped duties with the Scots Guards. The Welsh Guards Band were originally due to do the Chapel service, but they had an engagement elsewhere; they were standing on the platform at a London station (possibly Embankment or Fenchurch Street; accounts differ) when the bomb struck the Chapel. So the Coldstream Guards attended the service instead of the Welsh Guards, while the Scots Guards Band had just returned from the Changing the Guard Ceremony at Buckingham Palace. They had dismounted and were waiting for dismissal.

Lieutenant David Gurney, Scots Guards, was on Picquet duty that morning, and had chosen not to attend Chapel so that he would be available to attend to any incidents that might arise. He had already witnessed the plume of dust from the second V1 to land in Westminster that day, two hours before, and had been standing on the steps of the Officers' Mess, looking out over the parade ground and the assembled Scots Guards, when the third V1 hit the Guards' Chapel. He described what happened after the explosion:

> John Quilter [assistant adjutant, Scots Guards] ran out of the [Officers'] Mess towards the Chapel and I followed him. Dust was rising in a great column and the sun shone on this ghastly silent ruin. The whole roof had fallen in, including the arches and pillars. The four walls were standing, and the east end quite undamaged. The cornice and pediment fell down (both far too heavy for the structure) and the buildings nearby were much damaged by blast: windows destroyed, inner walls broken, tiles off the roof etc. As soon as the bomb fell, the Regimental Band (Scots Guards) were fallen-in by the Band Sergeant and they began the rescue work. This was complicated by the fact that the falling masonry had blocked all the entrances.

Contemporary accounts of the incident include vivid details. Several describe the bishop of Maidstone and a 16-year-old drummer boy emerging from the sanctuary, apparently unhurt. 'One survivor told of a loud buzzing that turned into a high pitched whine followed by the explosion. After that everything went quiet until he heard a woman's voice in the darkness; she was singing "The Rose of Tralee"'. Another account in a local paper described two men being thrown right to the top of the one remaining wall by the blast; they were dead by the time the rescuers reached them.

Several rescuers and survivors later recalled that the silver altar cross had been untouched by the blast and the candles continued to burn, while the six silver candlesticks remained unmoved and undamaged, despite the devastation all around. It is a very striking image, and one that has endured to this day. Many later accounts of the Guards' Chapel incident mention it, suggesting that the candles remained burning as a symbol of hope for the future. I have been unable to locate a first-hand account that gives specific details; moreover, and somewhat prosaically, I would have expected the candles to be extinguished swiftly by the rescue parties because of the risks involved, such as a gas leak. Interestingly, there are several significant pieces of evidence that together seem to give credence to the story. The first is that the apse survived intact, as did the bishop of Maidstone, who was seated near the altar. Another supporting factor is the random nature of the blast after the explosion; some victims remained apparently unharmed, like waxworks (such as the bandsmen mentioned below). To me one of the most conclusive pieces of evidence is a film showing stills of front line London (http://www.britishpathe.com/video/stills/front-line-london). The Guards' Chapel rescue attempt is shown from around three minutes into the film. Shots 207–210 show the altar and candles, seemingly untouched. Even the flower vases are intact, complete with contents. By the time of filming, the candles had been extinguished. However, there is no blast damage to be seen. (The cross and candlesticks are still in use today, more than seventy years later.)

An article in the *Daily Telegraph* of 9 July 1944 adds further details. It says that none of the altar furniture (cross, candlesticks, altar book and alms dish) was damaged or even knocked from the altar. However, it does note that the alms dish 'was slightly dented'.

George Laity, a lieutenant in the RNVR (Royal Naval Volunteer Reserve) and a duty officer at Queen Anne's Mansions (home to the Medical Department of the Royal Navy) that morning, helped with the rescue effort:

> One of the doctors told me how he was amazed at how lifelike the dead Guards' bandsmen looked. They were playing in the gallery around the side of the Chapel, where the blast had probably killed them by bursting their lungs, but they were in their original positions, holding their instruments, in natural colour as if made of wax.

Two ATS girls had witnessed the flying bomb coming over. They were on the top floor of a building near Buckingham Palace and were on catering duties. They heard the bomb approaching, and immediately set off down the external staircase towards the ground. When they were part-way down, the flying bomb exploded. All they could do was cling together, screaming, as they waited to discover whether their building would collapse. They survived, but the horror of that day was still vividly remembered by the woman who told me about it at the memorial service in 2014. (She was a friend of Valerian Peacock, also ATS, who died in the incident.)

Dr R.V. Jones had been close by when the bomb exploded. He hurried to see what had happened, but by the time he arrived the rescue work was already underway, and he realised there was little he could do. The first bodies were being carried out. He remarked upon the unusual appearance of Birdcage Walk; the road surface had disappeared, buried beneath a sea of fresh plane leaves stripped from the trees by the blast. The smell of fresh sap was very strong and would later be described as one of the distinctive and unusual features of V1 attacks.

David Gurney noted that once a couple of small holes had been made in the walls, and one of the doors had been cleared, a number of people were brought out alive; he estimated there were about 40. He mentioned that the bishop of Maidstone, who had been waiting to preach, was able to walk out over the rubble. A number of men in the choir also escaped with their lives; one of these was Keith Lewis, although he was not rescued for some hours. The chapel keeper and his orderly both emerged safely from the vestry, where they had gone to deal with a ringing telephone just before the V1 exploded.

The chaplain to the Forces, Leslie Owen (1886–1947), who had been appointed bishop of Maidstone earlier that year, had been invited to preach the sermon at the morning service; he was one of the very few left apparently uninjured. He was waiting to preach, and had been sitting in a throne-like seat in the sanctuary, near the altar; this was out of the way of the blast. He escaped with a slight scratch and, although very shaken, was able to make his way over the debris to the vestry. Bravely, he then threw off his cope and assisted in the rescue work. Once more workers arrived, he was advised to go home. He later collapsed from shock and was confined to bed for several days.

William Sansom described the immediate aftermath of the incident from the viewpoint of the rescue services:

> To a first aid party that soon arrived the scene in its subsiding dust looked vast and boxlike, impenetrable: sloping masses of the grey walls and roof shut in the wounded; the doors were blocked, the roof crammed down; it was difficult to find any entrance: but there was one – behind the altar … Doctors and nurses … scramble[d] up and down … in between the large intractable slopes and walls of chunked concrete … [There was] lung-choking dust [and] material had to be man-handled off casualties. While doctors were plugging morphia and nurses and first aid personnel were feeding bicarbonate solution and wrapping on … dressings, all rescue services together with soldiers from the barracks began prising up the debris-blocks and carrying out those freed.

The chief warden of Westminster was swiftly on the scene; he had been nearby, attending the earlier Rutherford Street incident. He described what he saw and how he set in motion the rescue effort:

> The whole floor was covered by debris, which blocked the portico entrance; on both sides the debris rose to 10ft, lessening in the centre. Apart from some movement at the east (altar) end there was a ghostly stillness over the whole scene. I appreciated at once that the incident was a rescue job from first to last. Doubling the length of the barrack square to the officers' mess, I spoke over the telephone to the Deputy Heavy Rescue Officer at Control, gave him a word picture of the scene and suggested Heavy and Light Rescue parties, mobile cranes and ambulances. Two senior Rescue Officers with parties, ambulance and cranes were quickly on the scene and rescue operations then put in hand continued without a break for 48 hours.

William Sansom noted the extra help available at the scene from the military:

> At that time the King's Guard had just dismounted and were waiting for dismissal in the Barrack Square. There were thus extra hands on the spot, and a regular military liaison was set up in conjunction with other

services. Outside in Birdcage Walk a Mobile Aid Unit had driven up. Nurses also dealt with the wounded in an undemolished room at the end of the chapel. An Incident Inquiry Point again dealt with the many enquiries that resulted from this catastrophe, of such large scale and involving so many prominent personages. Finally, notwithstanding its large amount, the debris was all removed and the last body recovered within 48 hours.

(It was in fact somewhat longer; the last bodies were not removed from the scene until late on Tuesday, 20 June, and the incident was not closed until 23.35 the following day.)

By this point in the war, the rescue services had clearly defined roles. (These will be described in more detail in the next chapter.) To summarise, the initial and vital role was that of the Heavy Rescue Service. They had the crucial task of extricating the casualties from the rubble, removing the chunks of concrete piece by piece, using cranes and other machinery, such as Kango hammers for breaking up concrete, while listening all the while to locate those buried and then dig them out. Their work continued day and night until all the casualties were located and removed. The Light Rescue Service then acted as stretcher-bearers, removing the freed casualties and carrying them out to the waiting ambulances. Those injured would then be removed to hospital as soon as possible by the ambulance service. The Mobile Aid Unit might stand by for many hours while casualties were extricated; they could then provide enough medical help to enable the patient to be fit enough to withstand the journey to hospital. The WVS (Women's Voluntary Services) set up an Incident Inquiry Point; this handled enquiries about people who were missing and coordinated details of the victims from the hospital and mortuary lists.

The official rescue effort began almost immediately, within minutes of the explosion. David Gurney reported:

> When I had seen that the work of rescue was in train, the heavy rescue parties were on the scene in eight minutes – and the other ambulances and appliances soon afterwards – almost filling the square. I went to the orderly room where John [Quilter] was busy trying to find out which officers were in Chapel. In a very short time he had a provisional list ... Major Tom Forde (CG) took command of the operations, and all the other officers began to work in the choking dust.

He went on to list some of the military dead:

> The Commanding Officer [Lord Edward Hay] was reading the lesson when the bomb fell and he was killed instantly by a large block of stone. The other officers killed were Lt Col. Ivan Cobbold (SG) Major Dickie

Thornton (GG), Major John Gilliat (IG), Major Windram (Director of Music Coldstream Guards), Capt Kemp Welch (GG), Lieut. Harold Dods (Assistant Regimental Adjutant – SG) and Michael Mitchell (ARS CG) who was killed with his mother and sister, also 2nd Lt James Duberly (SG). Harold's married sister Mrs Crampton had arranged to go to Chapel with Harold but her train was half an hour late. The Chaplain [Rev. Ralph Whitrow] was killed, with two Canadian officers [Major Clarence Baker and Captain John Gall], one ATS officer (Subaltern Gidley Kitchin – with her mother), an American soldier [Colonel Gustav Guenther], two Wrens [Joan Duncan and Edith Farmer] and one or two ATS auxiliaries [Private Kathleen Jackson, Valerian Peacock and Phyllis Potter]. About 40 Guardsmen lost their lives, chiefly Grenadiers and Coldstreamers. [The number was actually 50: 24 Coldstreamers, 15 Grenadiers, 4 Irish, 5 Scots and 2 Welsh Guards.]

The initial incident report at 11.32am spoke of 'free and trapped casualties' at the Chapel. At that time both Keith Lewis and Elisabeth Sheppard-Jones were trapped in the wreckage. Elisabeth, who had been towards the back of the Chapel, later wrote: 'I was scarcely aware of the chunks of massed grey concrete that had piled on top of me, nor did I realise that this was why breathing was so difficult. My whole being was concentrated in the one tremendous effort of taking in long struggling breaths and then letting them struggle out again'. At that point she did not know that her childhood friend, Pauline Gye, who had accompanied her to the Chapel, was already dead; Pauline had been killed outright by the same block of stone that had broken Elisabeth's spine. All Elisabeth could do was to wait for help to arrive.

Keith Lewis was some distance away in the choir area:

I found myself tightly rolled up like some hedgehog with my head between my knees. How long I was trapped there under a mountain of rubble I do not know but it was a long time. My immediate problem was breathing. There was obviously a shortage of air but an abundance of dust.

Every Guardsman knows that his belt has to be as tight as possible. Mine was also tight but because of my position it had been forced onto my lower chest. I remember cursing the marmalade I had eaten at breakfast because I imagined that was the cause of the slime in my mouth that was helping to choke me.

The only movement I was able to make was with my hands which were somehow near my face. Such movement was however very restricted but enough to feel the extended hand of my friend on my left. Later I noticed that this hand was not typically warm. One would normally assume that panic would have been the natural state in such a situation, but such was not the case. I was fully conscious and inexplicably calm. So was the Coldstream sergeant on my right. I hope that he too survived.

It would be another three hours before he was rescued.

The flying bomb had also caused a considerable amount of blast damage in the area. There were some casualties at Queen Anne's Mansions, home of the Admiralty Medical Department; some Wrens had been injured. Vandon Street and Vandon Court were damaged; Hettie Neilson and Ada Cattarns, two of the Guards' Chapel victims, had lived there. The Adam and Eve pub and the London Passenger Transport Board building were both damaged. Petty France and Palmer Street were affected, as were the St Ermins Hotel (used for covert operations for SOE, with MI6 two floors above) and Broadway Buildings (headquarters of the Secret Service, where Dr R.V. Jones worked). If the bomb had fallen about a hundred yards to the north or south, the damage to personnel in Downing Street or in the buildings used by a range of military intelligence organisations could have been very significant.

Nearby mansion flat blocks were also affected, including one used by Walter Cronkite (1916–2009). He was a well-known US news correspondent, who had just returned from reporting on the Normandy landings, and was living near the Guards' Chapel. When he heard the approaching noise, he realised this would be his first opportunity to see a V1:

> I threw open the window of my flat living room and leaned out to see what I could see … I could see all the Guardsmen leaning out their windows only a few yards from me watching it approach. Then I saw them duck back into the barracks and at the same instant the motor of the damned thing stopped … I turned and started running like hell for the main corridor of the apartment building.

He heard the tinkle of falling glass. 'I felt like someone had slapped me but hard on the back, and then shoved me but hard on the chest. The front door of the flat to which I was heading instead came over to me'. The flat sustained significant damage and he had to move elsewhere.

Progress of the rescue effort can be traced in the urgent, terse exchanges between the ARP and Westminster Control, some of which are given below.

At 11.32am a Heavy Rescue Party was sent from Dolphin Square depot in Pimlico, as well as two from Kingston House depot in Knightsbridge. (This was to assist with clearing the rubble inside the Chapel and releasing trapped casualties.) At 11.35am ambulances were requested at Queen Anne's Mansions, home of the Admiralty Medical Service; some of the Wrens there had sustained injuries from flying glass. Ten minutes later, a message was sent noting that Palmer Street and Petty France were partially blocked by debris; presumably the rescue services would have to make a detour.

As the Heavy Rescue parties began to clear some of the debris and remove the first casualties, there was a request for six ambulances and three Light Rescue parties to help take the injured to hospital.

A report noted that the Heavy Rescue parties were already on the spot. Four ambulances immediately made their way to the Chapel, arriving at about midday.

At 12.15 there was a request for a mobile crane to help remove some of the rubble.

Meanwhile, during those first few hours, a Coldstream Guards drummer, Harold James Evans, had a miraculous escape, as described in the *Daily Mirror*:

A solitary figure was seen to rise out of the mountain of debris. It was Drummer Evans. Briskly he brushed himself down, straightened his tunic, marched forward and saluted an approaching officer with parade ground precision.

Through the daze in his mind, Drummer Evans heard the officer ask what had happened.

'I had been detailed for the choir this week', he said 'and it was only this that saved me. I was standing at the back of the chapel and most of the debris fell near the entrance.

'I heard the plane come down. I slipped out of my pew and knelt on the ground. Then it landed.

'When I had gathered my senses I was buried face downwards under a pile of debris. At the back pinning down my legs I could feel the body of another guardsman.

'Then I heard the rescuers working overhead, and in twenty minutes I was sitting on top of the debris – and found that I had only a slight cut on the back of my head.

'I certainly could not have been more fortunate.'

His fiancée, Hazel Ord, had been nearby and saw the V1 fall. She knew he was detailed for church parade. She went to the barracks to make enquiries; she was told he was injured and had been taken to hospital, but he did not appear on the hospital list. Fortunately she was soon able to locate him; as he said with commendable understatement, 'it was not hard to see she had never been more pleased to see me before'.

They married on 7 August 1944 in Durham and had four children; Harold, generally known as Jim, lived on until 2005, and was buried in Merrow (St John the Evangelist) Churchyard, Guildford, with his wife who had predeceased him in 1997.

Gradually the news of the incident began to spread. People began to telephone or visit the WVS Incident Inquiry Point to ask for news of their friends and relatives. The military kept a list of those known to have been or believed to have been involved; their record-keeping was meticulous, and they were able to keep a tally of those who had attended in uniform by checking their shoulder flashes. The WVS kept records of the requests for information; some of these related to the military, while others were for relatives or friends of the Guards.

It was less easy to identify the civilian casualties, whether dead or injured. Many were removed from the Chapel unconscious, and all were covered in a coating of thick grey dust, so it was hard to establish such basic details as age or hair colour; many appeared far older because of this. In the chaos after the explosion, women became separated from their handbags, which would have contained their identity cards or discs. Because of clothes rationing, laundry labels and nametapes could no longer be relied upon as conclusive sources of identification, as might have been the case before 1939. When one victim was finally identified, she was found not to be wearing a single item of her own clothing; everything had been borrowed from colleagues. Another victim was wearing a shirt that had laundry marks relating to a previous owner who had died in 1915. It was also hard to know for sure who was missing; the hostel and YWCA supervisors acted in *loco parentis* and were swift to make enquiries, but in other cases, such as Pauline Gye, non-appearance at work the next day did not automatically cause concern. It was only once Elisabeth Sheppard-Jones regained consciousness in hospital that she was able to raise the alert for her friend. In one case, a Guards' Chapel victim was never formally identified; she remains anonymous to this day.

Towards lunchtime, Patricia Clewett, a nurse at St George's Hospital, had the first intimation that a serious incident had occurred. She had heard the earlier V1 explosion, but nobody was sure of the point of impact. Before long many ambulances began to arrive, but as she and her colleagues were working, they accepted it as 'just another hit'. At about midday she was asked to help on another ward as they were very busy. It was then that she realised most of the emergency admissions were very badly wounded Guardsmen from the Chapel. As soon as she could be spared she went round the wards to see if her friends had been brought in. Mary was in a ward upstairs; she had been knocked unconscious by falling masonry, was still very confused and had been badly cut about the head, but she was alive. Anne had escaped without significant injury. She told Patricia that Beryl had last been seen on a stretcher, where she was being given an injection. Anne had lost sight of her in the confusion after the bomb exploded.

Elisabeth Sheppard-Jones was still buried in the rubble of the Chapel:

> I was suddenly aware that somewhere far above me, above the black emptiness, there were people, living helpful people whose voices reached

me, dim and disembodied as in a dream. 'Please, please, I'm here', I said, and I went on saying it until my voice was hoarse and my throat ached with the dust that poured down it ... Someone frantically scraped away the rubble from around my head ... Somewhere not far from me someone was screaming, screaming, screaming, like an animal caught in a trap – and with the pain of that dreadful sound ringing in my ears came realisation of the awfulness of what had happened. I could not fully take in the scene of desolation around me, but my eyes rested in horror on a bloodstained body that, had my hands been free, I could have reached out and touched. It was the body of a young Canadian soldier whose eyes stared unseeingly at the sky ... I tried to convince myself that this was truly a nightmare, one from which I was bound soon to wake up. I think I must have been given a morphia injection for I still felt no pain, but I did begin to have an inkling that I was badly injured. I turned my freed head towards a Guardsman who was helping with the rescue work and hysterically I cried out 'How do I look? Tell me how I look!' The Guardsman's response was made with that traditional diplomacy for which the Brigade is famous ... 'Madam', he said, 'you look wonderful to me!'

Elisabeth was taken to the casualty department of St Mary's Hospital, Paddington; as an officer, she was then moved to a private room in the Lindo Wing. The casualty list described her as dangerously ill; her spine was fractured and her spinal cord damaged. She would never walk again.

At 12.30pm the first brief summary of the incident was issued:

400–500 casualties. Already on spot: 6 ambulances, NFS [National Fire Service], Military, 6 LRP [Light Rescue Parties], Police, 2 HRP [Heavy Rescue Parties], mobile crane. Some slight casualties at Queen Anne's Mansions where Admiralty Services are in charge.

The casualty numbers were eventually found to be an overestimate, but the fact that such a large number was given provides some indication of the scale of damage involved.

A few minutes later there was a further request for Light Rescue parties; another three were required. Their role was to act as stretcher-bearers; those extricated from the rubble by the Heavy Rescue parties were then removed by stretcher to the ambulances parked on the square, where the casualties' condition would be stabilised before they were despatched to hospital.

The damage report just before 1.00pm from Westminster to Group One gave more detail:

Direct hit on Guards Chapel. Widespread blast damage including superficial damage to Broadway Buildings, 13 Cartaret Street and Queen

Anne's Mansions (Admiralty). Casualties 400/500, including some trapped.

The first intimation of the appallingly heavy death toll came a few minutes later, at 1.20pm, when there was a request to send more shrouds, along with a Light Rescue party from Berkeley Square to take on the shrouding duties. Many blankets were also required.

Lunch was served as usual in the Officers' Mess, at the other end of the square from the Chapel. The atmosphere was very subdued. People were constantly looking to see who was coming in. One man who had missed the service because of an unexpected duty waited in vain for his friend; they normally sat together in the Chapel. 'Had he been there? He had'.

Sunday afternoon

The news quickly spread. The prime minister was working, but his wife Clementine had been to visit their daughter Mary, who was serving in the ATS with an anti-aircraft battery in Hyde Park. She returned and told him 'The Guards Chapel is destroyed'. Churchill promptly gave orders that the Commons should move back to Church House (a modern steel structure) for more protection. Later that evening he visited the Chapel site and was moved to tears by the scale of the devastation.

Greville Gidley-Kitchin was serving in the Grenadier Guards; he was camped at Charing in Kent with his battalion and all their Churchill tanks and was shortly to embark for France. He had tried to telephone his mother, whom he knew was staying in London on that Sunday, but failed to get a proper reply. He heard talk from the other officers in the 4th Battalion of a bomb having been dropped on the Guards' Chapel. He later found out that his mother and sister Rosemary had been among those killed; ironically, they had probably gone to the Chapel to pray for his safety. He went up to London by train and helped his father with the various arrangements that had to be made, including identifying the bodies. There was a funeral at St Marylebone Church on 24 June followed by a burial service later that same day at Ewshot, in Hampshire.

Hettie Ruthin Neilson had left her daughter's home in Northwood the day before to attend the Guards' service, because in doing so she felt near to her son, Andrew, who was fighting in Italy with the Scots Guards. She was planning to go to Beaconsfield for lunch with her other daughter, Mary, but had telephoned just before she went to the Chapel to say she might be late. When she did not arrive her son-in-law, John Elston, travelled immediately to London. Hettie's daughter, Margaret, and her husband, John Curtis, left Northwood for London in the early afternoon, after hearing the news of the flying bomb. John Curtis identified his mother-in-law's body the next day.

Dorothy Allfrey was due to have lunch with a friend in Lowndes Square; when she didn't appear, Mrs Bradshaw contacted the WVS Incident Inquiry Point. Miss Rendall, a neighbour, also asked after her and gave a description.

Mary Sargent normally went to the YWCA on Earls Court Road for lunch after the service; when she did not appear, a friend contacted the Incident Inquiry Point to say that she had been heard in her flat that morning, and normally sat just inside the Chapel by a pillar. Both she and Dorothy Allfrey were killed by flying masonry.

When my mother's friends had not returned for lunch, Lucy Lane, the YWCA warden at Penywern Road, lodged an enquiry with the IIP about them. Ellen Norris, her cousin Beatrice Gardner and Marjorie Souter were missing, along with Barbara Howard, another resident, and Jessie Souter, Marjorie's younger sister. The following day Miss Lane learned that Barbara and Jessie were in hospital, one at Brompton and one at Westminster. The other three, as my mother said, 'never came back'.

By 2.00pm there were eight ambulances in the square: two from Paddington, two from Hammersmith, two from St Marylebone and two from Dolphin Square depot. This gives an idea of the demands large incidents made on the resources available. Meanwhile, the military were updating their records, as were the WVS. The Metropolitan Police maintained air raid casualty lists, arranged by date and hospital or mortuary. The hospital lists gave casualty names and addresses, where known. The mortuary records provided brief details to assist in identification of the casualties.

As the day moved into early afternoon, Keith Lewis was struggling to survive in the choking dust:

> At some later point it was clear to me that my time was limited. I could feel myself becoming weaker, mostly I thought through my failing ability to breathe. Although I was unaware of it at the time, I had also lost a lot of blood as a result of a serious head injury. I remember telling myself that it wasn't so bad – I had had a good life (at the age of 18!), but I was sorry that I hadn't written home often enough and that my mother would grieve at my going and that bothered me.
>
> When I had reached the stage where I was convinced that I wouldn't last a further five minutes I heard faint shouts and movements above me and the next thing I remember was being free to the waist and gulping air and noticing how those wonderful civilian rescue people tore at the stones with their bare hands. Then the greatest physical pain I have ever experienced, before or since, took charge of my body. Through the mist I remember my shoulder being dusted off and someone saying 'he's a Grenadier', then finding myself on a stretcher with the corporal in waiting asking for my name and number. In my state to me this was a

tortuous unnecessary extension of my pain, but in reality it was good logic and Guards discipline.

Keith Lewis was extracted from the rubble at about 2.30pm, more than three hours after the explosion. His ordeal was not yet over:

Then I was in an ambulance on Birdcage Walk, but still waiting. The ambulance was able to take six stretchers but I was only the second to be put on board. The ambulance would not leave until it was full and my pain was becoming more and more unbearable. [He was taken to hospital at about 2.40pm.]

I was still unaware of any injuries except that I noticed a flap of skin on my forefinger and thought 'they'll see this and just rip it off and it'll hurt.'

My next memory was being taken down a slipway somewhere at St Thomas Hospital. Then my hair was being snipped off as I was put out by an injection.

Keith Lewis had been in the choir; some of them were seated towards the apse and escaped the worst of the blast. The Coldstream Guards Band and their director of music were less fortunate, however; they were playing up above the congregation on a balcony. This collapsed as a result of the explosion and caused multiple casualties. Five of the musicians were killed outright by the blast; another fourteen were taken to hospital, seriously injured. Major Windram died in St George's Hospital soon afterwards; he had been suffering from angina and other heart problems for some time, and had sustained a serious leg injury in the Chapel. He died on the operating table as they were about to amputate his leg.

His wife Olive had attended the service that morning, to see her husband conduct the band. She was trapped in the wreckage until 2.30pm; she was then removed unconscious to St George's Hospital. She had sustained head injuries and it took her some months to recover. She was still seriously ill in hospital a week after the incident, and was unable to attend her husband's funeral on 26 June.

While locating and extricating casualties was the priority for the rescue services, there were other objects to be rescued. Bryan Jones wrote: 'My father Coldstream Guardsman William Trevor Jones was one of the soldiers that arrived shortly after the impact and apart from helping the injured and trapped people was one of the soldiers that rescued the colours from the chapel carnage.'

At 2.45pm there was a message from Cannon Row Police Station about a barrow load of metal sheeting from the V1; it was at the police station. The sheets had been removed to 'prevent unauthorised looting'; please could someone collect them?

Two further Heavy Rescue parties arrived soon afterwards, closely followed by four Light Rescue parties. At this stage, the nearest hospitals (St George's, Westminster and St Thomas') were starting to be overwhelmed by the increasing influx of seriously injured casualties requiring urgent medical treatment; there was a request for all further casualties to be sent to Brompton Hospital. The death toll continued to rise. News began to come in that some of those taken to hospital that morning had died of their injuries.

As the afternoon wore on, more and more enquiries were received by the WVS. Mrs Dorothea Sealy asked about Mrs Violet Wilson (her mother), who would have attended the service with Mrs Thorn; both died at the Chapel, along with Mrs Thorn's son, back from service abroad in the Royal Engineers, and his wife who was a section officer in the WAAF.

Sir Thomas Lumley-Smith asked about his wife, daughter and sister, Mrs Keane; all of them were known to attend the Chapel. All three died.

Colonel James Attenborough made enquiries about his wife, Phyllis; he discovered her handbag had been found in the Chapel. She was found semi-conscious with multiple injuries at 3.15pm; she was taken to Brompton Hospital at 3.50pm once her condition had been stabilised. (She lived on until 1990.)

That afternoon, Colonel George Tyrie Brand Wilson contacted the IIP about his wife, Adelaide. She was originally thought to be a casualty in hospital. She had attended church with Isabelle Dewar-Durie, a friend; both died at the Chapel.

Wounded Guardsmen continued to be rescued throughout the afternoon. Two musicians were taken to hospital at 3.40pm.

As the news spread, more and more enquiries came through. Agnes Moscrop was attending a Morse training course in London, along with Ida Thomson. The warden of Agnes's hostel was swift to ask about her once she realised Agnes had gone to the Chapel and not returned. Sadly both girls had died at the Chapel.

Two hospitals asked after their nurses: Peggy Arnold from Westminster and Beryl Clark from St George's. Two ATS girls, Valerian Peacock and Kathleen Jackson, were known to have attended the service; their Signals section at Catherine Place made enquiries. Two of the Millen sisters had gone to the Chapel that morning; their sisters made enquiries about them later that day, all to no avail. All six of them had died.

Gwen Horton's husband, Gray, telephoned from RAF Uxbridge; he was a lieutenant colonel in the Scots Guards, commanding RAF Regiment No. 85 as part of the Allied Expeditionary Air Force. Gwen had been staying at Claridges on Saturday, 17 June, possibly so that she could attend the service on his behalf. He described her as wearing a black coat with an unusual Scots Guards star in white gold with diamonds, by Cartier. He found out later that evening that she had died in the Chapel: the same Chapel where they married fourteen years before, and where both their children had been christened.

At 3.15pm, Chief Commissioner Ferguson of Alexander House asked about two ATS officers, Miss Hunt and Miss Gidley-Kitchin, who were known to have left for Chapel with Mrs Gidley-Kitchin. Only Miss Hunt survived; she was taken to St Thomas' Hospital suffering from shock.

At 3.00pm Major Paul Hitler, deputy provost marshal in charge of US military personnel, made enquiries about Colonel Gustav Guenther. (Major Hitler was to change his surname to Harrison in 1945, for understandable reasons.) Colonel Guenther was an American Army colonel and a friend of General Eisenhower. He had previously worked in special operations in Cairo and been chief of Special Operations Branch in London, before joining the US Army's psychological warfare branch there, where he was the public relations chief. He died at the Guards' Chapel that day.

A colleague from the Australian Embassy made enquiries about Arthur Berry, a member of an Australian trade delegation. Mr Berry was another casualty.

Two young Free French soldiers also attended the service. Pierre Gras and Martin Bacchiolelli were removed alive from the rubble and taken to St George's Hospital, where they succumbed to their injuries later that day. Two Canadian soldiers, Major Baker and Captain Gall, also died, as did an Australian padre serving with the RAAF, Squadron Leader Wood; he had been due to fly home the following day.

'Every top civil servant or society hostess knew someone in the Brigade who might have been at Wellington Barracks that morning,' wrote Jane Gordon, wife of the writer Charles Graves. 'All day, we kept hearing of more people we knew who had been killed.' One of her best friends, Rosemary, was married to a young Guardsman, Dick Thornton, and the four of them regularly played bridge together. That afternoon Rosemary called her, distraught, to say that Dick had gone to the Chapel for morning service and not returned; could Charles please make some enquiries? Jane and Charles both went to Wellington Barracks; Charles spoke to the orderly who said he 'knew just where Dick would have been sitting, as he always sat in the same place ... and it would be some hours yet before they could hope to rescue him'. Over the next couple of days, Jane, who was a children's nurse, was caring for the daughter of one of the Heavy Rescue workers; he told her about the rescue effort in graphic and distressing detail. Dick's dead body was not recovered until Tuesday night, one of the last to be brought from the rubble.

David Gurney continued his account:

I remained in the Orderly room all the afternoon answering the constant summons of the telephone, this continued all the evening as well when more and more people began to hear of the disaster. The private secretary of the Minister of War telephoned for inquiries. The Air Minister [Sir Archibald Sinclair] also made enquiries about his son Angus who was at a Church of Scotland service at the time and who worked at rescue [in the Chapel] all the afternoon. The Major General commanding London District (Sir Charles Loyd) came with the Brigade Major (Col. Tim Nugent).

At 4.38pm a mobile canteen was requested. The next report to Westminster Control, at 5.20pm, stated: 'Sit[uation] well in hand. Civilian casualties to date: 6 injured, 21 dead. Work still proceeding.'

Sunday evening
Just before 7.00pm, there was a message:

NFS [National Fire Service] will send complete emergency tender with cluster of lights to report to Capt. Rogers RE WB [Royal Engineers Wellington Barracks] at 22.30 hours. Apparatus is similar to that recently sent to St Pancras and generates own power.

This meant that the rescue effort could continue all through the night. (Wartime use of double summer time meant that sunset would not be until about 22.20.)

Shortly afterwards, it was noted that there were 11 civilian war dead for removal to Glasgow Terrace (the City of Westminster mortuary), and a mortuary van was requested; they were removed the following morning.

Just before 7.25pm, there was a message stating that the Incident Inquiry Point would be wanted at 8.30am on Monday, 19 June. Meanwhile, the work continued in the Chapel. Three Heavy Rescue parties and one supervisor would be working from 9.35pm until 12.00am. At midnight, three new Heavy Rescue parties would come to relieve them. A supervisor from the Adelphi would relieve the supervisor from Rutherford Street.

A further incident report at the end of the day summarised the situation to date. So far, 94 people had been known to be killed: 53 military, 41 civilian. Of those trapped, 104 had been released and about 50 remained trapped.

Sunday night
David Gurney's description is as vivid as a nightmare:

When night fell, lamps were strung across the Chapel and the work continued all night. From Queen Anne's Mansions (which were only superficially damaged) the place looked like a film set – of a rather ghastly kind as bodies were being brought out all the time as the rubble was cleared from the floor.

The men worked in four hour shifts, each shift under the command of an officer and I was told that the early morning shifts, with the flying bombs flying overhead and bodies being dug out were almost unbelievably nerve racking. The Prime Minister and Air Marshal Tedder visited the ruins on Sunday evening. The whole Battalion slept underground and I slept in the basement of the Officers' Mess though continually being woken by people making enquiries about casualties.

The news of the incident spread. James Lees-Milne heard about it from a friend at his club, and after dinner they went over to survey the scene. Crowds of people were looking at the Chapel, across Birdcage Walk, which was roped off. The Chapel had no roof at all. As they watched, a body was carried out on a stretcher, just as the air raid siren went and everyone scattered. 'I felt suddenly sick. Then a rage of fury welled inside me. For sheer damnable devilry what could be worse than this awful instrument?'

Monday morning, 19 June, 1944

The work went on all night, and at 8.30am on Monday, 19 June, the WVS Incident Inquiry point reopened for business. If anything, there were even more enquiries about missing relatives and friends that day. People had not turned up at their place of work, family members had not returned home, friends had failed to appear as expected; all of this was out of character and required action to be taken. Contacting the Incident Inquiry Point would be the first step.

An hour earlier, five Heavy Rescue parties had already made their way to Wellington Barracks, to continue with the work of clearing the chaos in the Chapel and removing casualties from the rubble. They continued to work in shifts and were prepared for at least another 24 hours of work. At just after 9.00am, the 11 civilian dead were removed to Glasgow Terrace mortuary.

At 9.30, the Incident Inquiry Point was trying to establish an authoritative list of casualties, but the casualty lists were coming through very slowly. The military casualty list was being built up in the orderly room at Wellington Barracks. One of the problems was the piecemeal nature of the information. Although the IIP tried to maintain accurate records, the scale of the operation meant that inevitably there were some discrepancies, either in stating which hospital had received which casualty, or in knowing whether a casualty was alive or dead. There were police lists of those in hospital and descriptions of those received at the mortuary; these bulletins were issued at regular intervals by Cannon Row Police Station. At least five hospitals were involved initially, with some of their patients later dispersed to hospitals outside London for safety, once they had been assessed at the main inner London hospitals; some of the musicians were sent to Slough, and Mrs Windram was eventually moved to Windsor.

The approximate casualty list at 9.30am on Monday was 53 military dead and 41 civilians, a total of 94; 50 military personnel had been seriously injured, along with 10 civilians, a total of 60. That made a grand total of 154 casualties, but rescue work was still in progress.

An article appeared in *The Times* that day:

> The morning service had just begun in a Southern England church yesterday when a flying bomb crashed through the roof, demolishing the building except for the east wall where the altar stood undamaged. A number of worshippers were killed, but the clergyman who was to have preached and was standing in the sanctuary was unhurt.

The full story would not be published until 9 July, when censorship was relaxed.

There was another situation report at 10.16am. This stated that the total number of persons involved was 200, with about 50 per cent of those being civilians. Some 150 persons had been removed from the Chapel: 90 were dead, and the remaining 60 had been taken to hospital. The rescue work was going ahead steadily. The services on the spot at Wellington Barracks included six Heavy Rescue parties removing the rubble, five Light Rescue parties carrying out the casualties, two ambulances to take the injured to hospital, and two mobile cranes to assist with the heavy lifting and clearing.

The work of the IIP continued. People who had made initial enquiries on the Sunday returned with more detailed information, while others had begun to realise that their friend or family member had not been heard from since that fateful Sunday morning. Mrs Worrall had been seen on her way to church; Bryn Davies and Mabel Maultby both normally attended chapel. Clara Deadfield's brother made enquires about her, and Ada Cattarns' sister did the same. Kay Garland's brother asked after her; she had changed shift at the Ministry of Information so that she could attend the service. Lucy Lane, warden at the YWCA, Penywern Road, asked again after Beatrice, Ellen and Marjorie. Sarah Courtney, mother of the Coldstream Guards' sergeant major, was missing. Colonel Astill of the Grenadier Guards made enquiries about Olive Penn, sister of their regimental adjutant, Arthur Penn. Even David Gurney had an enquiry to make; Lady Gordon-Lennox normally attended church and her niece was asking after her. Lady Evelyn Gordon-Lennox was the widow of a Grenadier Guardsman, Lord Bernard Gordon-Lennox, who was killed in action in 1914, and her son George was the commanding officer of the 5th Battalion of the Grenadier Guards. All of those named here as missing proved to be among the dead, and the process of formal identification began.

Beryl Clark, a nurse from St George's Hospital, was still missing. Matron Helen Hanks asked Beryl's friend, Patricia Clewett, to go with another nurse to look for her. They took a taxi to Scotland Yard, but could not find her name on the lists of victims held there. Allegedly, if she had been taken to any of the London hospitals, Matron Hanks would have been informed. Had they tried the mortuary at Glasgow Terrace? The two nurses were appalled, but obeyed. At the mortuary they were each given a large glass of brandy before being taken to view a body. Initially they could not identify her, but as they turned to go they heard an ornament fall to the floor. It was the small tortoiseshell clip that Beryl used to wear in her hair.

So many relatives and friends would have had to go through the same distressing process, either that day or in the days to come. Once the bodies had been identified, relatives had to register the death with Westminster Council and acquire a death certificate before the funeral could be planned. Cause of death was simply given as 'by enemy action', with no need for a post mortem.

The chief of imperial general staff, Sir Alan Brooke, later Lord Alanbrooke, was a friend of Ivan Cobbold, and they would regularly go shooting or fishing together. He recorded in his diary his 'great grief' at Ivan's death; on his desk that Monday morning was a letter from his friend, written on Saturday.

> The death of Ivan Cobbold was a ghastly blow to me. I had grown to know him very well … and had grown very fond of him … When Bryan Boyle was telling me of his death, I was actually picking up Ivan's letter … His invitation to lunch with him that week made a very large lump rise in my throat.

David Gurney continued to liaise with the relatives and friends of those missing. Early on Monday morning, the body of Harold Dods was brought out; he was a fellow lieutenant in the Scots Guards and David had come to know him well. Now he 'had the sad task of ringing up Mrs Crampton to tell her the sad news.' [Mrs Crampton was Harold's sister, and had originally intended to attend the service with him, but her train had been delayed.]

Monday afternoon
Later that day, just before 3.00pm, there was a request from the chief warden for a sprinkler to lay the dust; this was continuing to impede the rescue effort. The National Fire Service sent a pump at once.

The headquarters of both the Coldstream and the Grenadier Guards had to be moved after the incident; they went to Eggington House, 25–28 Buckingham Gate, on Monday, 19 June. Within five days that location was also bombed; the Grenadier Guards HQ stayed on despite this, but the Coldstream HQ moved to 73 Ashley Gardens, Ambrosden Avenue, on 23 June 1944 and stayed there until 17 May 1946.

The V1s continued to come over, day and night. At about 4.00pm on Monday, 19 June, one of them exploded at Bankruptcy Buildings, Carey Street, near Clements Inn. Some of the rescue effort at Wellington Barracks had to be diverted to the area, where 3 people were killed and 12 wounded.

At 4.35pm, the next progress update was issued: 'Casualties to present 46 civilian dead, 53 military dead. Injured 53 including civilian and military. Rescue work proceeding.' Another Heavy Rescue party was ordered from St Marylebone to take over the evening shift.

Monday evening
Another update was given four hours later. There were 87 troops belonging to [Wellington] Barracks in the Chapel and 53 had been recovered dead. Some 49 civilian dead had been recovered. There was 1 more dead 'not known'. A total of 68 wounded had been taken to St George's Hospital; it was known that 1 had died since at 1700 hours. An estimated 15 of the 68 were civilians. 'Post Warden will endeavour to get further analyses and report again, probably not able to get further results till morning.'

The figures continued to vary. At 10.00pm, Cannon Row Police Station estimated the total at 99 dead plus 1, 68 injured. (Injured: military approx. 60, civilians 12–18). A few minutes later, another estimate stated 53 military dead, 47 civilian dead, 81 persons injured (does not include hospital dead).

The rescue effort continued through the night. Just before 1.00am on Tuesday, 20 June, the lights that were needed for rescue work had to be switched off; the current was cut because of an alert. The engineers had put up temporary lights. In the end the civilian rescue services liaised with Wellington Barracks to ensure that the work could continue, alerts permitting; the V1s continued to come over in large numbers.

Tuesday morning, 20 June 1944
By mid-morning, there was another situation report: 106 dead, 53 wounded, with two Light Rescue parties, four Heavy Rescue parties and two mobile cranes on the spot. Work was proceeding satisfactorily. Half an hour later, there was a request for an ambulance; someone had been recovered alive after almost 48 hours. This may relate to the account given in the *Daily Mirror* of 10 July, which spoke of a 'buzz bomb miracle':

> 36 hours after the bomb fell rescue workers freed another Guardsman of infinite discipline. He was still alive though badly injured.
>
> Without help, he stood upright painfully, dazed, and began to march stiffly out of the wreckage. Guardsmen helpers rushed to greet him and shake his hand. Stiffly and wordlessly he shook hands, then marched with dignity to the waiting ambulance. Not until he reached the very door did he finally lose his strength and collapse.

David Gurney's comments may refer to this incident:

> Disturbing rumours circulated to the effect that even 48 hrs after the explosion people were brought out alive. Verisimilitude is given to this idea by the story that a girl of 16 asked for a cigarette as soon as she was brought out. However there is no confirmation of this rumour ... All the military bodies were taken to Chelsea where the contracted undertaker began to place them in coffins on the evening of Monday. I was detailed by the Adjutant to supervise this work.

Just before lunchtime there was a request for a mobile canteen for about 60 people at Wellington Barracks, so that the rescue workers could have refreshments when they had finished working. Several articles remarked on how well the various rescue teams worked together and demonstrated team spirit; a flying column with loudspeakers helped to coordinate the work.

Captain Pearson telephoned Lady Eileen Duberly, Second Lieutenant James Duberly's mother, at midday on 20 June. 'I told her that James was missing as a result of enemy action on Sunday 18th. I said that I could offer no hope of his still being alive.' His body was not found until later that evening.

Tuesday afternoon
Later that afternoon there were two more requests for mortuary vans, one for a military casualty and one for 4 civilians. By now the military dead were starting to be transferred to Chelsea Barracks before the funerals at Brookwood Military Cemetery on Friday, 23 June; as a mark of respect, their coffins would lie in the garrison church overnight beforehand.

The death notices began to appear, in *The Times* and *Telegraph* or in local papers. The wording was deliberately vague: 'recently, by enemy action'. This was to ensure that the Germans could not tell where the V1s had landed or guess the size of the death toll. There was no mention at that point of 18 June or the Guards' Chapel; it would be early July before the incident became common knowledge. As soon as death certificates could be issued, family and friends began to plan the funerals of those who had died. Some wished the victims to be buried in family graves, reunited in death with parents, grandparents and even in some cases their small children who had predeceased them. Others opted for cremation, at Golders Green or elsewhere. Some death notices made specific requests: 'no mourning' or 'no letters'.

Wednesday morning, 21 June 1944
On Wednesday, 21 June the first funeral was held, that of Mrs Mary Sargent at Golders Green Crematorium. The notice in *The Times* asked for 'no mourning, by request'.

Back at the Chapel there was a perhaps belated realisation of the architectural importance of the building. Prior to the V1 attack, it had housed over

2,000 memorial plaques commemorating both battles and the Guardsmen involved, as well as a large number of other items of regimental and architectural interest. The DRO of the Heavy Rescue Service, Westminster, wanted 'to draw attention of all ... supervisors to the necessity for preserving all architectural stonework and inscribed marble from further damage at the Guards' Chapel ... Such articles of value should be referred to the office in charge on the site who will make arrangements to have them stored outside the Guards' Chapel.'

Wednesday afternoon
By late afternoon, the work was drawing to a close. There were still two Heavy Rescue parties and one Light Rescue party on site.

Wednesday night
At 23.35 on Wednesday, three and a half days after the explosion, the incident was declared closed. The total of those who died was thought to be 119, with 64 people injured (the latter number was later corrected to 81).

Thursday, 22 June 1944

On Thursday, 22 June, there was another attempt to agree a casualty figure/ toll between the civilian and the military authorities. The civilian total was as follows. Dead: service (including Wrens, US officers, etc) 59, civilian 59, total 118. Injured and taken to hospital: service 58, civilian 8, total 64. This figure was felt to be probable, but there was the issue 'about the one dead person extra in our [Wellington Barracks] casualty figures'.

This extra person has continued to cause debate for more than seventy years. Later figures have suggested 121 people were killed. I believe 123 people died at the time, in the Chapel or in hospital; Guardsman Gibson was missing from the original typed list of 121 names I was given by the Chapel, and there was also a woman who died at the Guards' Chapel and was buried in Westminster City Cemetery on 29 June who remains unidentified. The final victim was Musician Jock Hart, who died of his injuries the following April. The total then becomes 124: 65 military dead and 59 civilians.

There may even be another victim, Evelyn (or Barbara) Baildon Hole, who died in Westminster Hospital on 19 June; she appears on one handwritten Guards' Chapel list with two other known civilian casualties from the incident, but I have been unable to find conclusive proof that she sustained her injuries there. She is listed on the CWGC record of Westminster civilian dead, but their record does not state where she was injured. I am therefore omitting her from the list of known victims.

There were a few more funerals at Golders Green on Thursday, including those of Lady Evelyn Gordon-Lennox, Violet Wilson and George Kemp-

Welch, but the main day for the ceremonies for the Guards' Chapel victims was Friday, 23 June.

Friday, 23 June

The services at Brookwood Military Cemetery were carried out at 2.30pm with all due ceremony; the victims were deemed to have died on active service. Their relatives were conveyed there by special train. The thirteen CWGC headstones for the Guardsmen and Private Phyllis Potter lie in two rows near the entrance to the cemetery. The two Canadian servicemen were buried that day in the Canadian section of the cemetery, and the Reverend Wood was buried in the Australian military section. Martin Bacchiolelli is in the French section.

Many other funerals took place on 23 June, including that of the two Wrens who were close friends, Joan Duncan and Edith Farmer; they were buried together at Romford. Elizabeth Thorn and her younger son were cremated at Golders Green. The Reverend Ralph Whitrow was given a requiem in Winchester Cathedral, where he had been an honorary canon, and then a funeral service at St Paul's Church, Weeke, where he had formerly been rector. Lieutenant Harold Dods was buried at Donington; his family gave three maple trees to the Guards' Chapel garden in his memory.

Saturday, 24 June

There were further funerals on Saturday, 24 June, but by the end of the weekend memorial services were starting to be arranged for some of the more prominent members of the Guards' Chapel congregation.

Monday, 26 June

A memorial service was held in the King's Chapel of the Savoy for Lady Gwendolen Lumley-Smith and her daughter Moya.

Tuesday, 27 June

A service for Mrs Lumley Keane, Gwendolen's sister-in-law, who had attended the Chapel service with them, was held at St Michael's, Chester Square.

The Westminster City Cemetery funerals were organised by Westminster Council for those who did not have close friends or family nearby to arrange the funerals. They were held at Westminster City (now Hanwell) Cemetery from 27–29 June. The services were dignified; each had a minister provided whose religion matched that of the victim, coaches were laid on to take friends and family to the cemetery, and the coffins were covered by union flags. Later the names of the victims were inscribed on the Second World War civilian war memorial in the centre of the cemetery.

Friday, 30 June

Memorial services were held for George Kemp-Welch and Ivan Cobbold. Sir Alan Brooke attended the latter; 'I do not remember going to a memorial service that upset me more. I miss him most awfully'.

The Guards' Chapel incident was just one of the many V1 attacks that summer. Without the prompt assistance of the rescue services, many more people would have died. The next chapter deals in more detail with the role of all those who came to deal with the aftermath.

Chapter 4

The Rescue Process

Who Did What

This section on the rescue services gives specific details of how the process operated in the City of Westminster. However, the general outline of services in wartime Britain also applies to other London boroughs, as well as elsewhere in the UK.

The basic civil defence hierarchy was as follows. Once an air raid warning sounded, the local air raid wardens were tasked with ensuring that local residents sought shelter. Once the bombs began to fall, the wardens had to notify the Report and Control Centres of bombs, damage and casualties. This would enable appropriate action to be taken. The Report Centre reported to Group Control, and further resources could be requested if needed. The next level was Regional Headquarters; for London Region, this was located in the Geological Museum in South Kensington. The control room was in a fortified pillbox in the garden of the Natural History Museum, linked to the Geological Museum by an underground passage. This dealt with all the resources in London Region, Region Five (an area roughly equating to London and the Home Counties). The London Civil Defence Region was so massive in area that it was subdivided into nine groups. Group One included the City of Westminster and the boroughs of Fulham, Hammersmith, Chelsea and Kensington. Overall responsibility rested with the Ministry of Home Security, based in the Rotunda near Horseferry Road.

Report Centres

The Westminster Report Centre was in Westminster City Hall. When a wardens' post telephoned its message through to the Report Centre, this went to the basement at City Hall, where there were all the resources required to pinpoint where an incident had occurred. The officer in charge was supported by telephonists, messengers, the city engineer, the medical officer of health, the chief warden (Air Raid Precautions, or ARP), and the various deputies. Thus everyone could be consulted. The idea was to coordinate all messages so that the necessary services could be called out and information could be shared. Communication was essential; there were banks of telephones and messengers to link to the wardens' posts, fire and ambulance services, and the utility services. The borough surveyor had plans showing the exact location of pipes, wires and cables under every road, as well as detailed maps of the area.

In this way, the location of bombs could be notified, and the police could be kept informed of all incidents. Swift decisions could be made. If there were un-exploded bombs, for example, the Royal Engineers' UXB (unexploded bomb) disposal team could be called out to deal with them. The City of Westminster Archives Centre holds a detailed set of forms relating to many of these incidents; these demonstrate the complexity and frequency of the messages involved, giving regular updates on a situation and recording the resources on site to deal with it. There could be as many as 400 messages an hour at busy times.

Rescue services in Westminster: a general outline

The area covered was the whole of the City of Westminster: going east as far as Temple and Fetter Lane, north to Oxford Street, west to Kensington, and south as far as the Thames, all the way from Chelsea Bridge to Temple Pier.

Westminster had four large depots where First Aid parties, Heavy Rescue parties and ambulances were co-located, along with some mobile canteens run by the WVS (the Women's Voluntary Services). These were in the huge underground garages and basements of: Kingston House, Dolphin Square, Berkeley Square House (not far from the Royal Academy and Green Park) and the flats of the Adelphi (the Art Deco buildings dating from the 1930s near the Strand). At Berkeley Square there could be up to 230 staff present at any one time; this could include Heavy Rescue, Light Rescue, ambulance staff and the WVS. There was a canteen and dormitories, so that people could be fed after they finished their shifts and could sleep over in readiness for an alert.

The Heavy Rescue Service

This was organised by the London County Council and directed by West-minster Control. It was a new service that had not existed before the war; until then there had been no need for it. It was staffed by a 'buccaneering blend' of men, often with little formal education but dogged and determined to succeed in their task; this was 'rescuing people who were slowly dying and whose lives depended on the … action of the Heavy Rescue Team'. These men, with lorries and digging equipment, extricated casualties from the rubble. This work was the priority; once the casualties were rescued, the Light Rescue Service (stretcher-bearers) could take over and set about organising the next stage in the rescue process, normally operating a triage system.

The Heavy Rescue teams learned as they went along: how to walk on debris carefully, and above all to listen. There would be a call for silence: everyone would stop talking, vehicle engines would be switched off, and then the rescue caller would call, listening for a faint tapping or a muffled cry from those trapped – then they would know where to direct their efforts. Special equipment was often required: this might include air compressors, Kango hammers to break up concrete, including large concrete slabs, and cranes to lift girders, blocks and other heavy material. They also had heavy timber for shoring up buildings. They would beg or borrow any further items as required; the demands of the rescue took precedence over any paperwork. Teams would work in eight-hour shifts; they would work through the night, using powerful arc lights, racing against time to rescue those trapped.

They were really builders in reverse: they helped stabilise the devastated area to allow the Light Rescue Service safe access to trapped civilians. The Heavy Rescue Service got their name from the equipment they used, heavy winching and lifting gear that was carried round in the back of an old pick-up truck; the Light Rescue Service got their name from the light gear they carried round, ropes and stretchers and first-aid kits.

The men tended to come from the building and engineering industries, as they needed the knowledge and experience to predict how buildings might behave under the erratic strains and stresses that followed bomb damage. Searching meticulously through the debris in search of casualties was a delicate art. They had to know how to cut through debris, so that they could shore up a working space; then, and only then, they could drag out the casualty.

Once the living had been removed, the job of the Heavy Rescue Service was primarily demolition and shoring-up. Buildings had to be made safe, and further collapse had to be averted. There was also the task of removing the dead who had been buried in the rubble. The whole process could take days. In the case of the Guards' Chapel, with the debris up to 10ft deep in places, it was more than 48 hours before the last body could be removed. The incident was not declared closed until just before midnight on Wednesday, 21 June, 84 hours after the explosion.

Light Rescue Service (stretcher-bearers)

These were based at the depot, along with the Heavy Rescue Service and the ambulances; originally they were intended as 'field stretcher parties'. The men wore overalls and steel helmets; the helmets bore the initials LR so that they would easily be identified. They were there to attend the wounded on the spot, to give initial first-aid treatment and to operate a system of triage; they decided which cases needed to go to hospital and then carried these on their stretchers from the ruins to the ambulances that accompanied them. The less seriously wounded would be directed to First Aid posts. The Light Rescue

Service worked in all conditions, including during concentrated bombing raids, through fires and in collapsing buildings, throughout the day and night.

They worked in parties of four men and a driver, using light cars carrying stretchers and first-aid equipment. Often they had to wait till the Heavy Rescue Service had extricated the trapped and injured. Rather than standing by and waiting, they learned how to help the Heavy Rescue teams. Thus they became a Light Rescue Service rather than just a first-aid party.

Usually casualties were treated for shock, then rapidly removed to hospital where they could receive proper medical treatment. If need be, they were sedated or given fluids. It was hard to make an accurate diagnosis so soon after casualties had been removed from the rubble; they would normally be covered in dust and might well be unconscious. The priority was to remove the casualties to a place of safety where they could receive skilled medical attention; the Light Rescue Service formed part of the human chain to achieve this.

Ambulance Service

A fleet of auxiliary ambulances was put together in wartime to supplement the regular ambulance service, using any available vehicle, from converted lorries to small vans. In Westminster, they were housed at the four large depots. They were painted grey, unlike the regular white LCC ambulances; they were often high-powered saloon cars, modified to provide high van-backs to accommodate stretcher rests. The cars were staffed with a driver and attendant, usually female, and went out day and night to collect the wounded. In theory, the task was to drive to the incident and carry the wounded away from it to hospital or a First Aid post. In practice, this might include driving through heavy bombing and waiting out in the open during a raid while the casualties were being extricated.

First Aid posts

These could be either static (fixed) or mobile aid posts, and they dealt with cases that were too severe to be 'patched up' either by wardens or at home, but not grave enough for hospital: the type of case that might be described as 'walking wounded', requiring a doctor. The fixed First Aid posts were at the four Westminster depots and at Westminster Hospital. There were five Heavy Mobile Aid posts in service in the area. Each had a large van and a driver, six auxiliary nurses, three orderlies, one trained nurse and a doctor. Light Units consisted of a car and two Red Cross nurses, one trained nurse and a doctor. These were used mostly at incidents where there was a considerable delay in removing casualties from a damaged building. Otherwise it was often better to send casualties straight to hospital. The Mobile Aid Unit (MAU, also known as HMU for Heavy Mobile Unit) might stand by for many hours while casualties were extricated; they could then provide enough resuscitation to ensure the patient was fit enough to withstand the journey to hospital. There was a Heavy Mobile Aid Unit at the Chapel within minutes of the blast.

The incident doctor provided on-the-spot diagnosis and treatment. Doctors and nurses might have to follow the Heavy Rescue team through tunnels of debris to help the injured or even amputate limbs on the spot in the dust and grime. They had to do what was possible for casualties who were trapped in the debris but otherwise accessible, such as using dressings and morphine. With trapped casualties suffering from dust inhalation, 'rescue workers would try to thread in a rubber tube of drinking water or soda-bicarbonate to ease their discomfort'. Sometimes they were able to provide warm tea from a spouted enamel feeding cup, but usually speed was of the essence: time enough for such refinements when the casualty had been removed from the often dangerously unstable rubble. The First Aid staff wore steel helmets with the initials FAP, so that they could easily be distinguished from other rescue services.

Another task was to organise the despatch of casualties by ambulance, either to hospital or to a nearby fixed First Aid post. Records were kept of casualties sent to First Aid posts, which is how we know that almost forty Guards' Chapel victims were treated there. In contrast, no records were kept of those who left the incident, but were later found to be suffering from delayed shock or injuries that should have been treated at the scene.

Casualties could be taken to the depot and treated on the spot at the fixed First Aid post; this prevented hospitals from having an influx of relatively minor cases. Once they had been treated, these casualties could stay the night in the warm rest room at the depot, rather than being discharged imme-diately. The posts were staffed round the clock on a rota system by a doctor, a trained nurse and first aid workers.

The decision about whether a casualty was alive or dead rested with the doctors and medical personnel, not with rescue workers. The death certificate would be issued by the duty doctor at the incident, or later by the doctor in attendance at the mortuary.

ARP (Air Raid Precautions) wardens

The wardens formed the first line of civil defence. They were responsible for keeping a register of residents in the area. Their first duty was to report air raid damage and assist the rescue and first aid services: to assess the area and the damage after a raid, including the type of bomb, whether there was a fire, the degree of damage to housing, and an estimate of the number and type of casualties. They needed to patrol their post area and know it well, so that they knew who would or should be there; normally the warden's report would be the first to be sent to Control, so s/he needed to be an expert. In the case of the Guards' Chapel, the Westminster chief warden reported the incident himself as he was one of the first on the scene, after attending a nearby incident. The warden would quickly telephone the details through to the borough command centre, who would then forward it to Group Control. Each group would mark it on their wall map, which had information on resources available. The whole process would start almost immediately; the rescue services were at the Chapel within eight minutes.

Westminster was divided into five districts; these were subdivided into twenty-eight posts, which were further divided into 250 sectors. (The Guards' Chapel incident was Post 18, Sector 169). Each post would have a post warden plus a deputy; it would then be split into sections of three to six wardens, plus a senior warden. Most of the ARP wardens' work was done during raids. The ratio of wardens varied; it was usually ten per square mile and one in six wardens was a woman. Both Pauline Gye and Isabelle Dewar-Durie, victims of the Guards' Chapel incident, were air raid wardens; Isabelle served with Post 13 in Eaton Square, and attended the service still wearing her warden's coat.

Other services

The Fire Service was nationalised in the summer of 1941, and was organised by the LCC. Westminster was served by the London Fire Service as a whole. Fire-watchers and fire-guards were a vast army of private and semi-public firefighting citizens. The City was divided into ninety-eight sectors, then sub-divided, and 6,800 fire-watchers per night were trained. They had to be near the building they were watching by dusk. If there was an alert, they had to be up on the roof keeping watch for incendiary bombs. (My parents fire-watched in Bristol as students in the early 1940s.)

The Metropolitan Police also had an auxiliary body of war reserve police, plus part-time special constables. In a raid the police dealt with traffic control, the movement of the public, and the general preservation of order. They also helped out generally and kept watch for looters. There were two main police stations in Westminster: the main police station in Savile Row, and the New Scotland Yard station by the Embankment.

Women's Voluntary Services

The Women's Voluntary Services were set up by Stella, Marchioness of Reading, widow of Lord Rufus Isaacs, in 1938, and provided essential links in Britain's civil defence effort. They were staffed by women who were exempt from conscription, but who volunteered unpaid to give extra help whenever necessary and whenever possible. This was the advantage of the WVS; it allowed women to contribute what hours they could. Their uniform was distinctive: green tweed suits with red piping and matching felt hats, and they had to pay for it themselves. By 1940, one in ten women was a member of the WVS. (Some 241 members of the WVS were killed in action on the home front during the Second World War. Seven of them were killed at the Guards' Chapel; one attended the service in uniform.)

WVS members helped at canteens or clothing stores, British restaurants or hostels. At the start of the war, they provided assistance in evacuating children under 5, people over 65 and expectant mothers. Later, they also came to wash up and cook for the 3,000 builders who volunteered to patch up London during the flying bomb campaign. They also cared for the temporarily home-less, knitted for men in the services, mended socks and even garnished camouflage nets. They helped with evacuees and refugees (such as those from Gibraltar), collected for salvage and organised volunteer car pools. They ran a housewives service to provide local help and support, sharing cooking facilities and providing hot drinks for the ARP wardens and people in shelters. It was a rare opportunity for older women to make a contribution to the war effort, and one they embraced.

The Westminster WVS was run from Gloucester House, Old Park Lane. They staffed six canteens and one mobile kitchen. They also took over the vital enquiry points at large-scale flying bomb incidents in the nearest available premises with a telephone; they ran the Guards' Chapel Incident Inquiry Point from a guardroom in Wellington Barracks. Two or three WVS staff would collate the 'location cards' and liaise with friends and relatives. They would be under the direction of the incident officer, who was in charge of the whole operation. They checked details of enquiries against the names of casualties recovered and would answer queries from anxious relatives confirming whether someone had been sent to hospital or escaped unhurt; sometimes, sadly, they had to take the relatives aside to break the news of a death, or accompany them to the mortuary.

Mortuaries, death certificates and funerals

Glasgow Terrace was the mortuary for the Guards' Chapel incident; the former St Gabriel's Church hall had been taken over for this purpose. Once the bodies were recovered, they were labelled by rescue workers or mortuary workers, ideally with as much detail as possible: name, address, sex, age, place and time of death, time and date of finding the body. They were then despatched to the mortuary by mortuary van.

However, when a body was first brought out of the debris it was often so covered with dust that hair colour and complexion were impossible to identify with certainty; it could be unrecognisable even to close relatives and friends (as in the case of Beryl Clark). Sometimes the person was wearing an ID disc or had placed a slip of paper inside his or her National Registration card, giving the name of a serviceman to contact in the event of injury or death in air raid. (Local authorities had stocks of postcards to send to armed forces personnel to inform them of the death of a relative, and they would normally be granted compassionate leave.) Women were harder to identify than men as they tended to carry everything in a handbag, which would often become separated from them.

At times a degree of detective work was required, using evidence deduced from the body, clothing and possessions, and also from an interview with relatives or friends who had come to look for the missing. The interviewing was done in offices attached to the mortuary. Officers were appointed to trace relatives, and were in immediate liaison with the police. The town clerk was empowered to register deaths; a certificate of death due to war operations was issued. The death was described as 'by enemy action', with no further detail. Special arrangements were made for interment in Westminster City's burial ground at Hanwell; it was the duty of the local authority to bury the victims of air attacks, although in about 75 per cent of cases the relatives opted to bury the victim privately. Westminster Council provided a minister in accordance with the victim's religion, as well as a coffin (draped with the Union flag), a hearse, bearers and a coach for the mourners.

The Metropolitan Police visited all the hospitals and mortuaries to take details of casualties. Lists were issued to all police stations so that relatives who had not had the chance to visit the IIP could ask at the local police station. The information was collated at Scotland Yard by the Casualty Bureau, and official reports were compiled at regular intervals and sent on to Regional HQ.

If a casualty died in hospital, the relatives would be informed by the hospital authorities. If not, it was the duty of the police to inform the next-of-kin as soon as possible. The local authority also had to inform the next-of-kin and to offer a message of sympathy.

By this point in the war, the various organisations involved worked quickly and efficiently to deal with the aftermath of any 'incident'; the previous years had given them considerable experience of these. The demands of V1 attacks, with their potentially heavy death toll and numbers of trapped casualties, were particularly challenging; nevertheless, the rescue services who arrived so promptly on 18 June 1944 worked swiftly and efficiently. Without their sterling work, many more might have died.

Chapter 5

'A Microcosm of Society'

Biographies of the Civilian Victims

The final tally of the casualties was 124 dead and well over 100 injured, many seriously. No fewer than fifty Guardsmen died, including the director of music and six musicians (another twelve were severely injured). There was an assumption that the victims were all from the upper classes, but in reality they came from all walks of life and from a number of countries; they were a microcosm of society. They ranged from a US colonel in Psyops to two young girls attending a telegraphy course, from the 84-year-old mother of a Royal Engineer to a 17-year-old in the Welsh Guards. Whole families were involved: a Guardsman died along with his mother and sister, wives perished while praying for the safe return of their husbands who were on active service, brothers and sisters died together as did parents and children. Their stories are provided here for the first time.

Because of the numbers involved, the biographies of those who died have been split into two chapters. There is also an alphabetical list of names at the end of the book, along with an index. This first chapter contains material about the civilian victims, while Chapter 6 deals with the military casualties. Some military biographies are included in this chapter where family members attended together:

Section Officer Cornelia Despard THORN, WAAF, and **Major Terence Conrad THORN**, MC, Devonshire Regiment, attached Royal Engineers, are listed with Major Thorn's mother.

Second Subaltern Dorothy Rosemary Marian GIDLEY-KITCHIN, ATS, is listed with her mother Dorothy.

Lieutenant Michael Bradstock Alexander MITCHELL, Coldstream Guards, is listed with his mother and sister.

Captain Leslie Edwin Gordon WALL, Grenadier Guards, is listed with his wife, Diana.

Friends

Dorothy Allfrey and Ada Cattarns came to the Chapel together. They were near neighbours; Dorothy lived at Almoners House, St James Court, 45–51 Buckingham Gate, while Ada had a flat in Vandon Court on the same street.

Mrs Dorothy ALLFREY, aged 65, was the daughter of Beville Ramsay (1834–1910) and Sarah Maria Thompson (1839–1923); they married in 1858 in Stratford-upon-Avon. Beville Ramsay was born in Boulogne, France, but was a British subject. In the 1871 census he was the JP for Northamptonshire, and a farmer of 350 acres employing twelve men and with seven servants. By 1881 he was living at Croughton House, Brackley, Northamptonshire. Dorothy was born in 1879, the youngest of eight children. (Her elder brother, Allen Beville Ramsey, (1872–1955), was the former Vice-Chancellor of Cambridge University and Master of Magdalene College, Cambridge.) She married William Shedden Allfrey (1858–1932), a widower, on 18 October 1910 at Brackley; he had three children by his first wife, Ellen Rickman. In the 1911 census, he was described as an 'independent gentleman' and they were living at The Priory, Chacombe, Banbury, with his daughter and niece; they had five servants, which suggests a degree of affluence. (Dorothy's two step-sons were both away at boarding school). He died in October 1932 at Brackley, aged 75. In 1939, she was living in Bournemouth and was described as a widow of private means. On 18 June 1944, Dorothy was due to have lunch with a friend in Belgravia, after she had attended the church service; the friend raised the alarm when she did not appear. Dorothy's funeral was at Golders Green Crematorium on 27 June 1944. She is commemorated on the war memorial in the churchyard of the Church of All Saints, Croughton, and is the only civilian casualty listed for the Second World War.

Miss Ada Ellen CATTARNS, aged 72, was the second daughter of Richard Cattarns (1846–1929), a solicitor and ship owner, and Anna Ellen Pratt; they married in 1868 in Greenwich. Anna died eight years later, in 1876, at the age of 27; Richard married again later that year. He had six children in total. Ada was born on 28 September 1871 in Edmonton, and baptised on 10 January 1872 at St Andrew's, Enfield. Her half-brother, Glanvill Richard Cattarns, Prince of Wales Volunteers (South Lancashire Regiment, 6th Battalion) was wounded in 1915, then killed in action on 12 February 1917 after serving at Gallipoli and in Mesopotamia; he was awarded the MC. Ada became a nurse, as did Catherine, her younger sister, and in the 1901 census was described as a medical nurse working in Lewisham Union Infirmary and living in Enfield. Her interest in nursing and hospital work continued throughout her life; in 1944 she was a member of both the British Red Cross Society and Westminster WVS. At the age of 72, she was head of the WVS Westminster Hospital Supply Depot. Her funeral service was at St Paul's Church, Knightsbridge, on 26 June 1944, followed by interment at Hither Green Cemetery.

Mabel Maultby and Edna Shooter were friends; they were both nurses, and often went to the Chapel together. (Some seats were usually reserved for nurses at Guards' Chapel services.) Edna had long ginger hair, while Mabel had black hair and grey eyes.

Miss Mabel Annie MAULTBY, aged 41, was a member of the British Red Cross Society, and in 1944 she was living in Pimlico, not far from the Guards' Chapel. She was the daughter of Mr and Mrs Sidney Skinner Maultby, of 94 Felhampton Road, New Eltham, Woolwich. Sidney Skinner Maultby (1866–1952) married Mary Jane Turner (1874–1956) on 8 May 1897 in Buenos Aires at St John's Anglican Cathedral; she was his second wife. In the 1911 census he and his family were back in England; by then he had become an assistant inspector of weights and measures and was living in Lewisham, while his wife was a confectioner and tobacconist. They had eight children. Mabel was born in the March quarter of 1903 in Edmonton. In 1919 she became a Post Office telephonist in London. In 1932 she was living with her parents and two of her sisters; at some point she decided to become a nurse, possibly when war broke out. By 1944, she and Edna Shooter were both working as nurses and had become firm friends. (When Mabel's family contacted the Incident Inquiry Point to make enquiries, they asked after both women, as they knew Edna had no family to make enquiries on her behalf.) Sidney Skinner Maultby's first cousin Joseph and his wife Susan were killed by a V2 in Holloway on New Year's Day 1945.

Miss Edna Mary SHOOTER, aged 34, was a nurse, working at King's College Hospital, Denmark Hill, Camberwell. She was the daughter of George William and Olive Shooter. George William Shooter (1881–1918) married Olive Farrant-Patey (1879–1926) on 14 November 1906 at Christ Church, Richmond. George was a decorator. Edna was born on 2 January 1910 in Richmond. Her father had served in the 1901 campaign in South Africa, but was now a painter. Her parents had six children, at least two of whom died in infancy; Edna was the eldest surviving child. Her father joined the RAMC in January 1915 as a private but was discharged five months later on medical grounds. His health continued to be poor and he died in 1918 in Richmond, aged only 37; Olive died there eight years later, leaving Edna an orphan at the age of 16. By 1939 she was living alone in Willesden as a bank clerk; she later became a nurse. She is commemorated on the Civilian War Dead memorial in Westminster City Cemetery, and was buried there on 28 June 1944. (Grave reference: 21A, grave 11B.)

My mother's friends at the YWCA

Beatrice Gardner and Ellen Norris were cousins and almost exactly the same age (they were born barely two weeks apart). Both were working in London, so it was natural that they would share accommodation at the YWCA. Marjorie Souter was somewhat older, and had come to London from Scotland to do war work, along with her sister Jessie who was staying nearby. They and another YWCA resident, Barbara Howard, all went to the Chapel; Barbara and Jessie were the only survivors.

Miss Beatrice Isabel GARDNER, aged 22, was the daughter of Ernest Harry Gardner and Louisa Kate Mehrmann of Wembley. Ernest Harry Gardner (1892–1971) married Louisa Kate Mehrmann (1885–1956) in 1918 in West Ham. Beatrice was born on 22 September 1921 in Hendon. She was the cousin of Ellen Norris; her father was the younger brother of Ellen's mother. Beatrice was probably named after her aunt, her father's younger sister, with her second name in honour of her maternal grandmother; she was of medium height, plump, with brown eyes and light brown hair.

Louisa's mother Isabella had a difficult first marriage; she married Andrew Mehrmann in 1882 and they had six children, but the marriage grew progressively more unhappy. Louisa was a great support to Isabella from a young age, and took care of her from 1908; Andrew was violent and would regularly threaten to murder his wife and children. Isabella finally petitioned for divorce on the grounds of cruelty in 1914. She remarried in 1918 and lived happily with her new husband and two eldest sons. By 1921 Louisa had moved to north-west London with her husband and family to be near her mother and brothers.

In the 1939 register, the Gardners were living at Hillfield Avenue, Wembley. Ernest was a plumber, joiner and labourer, while Beatrice was a shop assistant (tobacco and confectioner). By 1944 she had moved to the YWCA in Penywern Road and was working as a wages clerk; her father was working as a fitter's mate. She was living there with her cousin Ellen. They decided to go to morning service at the Guards' Chapel on 18 June with some friends; it was a decision that would cost three of them their lives. She was buried on 26 June 1944 at Alperton Cemetery, Brent, in the same grave as her grandmother Isabella, who had died in 1942. (Grave reference D/167.)

Miss (Margaret) Ellen NORRIS, aged 22, was the daughter of Mr and Mrs George Norris, of River, Dover, Kent, and was usually known as Ellen. George John Thomas Norris (1893–1968) married Margaret Gardner (1887–1969) in 1917 at Elham; George was a groom and gardener at the West Cliffe Hotel, Westgate-on-Sea, where he met his future wife, who was a housemaid there. Their daughter was born on 5 October 1921 in Eastry; she was the eldest of three children, one of whom died in infancy. She attended Buckland Girls' School. She was slender and fair, with grey eyes and light brown hair, and slightly taller than her cousin. In 1939 her father was a motor driver in the public service, while Ellen was an omnibus office clerk. By 1944 she and her father were working as clerks; he was working for the East Kent Road Car Company. She was living in London with her cousin Beatrice, and may previously have worked for the GPO in Dover. Her funeral was on 26 June. A local paper wrote:

> She was buried at Buckland, with her choral funeral service held in St Andrew's Church. Representatives of the East Kent Car Road Company were present, along with many friends. Floral tributes included those from the East Kent Road Car Company, the GPO and Buckland Girls' School.

Miss Marjory-Mary (Marjorie) Gordon SOUTER, aged 31, was the daughter of Mrs William S. Harvey of Kintore, Aberdeenshire. Her parents were Alexander Souter and Marjory Mary Meredith, and they married in 1911 in Aberdeen; Alexander was a farmer at Monymusk. Their daughter Marjory-Mary was born on 2 February 1913 and attended Sir Arthur Grant's School in Monymusk; she had a younger sister, Jessie (also known as Netta). Alexander died in 1933. Two years later Marjorie was on the electoral roll in London, at 264–268 Marylebone Road, a nurses' home, and in 1936 she was registered at the Freemasons Hospital, 237 Fulham Road. In 1939, her widowed mother remarried in Aberdeen, to William Still Harvey. By 1944, Marjorie was a munitions worker. She shared digs with Beatrice Gardner and Ellen Norris, who also died in the same incident. Her sister had joined her in London to do war work and was living nearby in Cranley Gardens.

Marjorie's funeral was at 2.00pm on Sunday, 25 June, at Monymusk church. The burial details described her as 'domestic servant, late of Dalbraidie, Monymusk'. (Grave reference: 21st line, no. 762.)

The *Aberdeen Journal* of 17 July 1944 ran a story: 'Kintore sisters in bombed Chapel'. Beneath photographs of the sisters, it said that Marjorie had been killed and her sister Jessie was injured and was still in hospital, nearly a month later. Both girls were engaged in war work in London. They were small and dark, and the photographs show a distinct family resemblance between the two.

Friends on a course: Agnes Moscrop and Ida Thomson

Agnes came from Newcastle and Ida from Edinburgh; they had come to London to attend a telegraphers' course at the Morse Training School and were both staying in hostels. It is believed they decided to go to the Guards' Chapel service together that day; perhaps they were planning to use their day off from studying to explore London?

Miss Agnes MOSCROP, aged 19, was staying at Hyde House (a hostel), Bulstrode Street, London W1, at the time of the incident. She was the daughter of James and Agnes Logan Moscrop of Newcastle-upon-Tyne.

James married Agnes Logan Graham in 1911 in Easington. He worked for the Post Office as a telephone linesman; by 1939 he was an inspector for the engineering department of the GPO. They had seven children, six of whom survived to adulthood. Their second daughter, Agnes, was born in the September quarter of 1924 in Easington. Like her father, elder sister and brothers, she worked for the Post Office in Newcastle; she liked the country-side, and was part of the Post Office rambling club. She was tall and had striking dark auburn hair; friends and family often remarked on it. Her boyfriend, Philip Henry Peel, was originally also in the Post Office but later joined the Royal Engineers as a lance-corporal; he was killed in a shooting accident aged only 23, two months after Agnes died at the Chapel. Agnes was working for the war effort and was due to move to a new office; while it was being made ready, she came to London to attend a telegrapher's course at the Morse Training School in Cornwall House. She and Ida Thomson were both students there. They may have been working on transmitting classified communications alongside the ATS. She was buried at Newcastle-upon-Tyne (West Road) Cemetery, on Saturday, 24 June. (Grave reference: section Q, plot no. 292.) All of her brothers were stationed abroad, so were unable to attend her funeral, although her best friend, Edna Mew, was there. Agnes's name is on the Post Office memorial plaque at the Team Valley Sorting Office in Gateshead; she is the only woman to be listed. All three of her brothers served in the Forces, but survived the war.

Miss Ida THOMSON, aged 18, was staying at 44 Mortimer Street, St Marylebone, at the time of the incident. She was the daughter of Robert and Janet Reid Thomson, of Edinburgh. Robert was born in Fife in 1893 and his wife was born in Buckie the same year; they married in New York in February 1922. He was a plasterer, and one of his last jobs was on the Empire State Building in 1931. Janet had family in the US. They had five children. Ida was the eldest, and was named after her mother's sister; she was born on 29 December 1925 in New York. Her family came back to Scotland in about 1935 and were living in Edinburgh in 1944. She came to London to attend a telegrapher's course at the Morse Training School in Cornwall House. She and Agnes Moscrop were both students there.

Adelaide Wilson and Isabelle Dewar-Durie

Adelaide Wilson and Isabelle Dewar-Durie were friends. Adelaide worked for the WVS, while Isabelle was an air raid warden; both were actively involved in the war effort, although they were in their early seventies. They lived relatively nearby, and would often attend church together.

Mrs Adelaide Louisa WILSON, aged 71, lived at 14 Morpeth Mansions. She was the second daughter of Robert Knox and Hannah Masterton, of

Edinburgh, and the wife of Colonel George Tyrie Brand Wilson, DSO. Robert Knox Masterton (1831–1882), a cotton merchant, married Hannah McLean (1831–1884) in 1863 in Glasgow. They had six children; Adelaide was the youngest. She was born on 22 December 1872 and married Lieutenant George Tyrie Brand Wilson (1867–1953) in 1896; they had two children. George served in the First World War as a lieutenant in the Highland Light Infantry and fought at Gallipoli. He was awarded the DSO in 1917 at the battle of Romani in Egypt. Their son, Adam Tyrie Wilson Brand (1900–1952) became a brigadier; he was the senior British Liaison Officer to the Chinese Expeditionary Force in 1944 and in 1945 was the commanding officer of the 2nd West African Brigade in Burma. During the Second World War Adelaide and her husband were twice bombed out of their home. She was a member of the Kensington WVS Housewives Service and Hospital Supplies Depot. (Elizabeth Thorn and Violet Wilson, who also died at the Chapel, were also Kensington WVS members.) She was known as Mrs Claude Wilson. Several people went to the Incident Inquiry Point to ask after her and her friend Mrs Dewar-Durie. Adelaide was known to carry an identity disc in her pocket.

Mrs Isabelle Elisa DEWAR-DURIE, aged 73, lived at 22 Eccleston Street, Eaton Square, SW1. She was the youngest daughter of Francis William and Harriette Rowsell. Francis William Rowsell (1838–1885) married Harriette Emily Lancaster (1837–1899) in 1866 in Paddington. He became Super-intendent of Naval Contracts to the Admiralty (1870–79), and finally British Commissioner for the Domains in Egypt (1879–85). He published *Recollections of a Relieving Officer* in 1885 and died later that year; he was a practising barrister and had been awarded the CB in 1879 and CMG in 1880.

Isabelle was born on 29 June 1870 in West Brompton; she was the third of three daughters, and married Norman Dewar-Durie on 28 February 1905 at St George's Hanover Square. He was born in 1873 and died in early 1916 at Forewood Cottage, Crowhurst, Sussex; he was the fourth son of William and Elizabeth Dewar-Durie of Craigluscar.

The 1939 Register shows Isabelle living alone in Eccleston Street; she had a flat over the National Provincial Bank. She was a full-time ARP warden for Westminster Council, although she was already 69 years old. She worked at Post 13, Eaton Square. Apparently Post 13 organised a Poultry Club in the gardens there; a group of air raid wardens purchased rationed feed for the hens and shared the eggs. Isabelle was wearing her warden's overcoat over her clothes when she attended the Guards' Chapel service with Adelaide Wilson on 18 June, and it was the post warden who made enquiries about her.

Her funeral was on 28 June 1944 at St Andrews, Farlington, Hampshire. There is a plaque in the church to Norman Dewar-Durie, and they are buried together in the churchyard.

Sisters: Elizabeth and Millicent Millen

Miss Elizabeth Amy MILLEN, aged 56, of 85A Knatchbull Road, Camberwell, was the daughter of Stephen George and Millicent Millen, and sister of Millicent (who died in the same incident). Stephen George Millen (1859–1924) married Sarah Millicent Silk (1857–1942) on 1 September 1883 at St Saviour's, Pimlico. Elizabeth was born on 4 September 1887 in Pimlico, and was one of seven children. Stephen had an interesting career; in 1895 he was a cashier and accountant, but by the 1901 census he was described as 'a law writer and professional singer at a theatre'; he and his family were sharing accommodation with a vocalist at the music hall and an artiste from the Mohawk Minstrels. By 1911 he was described as a law writer, with no further mention of his musical career. At that time Elizabeth was a general clerk, working at Barker's of Kensington, and her younger sister was still at school. In 1935 Elizabeth, her four sisters and her widowed mother were living together at 85A Knatchbull Road. The 1939 Register gives Elizabeth's occupation as 'shop assistant, drapery'; she was living with her four sisters at Knatchbull Road; her mother was over 80 and a patient in St John's Hospital Battersea (a geriatric hospital). They were clearly a close-knit family.

Miss Millicent Marjorie MILLEN, aged 49, was the daughter of Stephen George and Millicent Millen, and the younger sister of Elizabeth, who was killed in the same incident. She was born on 26 December 1894 in Tooting. The 1939 Register described her as a 'stenographer, road passenger transport'. Elizabeth and Millicent were both petite, with dark hair and hazel eyes.

Brother and sister: the Atkinses

Amy and Philip Atkins were the last remaining members of the Atkins family. Like the Millens, they lived together and were a close-knit family.

Miss Amy ATKINS, aged 73, was living at Flat 3, 152 Holland Road, Kensington, in 1944, along with her younger brother Philip; both died at the Guards' Chapel. She was the fifth and youngest daughter of Charles Atkins (1815–1874) and Caroline Louisa Ironside (1841–1924); her parents married on 27 May 1862 in Lewisham. Amy was born on 17 April 1871 in Lewisham; her father Charles, a surveyor and auctioneer, died three years later in February, the same month in which his son Philip was born. At the age of 33, Caroline was left with six children under the age of 10 to support. By the 1881 census she was running a school, with her four elder daughters and nine boarders, at 37 Elsham Road, Kensington. Ten years later, Caroline was 'living on own means' at the same place; Amy was a governess, and there were seven boarders. In 1892 Amy's eldest sister Isabel married Frederick Dixey and moved to Oxford; he became a college bursar, lecturer and Fellow of

Wadham College, Oxford. By 1911, Caroline was living with her remaining four daughters and son at 148 Sinclair Road West, Hammersmith; the elder daughters were governesses but Amy was a woman clerk. She worked for the Board of Education. Caroline died in 1924, aged 83; she and her husband are buried together in Ladywell & Brockley Cemetery. Amy enjoyed travel as she entered her sixties; in 1929 she went to Tangiers, in 1930 she visited Gibraltar and in 1933 she went to Marseilles. This may have been to join her brother there, as he travelled to the same area in other years. In 1939, she and her brother were living together in Holland Road with their elder sister Kate; Amy was a retired clerical officer. By 1944 Amy and Philip were living there alone. Their funeral was held at St John the Baptist, Holland Road, a few doors from their home, on Monday, 26 June 1944, followed by cremation at Golders Green. Their ashes were later buried in Ladywell Cemetery, and there is a memorial to them and their sisters Dora and Mabel. (Grave reference 4134.)

Mr Philip ATKINS, aged 70, was the youngest child and only son of Charles and Caroline Atkins. He was born on 17 February 1874 in Lewisham; his father Charles died in the same month. He was a bank clerk, according to the 1911 census; he worked for the Bank of England. Like his elder sister, he travelled to the Mediterranean in the 1930s. In 1930 and 1931, he travelled to Toulon. In 1932 he went to Gibraltar; in 1934 and 1935 he returned to Toulon; by 1935 he had retired from the bank. He and his sister had a joint funeral.

The Jamesons: wife and mother-in-law

Mary Jameson came to the Chapel with her mother-in-law, Phyllis. John Jameson, Mary's husband, was serving with the Grenadier Guards in Italy in June 1944, and was very close to them both. They went to the service to pray for his safe-keeping. He was devastated by the loss of his mother and his young wife; they were killed at the point where all their thoughts were for him, and it destroyed his religious faith. Because of the situation in Italy, John was refused compassionate leave at the time of the incident and was only able to return to England in October.

Mrs Mary JAMESON, aged 24, of Mill Brooks, Earls Colne, Essex, was the daughter of Dr and Mrs Joseph Frederick Trewby, of Henley-on-Thames, and the wife of Major John George Campbell Jameson, Grenadier Guards. Joseph Frederick Trewby was born in 1883 in Wandsworth and died in 1956; his father, Joseph Henry Trewby, was the chancellor of the Ottoman Embassy in New Park Road from 1860 to the early 1880s and became deputy chairman of the Ottoman Railway Company. Joseph was an anaesthetist and served in the First World War as a captain in the RAMC. He married Mary

Lilian Langworth (1881–1959) in 1912 in Westminster and they had two daughters. Their younger daughter Mary was born in the March quarter of 1920 in Marylebone, and married John Jameson in the March quarter of 1942 in Westminster. Her husband was born on 18 November 1919 in Kensington and attended Marlborough College 1933–37; he entered the Grenadier Guards as a second lieutenant (service number 149114) in September 1940, was appointed war substantive captain in February 1944 and temporary major in January 1945. He was serving with the 3rd Battalion Grenadier Guards in Italy at the time of his wife's death. In 1944, Mary was living with her mother-in-law, who died in the same incident; she was slim and had long red hair. They were both buried in Putney Vale Cemetery on 23 June 1944.

Mrs Phyllis JAMESON, aged 55, was the daughter of John Ward Baines (1851–1924) and Annabelle Hutchinson (1852–1942); they married in 1882 at St Mary Abbots and had two children. John studied at Marlborough and Wadham College, and was a barrister-at-law in Putney at the time of the 1911 census. Phyllis was born on 31 November 1888 in Kensington. She married George Dearden Jameson (1888–1951) on 1 December 1916 at St John the Evangelist, Putney; he was a captain in the RAMC. By 1944 he was a lieutenant colonel (retired). They had one son, named John, who was an officer in the Grenadier Guards. In 1939 she, her husband and son were all living at Mill Brooks, Halstead. On 18 June 1944, Phyllis and her daughter-in-law Mary went to the Guards' Chapel service; they came to pray for John, who was serving in Italy. Her daughter-in-law, Mary, died in the same incident. Phyllis was buried in Putney Vale Cemetery on 23 June 1944.

Nurses (see also Misses Shooter, Maultby and Cattarns)

Seats in the Chapel were frequently reserved for nurses from several London hospitals, and they would attend when off duty. On this occasion, nurses from Westminster, St George's and King's College Hospital were among the congregation.

Miss Peggy Louise May ARNOLD, aged 24, was the daughter of George Minter Arnold (1890–1923) and Dorothy M. Saunders of Highbury. George was a gas fitter in Walthamstow in the 1911 census. They married in 1917 in Lambeth. Peggy was born on 7 December 1919 in East Ham; she had a younger brother, born in 1922. Her father died in 1923, aged 32, leaving Dorothy with two children under the age of four to bring up by herself. In 1939 Dorothy was living with her two children in Islington; Peggy was working as a telephonist. Three years later, Dorothy married Albert Tongue in Islington. In 1944 Peggy was working as a hospital nurse at Westminster Hospital, and was living at the Queen Mary Nurses' Home in Page Street. She attended the service in her nurse's uniform; she was of medium height and had dark hair. She was buried in Walthamstow Cemetery (Queens Road). (Grave reference 1286 D.)

Miss Beryl Violet CLARK, aged 22, was a State Registered Nurse. Her parents were Philip Clark and Violet Laird, of Lee; they married in 1913 in Paddington. By 1939 Philip was a headmaster with the LCC. Beryl was born in the September quarter of 1921 in Lewisham, and was their only child. She was a nurse at St George's Hospital, Hyde Park Corner, and worked under Matron Hanks; an account by a former colleague described her as petite, with very dark curly hair, and an excellent nurse. Her fiancé had been killed on active service in Burma only a few weeks before. She went to the Chapel with two other nurses, Mary and Anne; Anne was unharmed, but Mary was seriously injured. Beryl's funeral was held a few days later, and a huge wreath of pink and red rosebuds was sent from all her nursing colleagues. (Matron Helen Hanks, an ardent spiritualist, remained convinced Beryl and her fiancé were both nursing posthumously.)

Miss (Dorothy) Pauline GYE, aged 24, was the daughter of Hugh Montague and Lilian Irene Gye, of Penarth, Glamorgan. Hugh Montague Gye married Lilian Irene Holway in 1917 in Cardiff and they had two children. Dorothy, usually known as Pauline, the elder, was born in the September quarter of 1919 in Cardiff. In 1944 she was working in London as a hospital nurse; she was also a part-time air raid warden. Elisabeth Sheppard-Jones was a friend of hers from childhood, and they would spend their free time together whenever they could. They decided to begin their Sunday off by attending morning service at the Guards' Chapel. Pauline was killed outright, while Elisabeth was left paralysed after the incident; she wrote a vivid account of it in her autobiography *I Walk on Wheels*.

Moya Lumley-Smith and Janet Lockett Mitchell were also nurses; their biographies are given with their families, as both were part of a family group.

Families
The Colemans: husband and wife
Captain Alan Fraser Coleman and his wife Edith attended church together.

Captain (Retired) Alan Fraser COLEMAN, aged 55, was a retired captain, living at 14 Woodstock Road, Chiswick, in 1944; he was the son of the Reverend George Worsley and Elizabeth Coleman of Nelson, Lancashire, and the husband of Edith Coleman (who died in the same incident). George Worsley Coleman (1851–1912, Chairman of Blackrod UDC 1907–10) and Elizabeth Heyes Boult (1862–1941) married in 1882 at St Margaret's, Dunham Massey, Cheshire. Alan was born in May 1889 in Nelson and was christened on 29 May at St Margaret's, Dunham Massey; he was the third of four children. He attended Bolton Church Institute School from 1897, when his father was Vicar of St Augustine's Church, Tonge Moor, Bolton (1893–1900), followed by a boarding school in Southport; he was working as a chemical improver in Liverpool at the time of the 1911 census. He married Edith King at Gravesend on 31 December 1914.

He served in the First World War; he joined the army as a private in the Manchester Regiment and was commissioned as a second lieutenant in the Lincolnshire Regiment on 25 September 1915. He served in France, and became a captain in the Royal Engineers before returning to civilian life. In 1927 he was a dyer's representative in Manchester. He and his wife lived in the Didsbury area near Manchester for many years. Alan and Edith had a daughter, Jean Marjorie (1921–1948); she served in the WAAF as a radar operator at RAF Jacka, Portloe, Cornwall in 1943, and in 1944 was at RAF Ashburton, Devon, as a radar operator. (Both were part of the Chain Home series of radar stations.)

The 1939 Register shows them as manager and manageress of the Queen's Hotel in Newbury. It is possible that they were managing the Grand Hotel, Southampton Row, in 1944; no details were available. Alan and his wife died at the Guards' Chapel on 18 June 1944. Both were buried in Westminster City Cemetery on 27 June 1944. (His grave reference: 21A, grave 12A.) They are commemorated on the Civilian War Dead Memorial there. He is also commemorated on Canon Slade School's war memorial website.

Alan's nephew, David Worsley Coleman, (son of Alan's brother, the Reverend Leonard Worsley Coleman, who died in 1943) died on 15 July 1944 while serving as a second lieutenant in Normandy.

Mrs Edith COLEMAN, aged 55, of the Grand Hotel, Southampton Row, was the younger daughter of Arthur King and Jane (Jennie) Warr, of Gravesend, who married in 1884. Edith was born on 16 May 1889 in Gravesend; she was the youngest of three children. Her father was the general manager of a waterworks in Gravesend at the time of the 1901 and 1911 censuses. In 1911 Edith was working as a lady's help to the wife and three children of Joseph Oakeshott, principal clerk of the Inland Revenue and member of the Fabian Society, in Berkhamsted. She married Alan Fraser Coleman on 31 December 1914. Edith died at the Guards' Chapel with her husband on 18 June 1944. She is commemorated on the Civilian War Dead Memorial in Westminster City Cemetery and was buried there, along with her husband, on 27 June. (Grave reference: 21A, grave 11B.)

The Mitchells: a mother and two of her three children
Miss Janet Lockett MITCHELL, aged 20, BRCS, was the only daughter of Major Alexander Black Mitchell, of Poulton Priory, Fairford, Gloucestershire, and Vera Margaret Mitchell (née Lockett); she was named after her

paternal grandmother. Her father was a major in the Somerset Light Infantry in the First World War. Janet was born on 7 December 1923 at Thornbury and named Lockett after her mother's family. She was nursing in London in 1944, but had been granted 24 hours' leave, so she and her mother decided to join her older brother at the Guards' Chapel service. All three of them died; they were cremated at Golders Green on 24 June 1944, and there was a memorial service for them at Poulton Church the following week. They are listed on the Poulton war memorial, the only casualties of the 1939–45 war. There is also a memorial window to them in Poulton Church.

Lieutenant Michael Bradstock Alexander MITCHELL, service number 186914, 3rd Battalion, Coldstream Guards, aged 22, was the elder son of Alexander Black and Vera Margaret Mitchell, of Poulton Priory, Gloucestershire, and was known as Mike to his family. He was born on 1 July 1921 in Thornbury, and was named Bradstock after his maternal grandfather, Garstang Bradstock Lockett, as well as his mother's younger brother of the same name who had died of wounds on 4 November 1918 in France. He attended Harrow (1934–39) and was a keen sportsman; he went on to Pembroke College, Cambridge, in 1939. In September 1940 he applied to join the Coldstream Guards. His reference from Harrow described him as 'a first rate fellow ... I found him reliable in every way'. His interview form summed him up as an 'excellent candidate'. He joined the Coldstream Guards on 17 May 1941. He was just over 5ft 11in tall. He went first to the Training Battalion, and was posted to the 6th Battalion on 24 October 1941, then to the Holding Battalion on 26 September 1942. He was posted abroad on 24 October, and disembarked in Egypt on 3 January 1943, when he was posted to 3rd Battalion. On 18 March 1943 he and several colleagues were badly injured by a mine during an attack on the Mareth Line in Eastern Tunisia. Michael's leg had to be amputated below the knee and he sustained multiple wounds; by 26 April he was described as dangerously ill. His recovery was protracted, but by early 1944 he had been fitted with an artificial limb; by February he was able to report for duty, and was given the post of assistant regimental adjutant with effect from 18 March 1944. He was still attending regular medical appointments at the time of his death. He is commemorated on Panel 3 at Golders Green Crematorium.

Mrs Vera Margaret MITCHELL (née Lockett), aged 50, WVS, was the wife of Major Alexander Black Mitchell, of Poulton Priory, Gloucestershire. She was the daughter of Garstang Bradstock Lockett (1857–1921) and Beatrice Augusta Edmiston (1864–1915); they married in 1887. Garstang (usually known as Bradstock) was a solicitor; he later became the chairman of the Northern Children's Union, and the Bradstock Lockett Hospital Home and School of Recovery in Stockport was named after him. They had four children; the eldest died in infancy. Vera was born on 20 May 1894 in Toxteth Park, Lancashire. She had one older brother, Archibald, and one younger, Garstang Bradstock. In the 1911 census she was at boarding school at Leatherhead Court, in Leatherhead. Her parents lived at Barnston Towers, Heswall, Wirral.

In May 1915, her mother died. On 4 November 1918, her brother Garstang, who was a captain in the Cheshire Yeomanry and had received an MC, died of wounds in France aged 21, a week before the end of the war. Vera married Alexander Black Mitchell (1881–1972), a company director for W.D. and H.O. Wills, in the June quarter of 1920 in the Wirral. Their son Michael was born on 1 July 1921. In September of that year her elder brother Archibald died aged 30; this was followed two months later by the death of her father. This made Vera the last surviving member of the Lockett family; she gave her daughter their surname when Janet was born in 1923.

Vera left Poulton to visit her daughter, who had been nursing in London for some time and had been granted 24 hours' leave that weekend. Major Mitchell remained at the Priory and was expecting a telephone call from his wife. It never came, so he called, only to hear that his son had been killed in action. There was still no news of his wife and daughter; he made enquiries and discovered they had been killed in the same incident.

The Gordon Walls: husband and wife

They attended the service together, both in uniform, died together and were buried together.

Captain Leslie Edwin Gordon WALL, service number 141033, Grenadier Guards, aged 45, had been living at 120 Mount Street, London. He was the youngest son of the Reverend Richard Wall, AKC, and Ethel Mabel St Quintin Wall, The Vicarage, Bobbing, and the husband of Violet Maude (Diana) Wall, who died in the same incident. The Reverend Richard Wall (1864–1950) married Edith Mabel St Quintin Graves (1865–1957) in 1893 in Canterbury, and they had five children. Leslie was born on 23 July 1898 at Walmer; he went to Faversham Grammar School, then Borden Grammar School and is listed on the Second World War memorial board at the latter. He was a private in the 14th Battalion of the London Regiment (London Scottish) from September 1916 to November 1917. He joined the Grenadier Guards (as did both his brothers) on 27 November 1917, and served with the British Expeditionary Force in France May–November 1918 and in Cologne, Germany, December 1918–April 1919. He divorced his first wife, Mildred, in 1928; he was a journalist and had been since the end of the war. He married Violet Maude Cambridge at St Martin's, London, on 26 July 1929. (They both loved skiing, and shared an interest in journalism.) The following day they set sail for Lisbon, Madeira and the Canary Islands, travelling first class on the *Alondra*.

His Grenadier Guards record notes that his travel was limited to quarterly visits to ski resorts in Germany and France. Since 1920 he had specialised in journalism, press, publicity and PR. For twelve years he had been the London editor for a New York newspaper, controlling correspondents all over Great Britain, France, Berlin and Vienna (35 in total). (This is why he was known to Peggy Graves, wife of Charles Graves, the journalist and writer, as they moved in the same circles.) In 1939 he was living with his mother-in-law (Susan Jackson, a retired farmer) at Haffenden, High Halden; his wife was at Mount Street, because of her work managing the salon at Elizabeth Arden.

In July 1940 Leslie joined the Middlesex Regiment; he was transferred to the Grenadier Guards on 3 May 1941. He was 6ft 1in tall. His former CO wrote: 'I shall be very sorry to lose him. He is an excellent officer.'

He was posted to Westminster Garrison Battalion as a captain on 25 November 1942. He was on active service when attending the Guards' Chapel incident on 18 June 1944, as David Gurney's account makes clear. The Household Brigade paid tribute to him, describing him as someone 'who worked so indefatigably for the comfort of others and whose cheerful and unselfish spirit was such a help to us all'. He was buried in Bobbing (St Bartholomew) Churchyard on 24 June, together with his wife. (NE Plot. Grave reference: Row 8, grave 5.) There was a memorial service for them at St George's, Hanover Square, on Tuesday 27 June. He is listed on the High Halden War Memorial, as is Diana's son, who died a month later.

Mrs Violet Maude (Diana) WALL, aged 52, was the only daughter of Mrs Susan Jackson, of High Halden, Kent, and the wife of Captain Leslie Edwin Gordon Wall, of Bobbing, Grenadier Guards, who died in the same incident. Violet Maude Neal was born on 24 January 1892. In the 1911 census her mother Susan was a widow and Violet was an artist, aged 19; they were living in Hammersmith. Violet (later known as Diana) had a son, William, in 1913, by her first marriage to Daniel Cecil Joseph Cambridge. Daniel was a chartered secretary. They had a daughter, Susan, who died in infancy in 1916. Violet suffered from severe post-natal depression, but recovered and went on to develop a very successful career.

She became assistant controller to Selfridges from 1918, and then became manageress of Elizabeth Arden, a post she held from 1926; she managed their salon in Old Bond Street, with over eighty staff. She was a keen sportswoman; she enjoyed skiing (as did her second husband) and canoeing, was a member of the Middlesex Ladies Athletic Club and wrote many articles about alpine sports. She divorced her first husband in 1928 and married Leslie Gordon Wall the following year. She belonged to the Women's Employment

Federation, and gave a speech to them in 1936 as Mrs Gordon Wall, London Manager of Elizabeth Arden Ltd. (Her fellow speaker was a female governor of the BBC.) In 1942 she gave a talk on 'Austerity and make-up' to the BBC Home Service, as Diana Gordon Wall. She was a member of the Westminster WVS Mobile Canteen team, and was in uniform when she attended the Guards' Chapel service; she was tall and dark haired, with light blue eyes. She and her husband died together at the Guards' Chapel and were buried in Bobbing (St Bartholomew) Churchyard. (Grave reference: Row 8, grave 5.) A notice in *The Times* described her as 'his devoted wife'.

Only a month later, Diana's son, Sergeant (Flight Engineer) William James Cecil Cambridge, service number 1896872, was killed in action. He was serving in the RAF Volunteer Reserve, 460 Royal Australian Air Force Squadron, and died in the early hours of 19 July 1944, aged 30, when his plane crashed at Roggel, Limburg, Netherlands after a bombing raid on the Scholven-Buer oil plant (he died along with five others). He was buried in the Jonkerbos war cemetery near Nijmegen. (Grave reference: 12.F.7.)

The Lumley-Smiths and Lumley Keane: mother, daughter and sister-in-law

Alice Lumley Keane was the elder sister of Sir Thomas Lumley-Smith; their mother had died shortly after Thomas's birth. She, her sister-in-law and niece regularly attended service together; this would be the last time.

Lady Gwendolen Muriel Maud LUMLEY-SMITH, aged 57, of 244 St James's Court, Buckingham Gate, was the daughter of the late Charles Edward Coles, CMG, Pasha, and the wife of Major Sir Thomas Lumley-Smith (1879–1961), DSO. Charles Edward Coles (1853–1926) served for forty years in India (including the police department) and Egypt; he was lent to the Egyptian government in 1883. He became inspector-general of prisons, Egypt. At one point he was commandant of the Cairo City Police. He married May (Mary) Emma Isabelle Alston in 1881. Gwendolen was born on 7 June 1887 in Williton; she married Thomas Gabriel Lumley-Smith in 1911 at Holy Trinity, Sloane Street, Chelsea. He was then a lieutenant in the 21st Empress of India's Lancers, based at Abbassia Barracks, Cairo, Egypt. They had three children; her eldest, Moya, also died in the Guards' Chapel (as did her sister-in-law, Alice Gabriel Lumley Keane). In the 1939 Register she and Moya were living on private means; her son Timothy was on the staff of the Halifax Building Society, and her husband Thomas was the Grand Secretary of Mark Master Masons (1923–1955) and a retired major.

Major Sir Thomas Lumley-Smith was born in 1879 and educated at Eton and Cambridge. He served in Egypt and Gallipoli in 1915, and then in France and Belgium; he was mentioned in despatches twice and received the DSO in 1918. He was knighted in 1937.

My mother, Enid Sykes, with a group of her friends from King's in 1944. Enid is at the back in the patterned dress. (*Author's collection*)

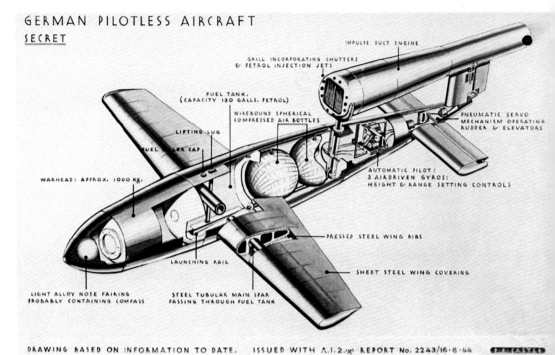

IMPULSE DUCT ENGINE

GRILL INCORPORATING SHUTTERS
& PETROL INJECTION JETS

FUEL TANK.
(CAPACITY 130 GALLS, PETROL)

WIREBOUND SPHERICAL
COMPRESSED AIR BOTTLES

PNEUMATIC SERVO
MECHANISM OPERATING
RUDDER & ELEVATORS

LIFTING LUG

FUEL FILLER CAP

AUTOMATIC PILOT:
3 AIR DRIVEN GYROS:
HEIGHT & RANGE SETTING CONTROLS

WARHEAD: APPROX. 1000 Kg.

PRESSED STEEL WING RIBS

LAUNCHING RAIL

SHEET STEEL WING COVERING

LIGHT ALLOY NOSE FAIRING
PROBABLY CONTAINING COMPASS

STEEL TUBULAR MAIN SPAR
PASSING THROUGH FUEL TANK

DRAWING BASED ON INFORMATION TO DATE.   ISSUED WITH A.I.2.(g) REPORT No. 2243/16·6·44

Cross-section of a V1. This is from an intelligence report dated 16 June 1944, just three days after the first V1s had landed in England. (*Crown Copyright*)

V1 hanging from the ceiling of the Imperial War Museum. (*Collection of Per-Olof Forsberg*)

Message Form for Use at Report Centres.

(For "IN" Messages. For the text of messages other than reports of Air Raid Damage only the "Remarks" space should be used.)

	Time at which reception of message was completed	Initials of Receiving Operator
Date:— 18/6/44	12.30	AO

AIR RAID DAMAGE — Designation of Reporting Agent (e.g. Warden's Sector Number) P18 S164

Position of occurrence:— WELLINGTON BARR.

*Type of bomb:— P A C   H.E.   Incendiary   Poison Gas

Casualties :— Approx. No. 400–500. Whether any trapped under wreckage F + T

Fire. (If reported, write word "FIRE") NIL

*Damage to Mains :— Water   NIL GA.   Overhead Electric Cables   Sewers

Names of any roads blocked   NIL

Position of any unexploded bombs   NIL

Time of occurrence (approx.) :— 11.20

Services already on the spot or coming :— 6 AMB, NFS MILITARY 3 LRP. Pol 2 HRP MOBILE CRANE

Remarks :—
DIRECT HIT ON GUARDS CHAPEL
HEAVY CAS.   I.O MURPHY

qort 12.50
N. A. ops

Serial No. of occurrence
1861

*Delete those NOT reported.

ARP form sent at 12.30 from Post 18. The statement that there are 4–500 free and trapped casualties, together with the number of services already on the spot, indicates the severity of the incident. (*Copyright Westminster Archives*)

The Heavy Rescue Services in action in the Chapel. (*David Gurney*)

The devastation inside the Chapel. The portico has remained intact, but the dust is still rising.
(*David Gurney*)

The rubble, looking out towards Birdcage Walk. (*David Gurney*)

The rescue effort continued for more than three days. (*David Gurney*)

Colonel John Murray (Ivan) Cobbold. His nurse nicknamed him Ivan, as in 'Ivan the Terrible', and he remained Ivan all his life. (*Private collection*)

Phyllis Margaret Roper had planned to meet a friend, Elsie Goodson, at the service on 18 June, but Elsie was late. (*Zena Carter*)

Lance Serjeant Sidney Walter Newbould and Betty Balegian; they met in Egypt in 1941 and had hoped to marry. (*John Anslow*)

Colonel Gustav Bismark Guenther was a cavalry graduate from West Point. He worked in intelligence, rising to become a senior officer in the US Army's psychological warfare branch in London. (*St John's Military Academy, Delafield, Wisconsin*)

Lieutenant Harold William Dods, Scots Guards. He played cricket for Lincolnshire before the war, and had become assistant adjutant at Wellington Barracks earlier in 1944; he had married Marigold Bird four months before the incident. (*John Holden*)

Agnes Moscrop out walking near Newcastle. She and many of her family worked for the Post Office; she was on a training course in London when she was killed. (*Jenny Jackson Jones*)

Ida Thomson in Edinburgh, 1944. She and Agnes Moscrop attended the same telegraphers' course at the Morse Training School. (*Robert Fairgrieve*)

Major Windram leading the
Coldstream Guards' Band.
(*Crown Copyright*)

Originally from Corsica,
Corporal Martin Bacciolelli is
buried in the Free French
section of Brookwood Military
Cemetery. (*Alan Gore*)

Brookwood Military Cemetery and a row of Guards' Chapel graves, beautifully maintained by the Commonwealth War Graves Commission. From the left, WO2 Nathaniel Turton, Guardsman Eric Curry, Guardsman Derek Weaver, Guardsman Henry Thornton. (*Alan Gore*)

Guardsman Dennis George Gibson, who died three weeks after his son was born. (*Barry Gibson*)

Guardsman Derek Weaver, August 1943. (*Gareth Watson*)

Gwen Le Bas, society beauty and sister of Edward Le Bas, the painter, in 1930; she became the wife of Lieutenant Colonel William Gray Horton, Scots Guards, later that year. (*National Portrait Gallery*)

Rose Sheridan and her four sons. Her husband, Guardsman James Sheridan, was due to attend the service with her, but was called away at the last moment. No fewer than eleven of her descendants attended the commemorative service in 2014. (*James Sheridan*)

WO2 Nathaniel Turton. He had invited his fiancée to attend the service with him, but she was Church of Scotland and declined. (*Katharina Miller*)

Drumhead service outside the Chapel on 25 June 1944.
(*Crown Copyright*)

Inside the Chapel, 22 June 2014; the view towards the portico also shows the plaque remembering the more than 2,000 memorials destroyed when the Chapel was bombed seventy years earlier.
(*Crown Copyright*)

The Bishop of London leading the sermon. (*Crown Copyright*)

The congregation listening intently. (*Crown Copyright*)

Keith Lewis, the last known survivor. (*Crown Copyright*)

Present and former members of the Coldstream Guards Band (Sergeant Darren Hardy and Alan Cooper) lay a wreath for fallen comrades. (*Crown Copyright*)

The relatives and the Bishop of London on the steps of the Chapel after the commemorative service, 2014. (*Crown Copyright*)

Gwendolen was cremated at Putney Vale Cemetery on 26 June, two days after her daughter. The funeral arrangements for her and her daughter Moya were private, but a memorial service for them both was held at the King's Chapel of the Savoy on 26 June.

Miss Moya LUMLEY-SMITH, aged 31, staff officer, SJAB Headquarters, was the only daughter of Major Sir Thomas Lumley-Smith, DSO, and Lady Gwendolen Muriel Maud Lumley-Smith, who died in the same incident. She was born on 2 January 1913 in Cairo, and was the eldest of three children; she was working for the St John Ambulance Brigade mobile ambulance unit at the time of her death. She was cremated at Putney Vale Cemetery on 24 June 1944.

Mrs Alice Gabriel Lumley KEANE, aged 67, of 8 Cadogan Court, Draycott Avenue, Chelsea, was the second daughter of the late Sir Lumley Smith, KC, Judge of the City of London Court and Lady Jessie Croll Smith (née Gabriel), of 25 Cadogan Square, and the widow of Colonel Richard Henry Keane, CBE, (1881–1925) of Cappoquin, County Waterford, Irish Republic. Lumley Smith (1834–1918) married Jessie Gabriel (1851–1879) in 1874 at All Saints, Wandsworth. Alice was born on 22 September 1876 in Kensington, the second of three children; her mother died three years later, aged 28, three weeks after the birth of her son, leaving her children to be brought up largely by their grandparents. Alice married Richard Henry Keane on 18 July 1906 in Chelsea; they had three children. He was the MD of the Cappoquin Bacon Factory, a former high sheriff and an MFH. Her husband was killed in a shooting accident on his estate in Ireland in 1925. Her son Robert Lumley Keane (1910–1946) was married to the novelist Molly Keane (1904–1999), and they lived in Ireland. In the 1939 Register Alice was living at Cadogan Court with her daughter Diana, who married the following year. Alice was the sister of Major Sir Thomas Lumley-Smith (1879–1961), and hence the sister-in-law of Gwendolen Lumley-Smith and the aunt of Moya Lumley-Smith; they were in the habit of attending morning service together at the Chapel. There was a memorial service for her on 27 June at St Michael's, Chester Square. She is listed on Waterford's Roll of Honour.

The Thorns: mother, son, daughter-in-law and Violet Wilson (who accompanied them)

Elizabeth Thorn, a friend of Violet Wilson, lived in the same hotel, along with Violet's married daughter, Dorothea. Terence Thorn was her younger son, and had been serving abroad; his wife Cordelia was in the WAAF. Both had leave that day, so the four of them went to the Chapel service.

Section Officer Cornelia Despard THORN, service number 4442, Women's Auxiliary Air Force, aged 33, of Abbey Lodge, Regent's Park, was the elder daughter of William Birkbeck Vanderhoof (1882–1950) and Estelle Despard Vanderhoof (1886–1968), and the wife of Major Terence Conrad Thorn, MC, Royal Engineers, who died in the same incident, as did his mother. Her parents married in 1907 in New York. They had two daughters; the elder, Cornelia, was born on 14 February 1911 in Bronxville, New York. The family went to Cherbourg from New York in 1924; William was in insurance. They gave their address as the Imperial Hotel, Torquay when they travelled back to New York the following year, and by 1928 seem to have settled in Devon. Cornelia and her father were popular in Torquay. He was a well-known yachtsman, as well as assistant district commissioner of the Boy Scouts. She was also a gifted yachtswoman and frequently sailed her father's yacht, the *Estelle*, in the Torbay competitions. In November 1934 she became engaged to Terence Thorn; he also loved yachting, and named his own yacht the *Estelle*. Cornelia and Terence married on 17 January 1935 at St Mark's Church, Torquay. The US Vice Consul certified the marriage. After the service, the local Scouts formed a guard of honour; about 300 guests attended the wedding reception, which was held at her parents' home, Lavernock House. The wedding cake was decorated with a model of the bridegroom's yacht.

Two days later Terence and Cornelia went to Gibraltar on the *Orontes* for their honeymoon, and returned on 22 March 1935 aboard the *Ranpura*. In the 1939 Register, they were living at Druid Cottage, Ashburton. By 1944 she had joined the WAAF and was working at Abbey Lodge, the Air Crew Receiving Centre. This was a mansion block near Regent's Park; the restaurant at London Zoo was used as a cookhouse.

She is commemorated on Panel 5 of Woking (St John's) Crematorium. There was a death notice in *The Times*:

> THORN.-In June 1944, by enemy action. SECTION OFFICER CORNELIA DESPARD THORN. W.A.A.F., beloved elder daughter of Mr. and Mrs. William B. Vanderhoof, of Torquay and New York. Funeral service St. Mark's Church. Torquay. 5 p.m. to-morrow (Saturday 24 June). Interment private. Please, no flowers. Contributions R.A.F. Benevolent Fund.

Mrs Elizabeth Amy THORN, aged 84, WVS, was the oldest victim of the Guards' Chapel incident. She was staying at the Pembridge Gardens Hotel, Paddington, and was formerly living at Ye Whyte Cottage, Selsey. She was the daughter of the late Richard and Eleanor Sennett, and the widow of William Thomas Thorn (1856–1923). Her younger son and daughter-in-law died in the same incident. Richard Sennett (1834–1898) married Eleanor Bradley (1839–1880) in 1856; he was a furrier. Elizabeth was born on 31 March 1860 in St Saviour, Southwark. She married William Thomas

Thorn on 1 August 1883 in Lambeth. He was a coach builder, according to the 1901 census, and died in 1923, leaving a significant fortune of almost £25,000. They had three sons; their youngest son, Dudley, was killed in action near Merville in France on 7 August 1918. Their two older sons also served in the First World War; William, the eldest, was in the Honourable Artillery Company and served as a lieutenant in Egypt. In 1944, she was a member of the Kensington WVS Work Party; these were groups of members who came together either in their own homes or at WVS centres to undertake knitting and sewing for the services, civil defence workers, evacuees and our allies overseas. Her son had just returned from abroad and was on leave, so she, her son and daughter-in-law all attended the Chapel service, along with a friend, Violet Wilson, who was staying at the hotel. All four died. Her funeral service, held jointly with her son, was at Golders Green Crematorium on 23 June.

Major Terence Conrad THORN, MC, service number 127713, Devonshire Regiment, attached Royal Engineers, aged 56, of Pembridge Gardens Hotel, Paddington, was the younger son of William Thomas Thorn and Elizabeth Thorn, and the husband of Section Officer Cornelia Despard Thorn (née Vanderhoof) WAAF, who was killed in the same incident. He was born on 15 January 1888 in Hampstead. He attended Merchant Taylors' School and became an engineering student. He served in the Indian Army Reserve of Officers in the First World War, and was awarded the Military Cross in March 1917:

> 2nd Lt. Terence Conrad Thorn, I.A.R.O. For conspicuous gallantry and devotion to duty, when he went out under very heavy rifle and machine gun fire and carried into safety a man who had been severely wounded.

He gained an aviator's certificate from the Royal Aero Club in 1929, at the age of 41. By 1944 he was a major in the Devonshire Regiment, living in Dorset. He was on leave from abroad when he attended church with his wife and mother. He and his mother were cremated at Golders Green Crematorium on Friday, 23 June. He is commemorated on Panel 3 at Golders Green Crematorium.

Mrs Violet WILSON, aged 74, WVS, of Pembridge Gardens Hotel, Kensington, was the daughter of the late Col. Charles Vanrenen and Anna Lumsden Roberdeau Conway-Gordon, and the widow of Major John Arthur MacLean Wilson, OBE. Charles Vanrenen Conway-Gordon (1834–1884) married Anna Lumsden Roberdeau (1840–1916) in Murree, Bengal, in August 1865; he served in the Bengal Staff Corps. Violet was born on 30 August 1869 in Murree, Bengal; she was the third of five children. She married John Arthur MacLean Wilson (1866–1936), possibly in India, and they had two children; their son Ronald was born in Bihar in July 1895. Her husband was born in Pietermaritzburg, Natal, in 1866, became a naval cadet in 1878 and served in the Indian Army in the First World War. His father, Henry Kenneth Wilson, was born in Port Louis, Mauritius in 1836; he was the governor of Gloucester County Prison in 1871 and was HM Inspector of Prisons in 1881.

Violet was widowed in 1936; in the 1939 Register she was living with her daughter and son-in-law in Amersham. During the Second World War she worked for the Kensington WVS. This included looking after Gibraltarian refugees in London. Most of the civilian population of Gibraltar was evacuated in 1940, and about 10,000, mainly women and children, ended up in the London area. The children had a reputation for being high-spirited; they were housed mainly in large mansions, in areas such as Lancaster Gate, and in the King's College buildings at Campden Hill. This must have been a challenging role for an elderly woman. By 1944, she and her married daughter, Dorothea Sealy, were staying at the Pembridge Hotel; Violet and Elizabeth Thorn were both WVS members and this may have been how their friendship began. They went to the Chapel service together. Her funeral was held at Golders Green Crematorium at 3.00pm on 22 June.

The Gidley-Kitchins: mother and daughter
They had gone to the Chapel to pray for the safety of Greville, their son and brother, who was about to embark for France. He was in the Grenadier Guards. Rosemary had joined the ATS less than six weeks before.

Mrs Dorothy Helen GIDLEY-KITCHIN, aged 55, of Audley House, Crane Street, Salisbury, Wiltshire, was the youngest daughter of the late Robert Nathaniel and Janie Hodges, of 123 Ware Road, Hertfordshire, and the wife of Colonel Edward Gidley-Kitchin, who was in the Royal Engineers. Robert Hodges was the chief engineer of the Indian State Railways; he and Janie married in 1873 at St John's, Meerut, India. Dorothy was their fifth child, born at Saharanpur and christened at Dehra Dun in December 1888. Her older siblings were Ethel (born 1874 and died aged 3 months), Robert William (born 1877, survived to adulthood), Mabel Louise, who was born in 1882 in Uttar Pradesh and died at sea in 1884, and Muriel Katherine, born 1885, who drowned on 21 August 1908 at Srinagar, Kashmir, aged 23, and was buried on 26 August.

In November 1915 Dorothy married Edward Gidley-Kitchin (born in November 1888 in India), at Peshawar (then in India, now Pakistan). He had arrived in 1909 with the Royal Engineers in time to be there for the Delhi Durbar and was stationed in India for the first part of the First World War. He then went to Syria as part of the special expeditionary force in General Allenby's campaign to prevent the Germans (who were allied with the Turks) from making their way south towards Egypt. During this period Dorothy stayed behind in India, where her parents were still living.

Dorothy and her husband had two children; the first, Greville, was born in England when they were home on leave in February 1921. They returned by sea via the Suez Canal when he was a couple of months old. The second, Rosemary (who was killed in the Guards' Chapel incident), was born in Quetta, now Pakistan, in 1922.

In 1937 Colonel Gidley-Kitchin was promoted from the Royal Engineers and took up the appointment of assistant adjutant general at Southern Command HQ in Salisbury. Audley House became the family home. In 1944 he was the Army council liaison officer in Bristol.

The reason why both Dorothy and Rosemary were in the Guards' Chapel that day in 1944 was primarily to pray for Greville, their son and brother, whom they knew to be in Kent, preparing to go to France with the 4th Battalion of the Guards Armoured Division; they would land in Normandy on 26 June to take part in Operation Overlord.

There was a funeral service at St Marylebone for Dorothy and Rosemary on 24 June, followed by interment at Ewshot Church later that day. They were buried in the same grave, number 116. Their memorial plaque in the church says they 'both lived courageously and together died for us all and their country on June 18 (Waterloo Day) at the Guards' Chapel, Wellington Barracks, London. Their ways are ways of pleasantness and all their paths are peace.' Dorothy is also listed in the Salisbury Cathedral War Memorial book.

Second Subaltern (Dorothy) Rosemary Marian GIDLEY-KITCHIN, service number 322124, ATS, aged 21, was the only daughter of Colonel Edward Gidley-Kitchin and Dorothy Helen Gidley-Kitchin. She was born on 16 September 1922 in Quetta, as her father was attending Staff College there. Known as Rosemary, she moved with her family back to England in 1925 or 1926; they lived first at Sutton-at-Stone where her father had a job connected with the Territorial Army, and later moved to Ewshot, Hampshire, where he was in charge of a battalion at Aldershot. They stayed at Ewshot when her father was moved to a job at the War Office in London. During this period Rosemary was educated at home by a governess, together with her older brother, until he went to prep school at the age of nine or so.

Rosemary moved to Bruges in Belgium with her parents for about a year while her father was on half pay awaiting promotion; she attended school there. When the promotion came through the family moved to a small house in Salisbury (Audley House, Crane Street). Rosemary then went to school as a day girl at the Godolphin School in Salisbury; she was one of five girls from the school who lost their lives on active service. Her father had a staff job at Wilton House nearby.

She joined the ATS on 12 May 1944, less than six weeks before the Guards' Chapel incident. Her mother was killed in the same incident. She is listed on the Scottish Roll of Honour. She was in C Company, 5 LD Group, and attended service with Kath Hunt, another ATS officer, who was injured in the incident. Rosemary was described as having fluffy fair hair and glasses. She and her mother were buried together in Ewshot churchyard on 24 June.

Women's Voluntary Service

Seven members of the **Women's Voluntary Service** attended the Guards' Chapel that day. They were: Ada Ellen Cattarns, who attended with her friend, Dorothy Allfrey; Vera Margaret Mitchell who came with her daughter and Guardsman son; Elizabeth Thorn and Violet Wilson, who came with Elizabeth's son and daughter-in-law; Diana Gordon Wall, who was there with her husband; Adelaide Wilson, who came with her friend Isabelle Dewar Durie; and lastly Hilda Worrall, who attended alone.

Mrs Hilda Mary WORRALL, aged 49, WVS, of 25 Kensington Gore, was the daughter of George Edward and Jane Emma Chambers, of 31 Mill Lane, Ryhill, Wakefield, Yorkshire. George Edward Chambers (1867–1944) and Jane Emma Dixon (1866–1944) married on 16 July 1893 at St Peter, Felkirk with Brierley, and had eight children. Hilda was the eldest and was born on 23 September 1894. Her father was a miner. She married Alfred Thomas Worrall (1904–1937) on 4 August 1930 at St James's Church, Ryhill. In 1934 Hilda and Alfred were living in Neasden Lane, Cricklewood. Alfred died in 1937 in Birmingham. By 1944, she was a member of Westminster WVS, helping by garnishing camouflage nets, and also a member of the WVS Housewives service. Hilda was buried in Westminster City Cemetery on 28 June 1944. (Grave reference: 20A, grave 13451.) Both her parents died later that same year.

People who came alone

More than seventy years later, it is hard to be certain why people came to the Chapel that morning in June. Their reasons will have been varied, from a love of fine music to a wish to give thanks for the success of the Normandy landings. As the service was one for Guards and their relatives and friends, it is reasonable to suppose that many of those attending had special links to the Guards. Some came from families with a strong tradition of military service; others were there because of husbands or sons.

These included Sarah Courtney, Lady Evelyn Gordon Lennox, Gwen Gray Horton (wife of Lieutenant-Colonel William Gray Horton of the Scots Guards), Annie Ellen Irving, Hettie Ruthin Nielson, who had come to the Chapel to pray for her son, Andrew, a captain in the Scots Guards, (the

Gidley-Kitchins and Jamesons had a similar motivation), Olive Penn, sister of the regimental adjutant of the Grenadier Guards, and Rose May Sheridan, wife of Guardsman James Sheridan, who was due to attend the service with her, but was called away to other duties.

People with Guards connections

Mrs Sarah Louisa COURTNEY, aged 72, of 5 Great Scotland Yard, Whitehall (the former Guards recruiting building, and presumably where her eldest son was living in 1944), was the daughter of Eliza Goodchild and the widow of Thomas Courtney. Sarah was born on 25 June 1871 in Marylebone. By 1881 she was living in Marylebone with her aunt and uncle. In 1891 she was working as a housemaid and in 1901, aged 30, she was a lady's maid to Theodosia, the wife of the Reverend Canon Edward Chapman, at Pauls Cray Hill. She married Thomas Courtney at Christ Church Chelsea on 19 November 1902. They had three sons, and were living at Baubigny Arsenal, St Sampsons, Guernsey, at the time of the 1911 census.

Sarah's husband, Thomas Courtney (service number 8958), was born on 1 October 1877 and joined the Coldstream Guards in February 1892, aged 14 years and 4 months. He was a drummer and later a sergeant. He served in Gibraltar and South Africa, and in Guernsey 1906–1913. He was discharged in 1913 on completion of 21 years' service. In July 1920 he signed up for the 13th Kensington Royal London Battalion and served for three years. His service record describes him as 5ft 10in tall, 145lb, fresh complexion, blue/slate eyes, brown hair.

In the 1939 Register, Sarah, her husband and her grandson (also named Thomas) were living at Burton Court, Chelsea. Thomas senior was a hall porter and their 16-year-old grandson was a motor works garage hand. In 1940 Sarah and Thomas's eldest son, Thomas Courtney (1903–), was the WO1 garrison sergeant major of the Coldstream Guards. His family were then living at 68 Braemar Avenue, Wimbledon. On the night of 20 October, the forty-fourth day of the London Blitz, a high explosive bomb fell in the area. Thomas Courtney (Sarah's husband) was killed outright; his grandson, Thomas George Courtney, aged 16, was injured and died at Wimbledon Hospital on 31 October. Seven neighbours also died in the incident. Thomas senior and his grandson were both buried in Gap Road Cemetery (Merton). (Grave reference R/B/271.)

At the time of the Guards' Chapel service, Sarah was staying with her daughter-in-law, Eleanor, at 2 Hasker Street, Chelsea; Boyd (1908–2002), her youngest son, was serving in the Middle East. Sarah was buried in Gap Road Cemetery on 23 June 1944, in the family grave. Thomas Courtney, the Coldstream Guards' garrison sergeant major, had now lost both his parents and his son to enemy action.

Lady Bernard GORDON-LENNOX, aged 67, of 631 Nell Gwyn House, Sloane Avenue, Chelsea, was the younger daughter of Baron Loch of Drylaw (Henry Brougham Loch, 1829–1900), and Elizabeth Villiers (1841–1938), of 44 Elm Park Gardens, West Brompton, and the widow of Major Lord Bernard Charles Gordon-Lennox. Her parents married in 1862 and had three children, two daughters and a son. Evelyn was born on 29 July 1876. She and her elder sister Emily were presented at court in May 1894; Emily was associated with the family of Helena, Princess Christian, Queen Victoria's fifth child, and was lady-in-waiting to Princess Christian until the princess's death in 1923. Evelyn often attended functions with her sister, and, when she married in 1907, the Prince of Wales and Princess Christian sent presents for her wedding. Her brother, Captain Lord Loch, gave her away; she had been a bridesmaid at his wedding two years before. She married on 25 July 1907 in the Guards' Chapel; NCOs of the Grenadier Guards lined the aisle during the service, and the music was provided by the band of the regiment. After her marriage she became the aunt of the Duke of Richmond. They had two sons: George Charles, born May 1908, later Lieutenant General Sir George Gordon-Lennox, and Alexander Henry Charles, born April 1911, later Rear Admiral Sir Alexander Gordon-Lennox.

Her husband was the third son of Charles Henry Gordon-Lennox, the 7th Duke of Richmond and Gordon. He was born on 1 May 1878 and was educated at Eton and Sandhurst; he joined the Grenadier Guards in February 1898, becoming lieutenant in October 1899. He took part in the South African War, being present at the operations in Orange Free State, including the actions at Poplar Grove and Driefontein, for which he received the Queen's medal with two clasps. From 1904–06 he was seconded for service with the Chinese Regiment at Wei-hai-Wei. He was promoted captain in 1909, and was ADC from November 1907 to July 1909 and assistant military secretary from August 1909 to November 1911, to the general officer commanding-in-chief, Northern Command. He was promoted to major in 1913.

The 2nd Battalion landed at Le Havre on 13 August 1914 as part of 4th Guards Brigade, 2nd Division with Major Lord Gordon-Lennox commanding No.3 Company. Major Gordon-Lennox served at Mons on 23 August and the subsequent retreat, as well as at the battles of the Marne and Aisne. In October 1914 the battalion moved north, arriving at Hazebrouck on 14 October. The battalion arrived in the Ypres sector, going into trenches at St Jean north of Ypres, on 20 October 1914. Major Gordon-Lennox was killed in action near Ypres by a high-explosive shell on 10 November 1914, aged 36. He was buried in Zillebeke Churchyard, Belgium. (Grave reference E.3.) For his services in the war he was mentioned in the Supplement to Sir John French's Despatch of 14 January 1915, published by the War Office in

April 1915. There was a small memorial plaque to him above the arcades on the north side of the Guards' Chapel, but this was lost when the chapel was destroyed in 1944. There is a South Chapel window in Boxgrove Priory in his memory. There is a memorial to him on the gates of Goodwood House. The St Michael Window in Gordon Chapel, Fochabers, is also dedicated to his memory, and he is mentioned on the Archangel Raphael window.

An obituary described him:

> He was a member of the Guards' and Turf Clubs, and was a thorough all-round sportsman, his principal recreations being shooting, fishing, cricket, and polo. By his death the Army has lost a keen and brilliant officer, and the world of sport an exponent of whom there were very few equals.

The Grenadier Guards continued to be a very significant element of his widow's life. Not only had her late husband served with them, but also her elder brother Edward; her elder son also joined them in 1928. In the 1939 Register, she was at Halnaker House, near Chichester, with her household; this included a number of servants, and a teacher. Her elder son's wife Nancy was there too. Her brother, Major-General Edward Douglas Loch, 2nd Baron Loch, died in 1942 after a long and distinguished career in the Grenadier Guards and elsewhere; his funeral was held at the Guards' Chapel in August 1942. She remained close to his widow and family in London; they were the first to make enquiries about her after the Guards' Chapel incident. With so many Grenadier Guards connections, it was perhaps inevitable that she would attend the service on 18 June. At the time her elder son was commanding the 5th Battalion of the Grenadier Guards; he had been wounded in the leg at Anzio in February 1944, but had made a good recovery. Her younger son, who was in the Royal Navy, identified her body.

She was cremated at Golders Green. Her funeral took place at Boxgrove Priory, Sussex, on 22 June 1944. She is listed on the Boxgrove Priory War Memorial, as is her husband.

There is now a plaque commemorating their elder son in the Guards' Chapel, on the right-hand side as you face the altar. It reads:

IN MEMORY OF / LIEUTENANT GENERAL / SIR GEORGE GORDON LENNOX / K.B.E., C.B., C.V.O., D.S.O. / JOINED THE GRENADIER GUARDS 1928 / COMMANDING OFFICER / THE FIFTH BATTALION 1943–1944 / THE SECOND BATTALION 1947–1949 / COMMANDER / 1ST GUARDS BRIGADE 1952–1955 / GENERAL OFFICER COMMANDING / 3RD INFANTRY DIVISION 1957–1960 / COMMANDANT / R.M.A. SANDHURST 1960–1963 / GENERAL OFFICER COMMANDING / SCOTTISH COMMAND 1964–1966 / COLONEL / GORDON HIGHLANDERS

1965–1978 / BORN 1908 DIED 1988 / BRAVE GUARDSMAN AND
WISE HIGHLANDER

Mrs Gwendolen Anna Le Bas HORTON, aged 43, of 23 Montagu Square,
St Marylebone, was the elder daughter of the late Mr and Mrs Edward Le Bas
and the wife of Lieutenant-Colonel William Gray Horton, Scots Guards.
Edward Le Bas (1863–1935) married Anna Maria Le Grand (1873–1943) in
1900; both were originally from Jersey. Edward was an iron merchant. They
had three children. Gwendolen was the eldest; she was the sister of Molly
Brocas Burrows (1903–96), the sculptor, and Edward Le Bas (1904–66), the
painter, and was always known as Gwen. She was born on 18 March 1901 and
baptised on 5 May 1901 at St Mary, Newington. In 1911 she was living at
2 Glebe Place, Stoke Newington. In 1927 she and her sister were debutantes
of the year, and they continued to attend society balls and other social events.
In 1928 she was described as a Rossetti beauty at the Empire Ball. By 1929,
she was living with her parents at 28 Bryanston Square, Marylebone. In April
1930, her portrait, painted by Howard Somerville, was displayed at the Royal
Academy, and she was described as a 'society beauty'. She married William
Gray Horton (1897–1974) on 30 October 1930, by special licence at the
Guards' Chapel; she was described as a 'tall, lovely bride' in white satin and
pearls. Her sister was a bridesmaid in silver tissue and silver net; there were
four pageboys and four little girl bridesmaids. Major Trappes Lomax, Scots
Guards, was best man. The honeymoon was spent in Paris and Biarritz.

Her husband William was the son of the American impressionist painter
William Samuel Horton and was usually known as Gray, his mother's maiden
name. He was educated at Harrow and Sandhurst. He joined the 1st Battalion
of the Scots Guards in May 1917. He was wounded in November and was
awarded the Military Cross in February 1918. He took part in the British
Olympic bobsleigh team in the Winter Olympics in Chamonix in 1924; his
team came fifth. He left the Army in October 1932 to help run the Le Bas
group of businesses, but rejoined in July 1939. Among a number of other
roles, he saw special service with the British Expeditionary Force in France in
1940, attached to the British Military Mission; he was evacuated from France.
He went on to command the 70th Battalion of the East Surrey regiment in
1941. He was local defence commander at a succession of RAF stations in the
south-east during 1941–1942, then became commandant and chief instructor
at RAF Hazlemere. He formed and commanded the legendary Fighter
Command Battle School, first at RAF Hazlemere and then at RAF Great
Sampford. He then commanded RAF Regiment No.85 Group as part of the
Allied Expeditionary Air Force in 1944, in England, Normandy, Belgium and
Germany, before ending the war as GSO 1 in the RAF's Berlin Air Command; he was mentioned in despatches in 1946. He died on 13 July 1974; his

grave is in the Scots Guards section of Brookwood Military Cemetery. His son-in-law described him as someone who 'loved life, and grabbed it with outstretched arms'.

Both their children were christened at the Guards' Chapel, and their daughter married at the chapel in the 1960s. The Hortons continued to live in Bryanston Square, but during the 1930s they also shared her parents' country home in Angmering, White Cottage (later White Lodge). They travelled to New York several times, once in October 1931 and once in December 1937.

In March 1939, Colonel Gray Horton bought Guilsborough Hall, a sixteenth-century house, formerly owned by the MFH of the Pytchley Hunt. In September, the 1939 Register shows them at 23 Montagu Square. She was a company director, her husband was a captain in the Scots Guards, and they had a lady's maid, a cook and a housemaid. Before the Guards' Chapel incident, Gwen and her husband had already survived the bombing of the Café de Paris in March 1941, during the Blitz.

On the night of 17 June 1944, Gwen was staying at Claridges Hotel, while her husband was based at Uxbridge, HQ 85 Group RAF. It is believed she attended the service the next day as his representative. She was dark-haired, tall and elegant, and was wearing a black coat, with a white gold Scots Guards star with diamonds by Cartier on her lapel. Gray made enquiries as soon as he knew of the incident, and was told of her death that same evening.

Gwen is listed on the family gravestone at Guilsborough Cemetery:

> Gwen Gray Horton
> Killed by enemy action at
> the Guards Chapel
> June 18th 1944
> aged 43
> in loving memory of Mummy
> from Daddy, Robin and Carlotta.

The family continued to place an '*in memoriam*' notice in *The Times* for her every year for more than ten years; she was clearly greatly missed.

Mrs Annie Ellen IRVING, aged 54, of 16 Theobald's Road, Holborn, was the widow of Ernest Irving. She was the daughter of Murry Wilson Goffe and Eliza Matilda Lines; they married in 1889. Annie was born on 28 March 1890 in Whitechapel. At the time of the 1911 census, she was a dressmaker in Chancery Lane, London; she was living with her parents and her younger sister Rose. Her father was a former soldier; he was working as a commissionaire in 1911. He was serving in the Coldstream Guards at the time of Annie's baptism; in 1891 he was a policeman in Aylesbury. By 1916, when he was a witness at his daughter's wedding, he was a police sergeant.

Annie married Ernest Irving on 24 February 1916 in Southwark. Ernest Irving, service number 8365, served as a sergeant major in the Coldstream Guards in the First World War. He was born in 1889 in Dalton-in-Furness; he joined the Coldstream Guards in April 1909 at the age of 20. He received a Montenegrin silver medal in 1916 for merit, and also the DCM in April 1918 'for conspicuous gallantry and devotion to duty'. He was killed in action on 27 September 1918 and buried at Hermies Hill Cemetery, near Arras. He and Annie had one child, Constance, born five months before Ernest's death; it is unlikely at that stage in the war that he would have been able to obtain leave to return home to see his daughter. In the 1939 Register Annie was living at 16 Theobalds Road and working as a 'housekeeper – offices'. She had links to the Coldstream Guards both by blood and by marriage; the service on 18 June would have been important to her.

Mrs Hettie Ruthin NEILSON, aged 63, of 78 Murray House, 3 Vandon Street, was the daughter of William and Mary Jane Sarvis, of The Garth, Hirwaun, Glamorgan; William (1841–1907) was a draper and silk mercer in the 1891 census, with a large family. Hettie Ruthin Sarvis was born on 5 February 1881 in Aberdare, Glamorgan; she was baptised on 6 October 1891 at Aberdare, aged 10. In the 1901 census William was a draper and silk mercer, employing eight assistants, including two of his elder children, and they had a 15-year-old female servant from Patagonia. By 1911 the family lived at The Garth, Penderyn Road, Hirwain; Mary Jane (1843–1921) was widowed and a draper. Hettie married Andrew Shennan Neilson (1888–1975) on 16 September 1915 at St Bride's Major, near Bridgend; he was a doctor of medicine aged 29, from Kilmarnock. They had three children: Margaret, Mary and Andrew. Hettie brought up the children by herself after her husband left home when the youngest were still in their teens. In 1939, she was living at Coddenham Lodge, St Stephens Road, Cheltenham, along with her widowed mother, her married daughter Mary and her husband, and the husband-to-be of her other daughter, Margaret. Andrew went up to Hertford College, Oxford, that autumn. The house in Cheltenham was later leased by the government, and Hettie then moved to London.

In August 1941, Andrew gained a commission in the Scots Guards as second lieutenant; he had already done basic training with the King's Own Yorkshire Light Infantry. He proved to be an excellent trainer of soldiers, and by late 1943 he was involved in running a very successful Scots Guards training camp in north Wales. The regiment began to leave for Italy, where he joined them in early 1944.

Hettie lived in a flat not more than five minutes from the Petty France gate of the Guards' Chapel; she went to morning service most Sundays as she wanted to feel near her son, who was commanding S Company in Italy.

She sent him parcels with books and candles, and he wrote to her regularly. He was badly wounded in the arm in late May, but after a hospital stay he was sent to Rome on sick leave to convalesce.

On Saturday 17 June, his mother left her elder daughter's house in Northwood to return to her London flat. She wished to attend Matins at the Guards' Chapel. Her daughter Margaret had tried to dissuade her, but she was resolute. Susie Roskill (Mary's daughter) relates that Hettie had planned to go to Beaconsfield for lunch with them on Sunday, 18 June, and had telephoned them to say that she might be late. When she did not arrive, her son-in-law, John Elston, travelled immediately to London. Hettie's daughter, Margaret, and her husband, John Curtis, had left for London from Northwood in the early afternoon, after hearing the news of the flying bomb from one of Hettie's neighbours, who knew she had gone to the Chapel. There are letters written to Andrew (later returned as he had died) which show clearly that Margaret had strenuously tried to prevent her mother returning to London – almost as though she blamed herself for her mother's death.

Hettie was cremated at St Marylebone Crematorium and her ashes were scattered in the Garden of Remembrance.

Her son Andrew was killed in action in Italy the following month. He was Captain Andrew Shennan Neilson (known to his friends as Jock), service number 219064, of the Scots Guards attached to the 2nd Battalion of the Coldstream Guards. He commanded the Scots Guards Company on 28 May 1944 at the battle of Monte Piccolo, with complete disregard for his own safety; his Brigadier said 'no one could possibly have done more or given more of himself'. He rejoined the battalion on 24 June. News of his mother's death reached him from a range of sources, both family and official; he wrote to his sisters and fiancée to say what a wonderful mother she had been. He was unable to take leave at the time. On 15 July, during the battle of Monte Lignano, he stepped on a schu mine and was severely wounded; one foot was blown off and the other damaged. He died early the following morning, aged 23, less than a month after his mother had died in the Guards' Chapel. He was buried in Assisi War Cemetery in Italy. (Grave reference: III F 12.) He was posthumously awarded the DSO in December 1944 for his action at the battle of Monte Piccolo.

Miss Constance Olivia PENN, aged 64, of 17 Eaton Terrace, was the elder daughter of William Penn, of Taverham Hall, Norwich. William (1849–1921) married Constance Mary Lucas (1855–1942) at St George's, Hanover Square, in the June quarter of 1877. William was a marine engineer in the 1881 census; he and his brother John employed 838 men. Constance was born on 1 August 1879 in St Martin in the Fields, London, and baptised at Great Bookham on 19 September 1879; the Penns were living at Hill Street,

Berkeley Square. She was one of five children. By the 1891 census she was known as Olive, possibly to avoid confusion with her mother. In the 1939 Register, she is at 34 Wilton Crescent with her mother, sister and brother and a number of servants. She and her younger sister were doing Red Cross work and first aid.

Two of her three brothers, Eric and Geoffrey, died in the same year during the First World War.

Eric Frank Penn, captain, 4th Battalion, Grenadier Guards, was born on 17 April 1878, in London. He died on 18 October 1915, aged 33, when a shell struck his dugout opposite the Hohenzollern Redoubt, Loos. He was at Eton, then joined the 3rd Battalion of the Royal Scots and served in South Africa, where he was injured in 1901. He went to Cambridge, and then became a member of the Stock Exchange. He transferred to the Grenadier Guards at the outbreak of war and went to the front. He was the husband of Gladys Penn (1881–1932), of Baldslow Place, Baldslow, Sussex, whom he married in 1906; their posthumous son, Lieutenant Colonel Sir Eric Charles William Mackenzie Penn (1916–93), also went into the Grenadier Guards. He was buried in Vermelles British Cemetery, Pas de Calais, France. (Grave reference: I.K.11.) Eric and Geoffrey are on the Roll of Honour, Nonington, Kent.

Geoffrey Mark Penn, second lieutenant, 6th Battalion, Rifle Brigade, was born 20 April 1886 and died 11 February 1915, aged 28. He was buried in Rifle House Cemetery (located in Ploegsteert Wood), Comines-Warneton, Hainaut, Belgium. (Grave reference IV.H.6.)

Her remaining brother, Arthur Horace Penn (1886–1960, and Geoffrey's twin), served in the Grenadier Guards in the First World War, and was awarded both the Military Cross and the Croix de Guerre. He rejoined his regiment in the Second World War and at the time of Olive's death he was their regimental adjutant; he later became the Queen Mother's private secretary and then treasurer. (It was he who identified Olive's body after the incident.) Thus Olive had links to the Grenadier Guards via two of her three brothers, as well as her nephew Eric. In a death notice in *The Times*, she is described as 'dearly loved sister of Marjorie and Arthur'. She was buried in Putney Vale Cemetery on 23 June 1944. Pew K in the Guards Chapel was given in memory of her and her brothers. The inscription reads:

THIS PEW WAS GIVEN / IN MEMORY OF / CAPTAIN / ERIC FRANK PENN / GRENADIER GUARDS / KILLED IN ACTION 1915 / IN MEMORY OF MISS OLIVE PENN / KILLED IN THE GUARDS CHAPEL 18 JUNE 1944 / AND IN MEMORY OF / MAJOR / SIR ARTHUR PENN G.C.V.O., M.C. / 1886–1960 GRENADIER GUARDS / 1914–18 AND 1939–45

Mrs Rose May SHERIDAN, aged 39, of 4 Queen Mary's Buildings, Stillington Street, Westminster, was the wife of Guardsman James Sheridan, Irish Guards (service number 2715064). She is believed to have been the youngest daughter of John Thomson; he married Elizabeth Tomlin in 1883. He was working as a lithographic printer for the Royal Engineers in Gillingham at the time of the 1911 census; he was a widower and eight of his children were living with him. She was born Rose May Thomson on 1 May 1905 in Medway, and married James at Westminster in the December quarter of 1933; they had four sons, the eldest of whom later followed his father into the Irish Guards. James is believed to have come from Northern Ireland, possibly the Belfast/Bangor area. In 1939 they were living in married quarters in the Tower of London. Her husband would have been at the service, but was called away to replace a Guardsman who had gone sick at Buckingham Palace. Rose was tall, with dark hair and blue eyes. She was cremated at Streatham Park Crematorium later that week.

Others

The unknown woman. So little is known about her that it is hard to provide any kind of authoritative biography. I was not aware of her existence until I visited Westminster City Cemetery and looked at their burial records. She is described as 'Unknown woman, died at the Guards Chapel'. So far nobody has discovered her name, age or circumstances. It is likely that she came to the service alone; otherwise surely a friend or relative would have made enquiries? She could not have been in uniform, otherwise the military records would have traced her, and she would not have been buried as a civilian; the military dead were well documented. Westminster Council waited ten days for someone to identify and claim her; when this did not happen, they organised a funeral, and she was buried in Westminster City Cemetery on 29 June 1944. Until recently, she was not counted as one of the Guards' Chapel dead; she brings the total who died in the incident to 124.

Mr Arthur Ernest BERRY, aged 38, of Australia House, Strand, and Rose Bay, New South Wales, was the son of Ernest William and Dorothy Berry (née Hoskin), of Ashfield, New South Wales, Australia; he was born on 10 June 1906 in Petersham, New South Wales. He married Sylvia Martha Gain (1916–1971) on 18 April 1936 in Ashfield; she was a milliner. They were living in Rose Bay in 1944 and they had a daughter. An article in the *Canberra Times* of 11 July 1944 states he was a member of a textile mission. Earlier that year, on 13 March 1944, he had flown to San Francisco from Sydney. The passenger list describes him as:

> Arthur Ernest Berry from Sydney Australia ... Australia Government official, going to stay c/o Australian Legation, Washington. Travelling

by US Army plane. He is senior officer, Division of Import Procurement, Dept of Trade and Customs on official business for the Commonwealth Government of Australia.

His will describes him as a civil servant. He was allegedly buried in Westminster City Cemetery, Hanwell, but cemetery records have no trace of him.

Mr John BOSTOCK, aged 74, was the husband of Annetta Bostock (1873–1960), of Hollrook, 100 Gloucester Road, New Barnet, Hertfordshire. His parents were John Bostock (1840–1926) and Sarah Quinn; they married in 1866 and had nine children. John was born in Tarporley, Cheshire, on 19 May 1870. He married Annetta Beeston in 1897; they had two children. In the 1911 census he was working as a valet (domestic) to Major Eustace Loder in Mount Street, London, SW1; Annetta was the housekeeper there, and their children were with them. (Major Loder (1867–1914) became a noted horse breeder. He began racing horses in the 1890s and later bought the Eyrefield Lodge Stud in Ireland; he was also a member of the Jockey Club from 1906, and a steward from 1912. He owned the 1906 Derby winner, Spearmint, and bred and owned Pretty Polly, who won twenty-two of her twenty-four races.) John was a butler at the time of his death; someone from St James's Palace made enquiries about him.

Herbert Vigers CALDICOTT, aged 70, was the managing director of H.V. Caldicott Ltd, 19–25 Argyll Street, W1; he was a freeman of the City of London, and was living at Berners Hotel, Berners Street, Marylebone, at the time of his death. (This was conveniently located for his firm's West End showroom.) He was the son of Thomas Parker Caldicott (1831–1907) and Eliza Vigers Lloyd (1835–1921); they married in 1871 in Camberwell. He was born in Brixton on 19 September 1873, the elder of two children, and later attended Haileybury School. In January 1888 he became an apprentice to John Wotherspoon, a leather seller. He attended University College, Oxford. Both Herbert and his father Thomas were ribbon manufacturers. In the 1911 census Herbert was described as a 'ribbon warehouseman' and was living with his widowed mother in Dulwich. He joined the RAF on 22 June 1918 and was discharged on 30 April 1920; he was 5ft 10½ins tall, with brown eyes and hair and a sallow complexion. He married Mabel Browne on 10 December 1913 at St Stephens, South Dulwich, but the marriage was dissolved in 1923 and a decree absolute was granted in 1924. They had been living at Wilminster Cottage, Remenham, Henley-on-Thames, but by 1923 he was at 36 Inverness Terrace and she was in Sussex. He travelled extensively on behalf of his firm: to Montreal and Quebec in 1936, to Capetown and Durban in 1937, and to Buenos Aires and Tenerife in 1938. The firm of H.V. Caldicott Ltd, set up by Herbert in 1908, survived for over 100 years; it continued to manufacture ribbons until its dissolution in 2010. *The Times* of 24 June stated that his cremation was private; a memorial service would be arranged later.

Mr Cyril Johnson COLEMAN, aged 49, of 38 Nottingham Place, St Marylebone, was the son of John Thomas Johnson Coleman (1865–1940) and Sarah (Sally) Hartall (1868–1942), of Cul-de-sac, King's Road, Bloxham, Banbury. They married in 1892 in Banbury. Cyril was born in the December quarter of 1894 in Bloxham, and was working as a GWR parcel porter at Bloxham Station at the time of the 1911 census; his father was a bricklayer. He later became a civil servant in the local tax office, and moved to London in 1936 to work for the Inland Revenue tax collection department, as an assistant collector. He was buried with his father and mother in Bloxham St Mary's Churchyard.

Miss Olive Louisa CROOKE, aged 73, of the Lonsdale Hotel, 23/24 Montague Street, Holborn, was the daughter of the Reverend Milward Crooke, CF, and Mrs Emily Crooke, of Morningside Park, Edinburgh. The Reverend Crooke (1828–1901) and Emily Hackett (1838–?) married in May 1860 at Parsonstown Church, Leinster, Ireland. Olive was born on 17 April 1871 in Newbridge, County Kildare, Ireland, and was one of eight children. Her father was chaplain to the Armed Forces throughout the Crimean war, and she came from a distinguished military family.

Three of her brothers were soldiers and died on active service: Lieutenant George Douglas Crooke (1865–97) died in action at Maidan on the north west frontier of India, Lieutenant Milward Crooke (1870–1901) of the 2nd Battalion Central African Regiment died of fever at Cape Coast Castle on the West African coast in May, three weeks after his father died in Edinburgh, and her youngest brother, Lieutenant Charles William Cantwell Crooke (1876–1906), drowned in West Africa while crossing a river; he was serving with the West African Frontier Force. Their uncle, Thomas Bernard Hackett (1836–80), had earlier gained the Victoria Cross at Lucknow in the Indian Mutiny, at the age of only 21. Her eldest brother, Thomas Leslie Crooke (1861–1943), was a physician and surgeon; he was Lord Tennyson's doctor on the Isle of Wight before emigrating to New Zealand. Olive was a pioneer pharmacist who studied under Dr Sophia Jex-Blake (1840–1912, physician, teacher and feminist) in Edinburgh before using her skills in the First World War as a hospital pharmacist in France. In 1901 she was living in Edinburgh with her parents and her younger sister Anne; both she and Anne were dispensary clerks.

When Olive volunteered with the Red Cross in 1918, she was living at the Apothecaries Hall, Blackfriars, and her age was given as 41 (she was actually 45 – did she deliberately suggest she was younger, so that she could be posted?); she had formerly been living in Forest Row. She served as a VAD (Voluntary

Aid Detachment) head dispenser from 4 February 1918 to 30 November 1918, and is listed on the British Red Cross Register of Overseas Volunteers 1914–1918; she served in France at No. 72 General Hospital at Trouville as head dispenser. This was a military hospital, which had 1,600 patients as of March 1918, and she was chief dispensing pharmacist; she was working full-time.

In 1923 she was returning from Bombay to London on the *Morea*; her occupation was described as 'pharmacist'. In 1929 and 1930 she was living in St George's Square, Pimlico. In June 1930 she sailed from Southampton to Mombasa on the *Ubena*; at that point she was allegedly intending to live in Kenya. In January 1934 she was back in London; she took the *Strathnaver* to Wellington, New Zealand, to be with her elder brother, Thomas. After he died in November 1943 in Christchurch, she decided to return to the UK. An interview in a contemporary paper described her as hale and hearty and eager to make a contribution to war work; she was clearly a very determined woman, with a lifelong tradition of public service. It would seem that travelling halfway across the world held no fears for her. The New York passenger list describes her as a chemist from Ireland, travelling from Christchurch, New Zealand, aged 73 years [*sic*.] 11 months, on the SS *Rimutaka* on 27 February 1944, arriving at New York on 31 March 1944 and at Liverpool on 18 April 1944: ironically, two months to the day before her death. She is commemorated on the Civilian War Dead Memorial in Westminster City Cemetery, and was buried there on 28 June 1944. (Grave reference: 21A, grave 11A.)

Mr Bryn DAVIES, aged 35, of 11 Kensington Place, Notting Hill Gate, was the son of the late (Aaron) James Davies and Ellen (Eleanor) Davies, née Connop, of Oaklands, Gorof Road, Ystradgynlais, Swansea, Glamorgan. They married in Leominster in the June quarter of 1896 and had at least three other children. James was a master plasterer in the 1911 census. Their son Brinley (Bryn) was born in the March quarter of 1909 in Ystradgynlais. James died in January 1944, aged 74. Bryn usually attended services at the Guards' Chapel; his married sister, Hannah, who was living in Harrow, contacted the WVS Inquiry Point when she failed to hear from him, and his brother-in-law Edward identified the body. Bryn was buried in St Cynog's Churchyard, Ystradgynlais, in the same grave as his father. (Grave reference: Row E, number 7.)

Miss Clara Georgina DEADFIELD, aged 53, of Berners Hotel, Berners Street, St Marylebone, was the daughter of George Henry and Elizabeth Deadfield. Her father George was born in 1846 in Bayswater and married Elizabeth Mary Banton (1851–1913) in Kensington on 24 November 1873 at St John, Notting Hill; he died in 1919 in Kensington. In the 1911 census he was described as a coal dealer and hawker, and they had seventeen children of whom ten were still living. Clara was born on 19 November 1890 in Chelsea and was baptised on 12 February 1891 at the church of St John the Evangelist, Kensal Green; she was the ninth of the ten surviving children. She was working as a dressmaker at the time of the 1911 census. Her elder brother Lionel Edward (1886–1918) joined up in 1915 and served with the 10th East Surrey Regiment in the First World War; he became a prisoner of war, was sent to Sennelager camp and died from influenza and pneumonia in Gevelsberg Hospital on 15 October 1918. In the 1939 Register, she was living in Willesden and working as a saleswoman (dresser). In 1944 she was working at Bourne and Hollingsworth; at that point the store dealt mainly with women's clothing and accessories. Fashion was important to her; she was slim and could carry off an elegant outfit. She was smartly dressed when she attended the Chapel, and wore a lace blouse and a grey pinstriped Harella costume.

Miss Edith Kathleen (Kay) GARLAND, aged 37, of 21 Pembridge Square, Bayswater, Kensington, was the younger daughter of Alice Elizabeth Jane Garland, of 43 Mackenzie Road, Beckenham, Kent. Alice Elizabeth Jane Peachey (1871–1950) married Herbert Edwin Garland (1863–1926) on 31 December 1897 in Bermondsey. Herbert was a grocer. By 1901 he was a commercial traveller and then an egg merchant in 1911. Kay was born on 12 September 1906 in Rochford, Essex, the youngest girl in a large family. In the 1939 Register, she was living at the Berners Hotel, Berners Street, so she may well have known Clara Deadfield or Herbert Caldicott, who also attended the Guards' Chapel service. At that point she was described as a secretary at the BBC; a number of BBC staff used to live at the hotel. Perhaps she moved jobs to the Ministry of Information when the BBC employees were evacuated from London? In December 1942 she was working for the Ministry of Information when she travelled to Cape Town en route for Egypt. *The Times* gave her role in 1944 as 'private secretary to Mr. J.H. Brebner, director of the news division, Ministry of Information'. (The Ministry of Information handled news and censorship; London newspapers and large news agencies had representatives there, and the MoI gave briefings to senior news staff.) She was normally known as Kay, and was a tall blue-eyed blonde. An article in *Time* about the Guards' Chapel victims refers to her as 'blond, gracious Kay Garland, known to every correspondent in London for her friendly labours in Britain's Ministry of Information'. She had changed her rota duty so that she could attend the service. Interestingly, she was the only civilian to be mentioned in the initial press coverage of those who died; this was on 10 July 1944, once censorship was relaxed. She was cremated at Honor Oak Crematorium on 24 June 1944.

Mr Albert William HALL (otherwise **William Albert Garland** [or Golland] BEER), aged 70, of 8 Bessborough Street (he was listed as William A.G. Beer in the England & Wales death index, 1916–2005), was born in 1874 in Cardiff. For a long time I was unable to establish anything further about him, until I consulted the Crime, Prisons and Punishment records for England and Wales. These describe someone known as Albert William Beer, with aliases of Albert Beer, Herbert William Beer, Albert William Hall-Beer, Albert William Golland-Beer, Albert Hall, William Albert Beer and William Beer; this person appeared at the Central Criminal Court, London, in 1931. He was about 5ft 8in tall, with grey hair and blue eyes (as was the man of that name who died in the Guards' Chapel); he had been sent to Dartmoor in 1931 for issuing a forged cheque, and was freed in July 1933, after which he was to work as a London salesman. However, he then opened Post Office savings accounts with worthless cheques and obtained money from the accounts; he was sent to Wandsworth gaol and released in 1935. Once released, he was going to Cardiff to work as an engineer. The records end at this point, so we have no way of establishing his conduct between 1935 and 1944.

The England & Wales Crimes, Prisons and Punishment index lists fifteen previous convictions and sentences for him. They include: stealing a watch, Cardiff, 1911; stealing mirrors, London, 1912; stealing rings, Manchester 1915 (as Herbert William Beer); stealing bicycle (1916); stealing clock (1920, as Albert William Hall Beer); stealing tankards, Derby, 1921; stealing dressing case (1924); stealing vanity box (1927); stealing sheets (1928), plus several counts of receiving and drunkenness. There may have been a mental health issue; at one point he was sent to an asylum, and as far back as 1921 he was referred for medical reports.

He is listed on the Civilian War Dead Memorial in Westminster City Cemetery, and was buried there on 28 June 1944. (Grave reference: 21A, grave 12B.)

Miss Ethel Annie JONES, aged 54, of 77 Castleton Mansions, Riverview Gardens, Barnes, was the daughter of the late David and Annie Jones (née Evans), of 21 Richmond Road, Cardiff. Ethel was born in Cardiff in the March quarter of 1890, and was one of eleven children. Her father was a tea traveller, who died in the December quarter of 1910, aged 63. In the 1911 census, Ethel was a governess, living with her widowed mother and maternal grandmother in Cardiff. One of her elder brothers, John Ivor Jones (1888–1916), served in the First World War with the 11th Battalion, Welsh Regiment (known as the Cardiff Pals); he was killed in action, aged 30, on 14 September 1916 at Salonika. He died while attempting to bring in wounded men from the previous day's fighting. Another brother, Stanley Ewart Jones (1881–?), was a major with the East Yorkshire Regiment; he was reported killed on 6 March 1917. In fact he had been taken prisoner, was sent to Switzerland and not repatriated until December 1918.

Captain (ret'd) Sampson Beamish LANE, aged 73, of 74 Inverness Terrace, Bayswater, Paddington, was the son of Major Thomas R. Lane, JP, of Arlandstown, Cork, Irish Republic; his mother was née Anne Barry and died in 1915 in London, aged 85. Sampson was born on 7 April 1871, and named Beamish after his paternal grandfather. At one time he lived in Cape Province, South Africa. He married Edith Maud Stoward (1870–1930) by special licence in Johannesburg on 26 August 1914. He was in the Rand Intelligence Corps and then the Royal Field Artillery in the First World War, when he served in France. His wife died in 1930 in Farnham. The 1939 Register shows him as an inmate of Suttons Hospital in Charterhouse; this was an almshouse, intended as a residential community of single men over 60 years of age. It was intended for those who could provide 'good testimonye and certificat of theire good behaviour and soundnes in religion'. The building was badly damaged during the Blitz in 1941, so this may be why he had moved to Bayswater by 1944. He was removed alive from the Guards' Chapel, but died in St Thomas' Hospital later that day from his injuries.

Miss (Marian) Daphne McDONALD, aged 40, of St John's Cottage, Kempston, Bedford, was the daughter of Gordon James McDonald, of Kenya, East Africa, and Marian McDonald (née Tomkins); they married in 1901 in Newport Pagnell and had two children. Gordon was described as a settler and planter in his passenger records. Marian may have been born in Kenya, as was her younger brother; she was known as Daphne, presumably to avoid confusion with her mother.

She made a will in 1935, leaving everything to her mother and brother; this included a house she owned in Farnborough. She had been living in Bexhill and appears to have been connected with Ancaster House, a school which closed that year; her mother and brother were living at Kempston. In 1944 her brother was a major in the army; he had joined the Royal Army Service Corps in 1933.

Mrs Diana MILTON-WILLMOTT, aged 46, of 117 Walm Lane, Cricklewood, Middlesex, who was the daughter of Frederick Wright, a major in the Royal Field Artillery; she was born in about 1898. On 30 October 1926 in Aylesbury she married Frank Percy Willmott (1897–1937), a musician whose stage name was Percy Milton, and adopted the name Milton-Willmott. They had a son the following year. Percy was a conscientious objector in the First World War; he had been a student at the Tate Gallery and was an accomplished watercolour artist as well as a gifted musician and theatre organist. He had played on the continent and in the provinces. In 1936 he decided to give up his work as an organist; he and his wife then opened a cafe in Dartford. The following year, while suffering from depression, he took his own life on Saddle Tor, Dartmoor.

In 1938 Diana was running a restaurant in Dartford, but she is missing from the 1939 Register. She is commemorated on the Civilian War Dead memorial in Westminster City Cemetery, and was buried there on 27 June 1944. (Grave reference: 21A, grave 11A.)

Miss Lilian NORTHING, aged 54, of 49 Gloucester Road, South Kensington, was the daughter of John and Elizabeth Northing, of the Murrough, Wicklow, Irish Republic. John Northing (1847–1915) and Elizabeth Clarkson (1853–1924) married in 1876 in Runcorn; he was an analytical chemist. In the 1910 Wicklow directory he was described as 'manager of Dublin and Wicklow Manure Co. Ltd (Manufacturers of sulphuric acid and artificial manures.)' Lilian was born on 24 June 1889 in Dublin and was one of four children. In the 1939 Register, she was living at 49 Gloucester Road and was a part-time typist and secretary. She made a will in early January 1941 (perhaps prompted by the London Blitz, which had resumed with renewed vigour after Christmas), which made specific provisions for her belongings; in particular, she was anxious to distribute her late mother's possessions among other family members. She wanted her grandfather clock to go to her only brother Herbert (1887–1954) in Natal, with the clock in storage at Harrods. She also left him her stocks and shares 'in appreciation of his kindness to me during anxious times'. Her mother's vase was to go to Lilian's nephew, while another nephew was left some monogrammed cutlery; a niece was left one of Elizabeth Northing's bracelets and a brooch. The will gives a vivid picture of someone who cared deeply for family and friends and was anxious to share out her belongings in a thoughtful way while honouring her mother's memory. Any remaining money would go to St Dunstan's charity for blind veterans. Finally, she stated: 'I desire a quiet funeral and I direct that my remains be cremated at Golders Green Crematorium and my ashes scattered to the winds'.

Miss (Edith) Winifred Cazenove OGDEN, aged 48, of Hanover Court, Hanover Street, Mayfair, was the daughter of Edith Armitage Ogden, of Cumberland House, Nassau, Bahamas, and of the late John Armitage Ogden. Her parents were first cousins once removed; John Armitage Ogden of Ashton-under-Lyne (1853–1912) married Edith Mary Armitage (1863–1953). Her father owned a tea plantation at Kirklees, Udapussalava, Ceylon. Edith was born in Badulla Uva, Ceylon and baptised at St Mark's Church, Badulla in about 1896; she was known as Winifred. In the 1930s she and her mother were living at Haydon Hill House, Aylesbury. In 1930 Winifred travelled to Bermuda; they also travelled together to New York in 1932 on the *Bremen*.

There was a notice in *The Times*:

OGDEN.-In June, 1944, by enemy action, Miss EDITH WINIFRED CAZENOVE ARMITAGE OGDEN, daughter of the late John

Armitage Ogden. Funeral Westminster Cemetery, Hanwell, Tuesday June 27 at 11.30. (American and Bahamas papers, please copy.)'

She was buried in Westminster City Cemetery. (Grave reference: 14, grave 13449.) She is also listed on the Caribbean Roll of Honour for the Second World War.

Mrs Phyllis Margaret ROPER, aged 59, of 33 Medway Street, was the daughter of the late Alfred Craven Fletcher and Emily Constance Fletcher, of Beech Lawn, Rose Hill, Bowden, Cheshire, and the widow of Garwood Roper. Alfred was a South American merchant. Alfred Craven Fletcher and Emily Constance Ogilby married in March 1883 at St Peters, Pimlico. Phyllis was born on 14 March 1885 in Altrincham, Cheshire, and baptised Phyllis Marguerite at Dunham Massey on 17 May 1885; she was the eldest of four children. In the 1911 census Phyllis was living with her aunt and uncle in Belgravia and was working as a shorthand writer and typist. She married Robert Garwood Roper (1880–1931) in the September quarter of 1915 in London; in the 1911 census he was living with his mother and sister in Woodford Green and working as an auctioneer. Later he became a surveyor.

Phyllis travelled abroad extensively in the last part of her life, but would return home regularly to see friends and family; she had a particular affection for her young nieces and nephew. She lived in France, at Villefranche, from 1925–27. In early 1927 she went to New York to stay with her friends Jack and Elsie Goodson; Jack was a theatrical manager. Phyllis's visa describes her as 5 feet 2 inches tall, with blue eyes and fair hair. She lived in California for three years. In 1930 she sailed from San Francisco to Honolulu. In 1932 she travelled to Malta from the UK. In 1933 she travelled to Malta again and was described as a journalist. In 1935 she travelled to Capetown, again as a journalist, and in 1937 she was on the *Windsorwood*, returning from Mauritius.

On the day of the Guards' Chapel tragedy, Phyllis was planning to meet Elsie Goodson there, as they had done before; Elsie arrived too late and found the Chapel doors already closed. After the incident, she waited for news of Phyllis; her friend had died instantly, crushed under a falling pillar. In her will, she stated that she wanted to be buried in the next plot to her father, at St Michael, Kirby le Soken, Essex.

Mrs Mary Josephine SARGENT, aged 65, of Flat F, 3 Bramham Gardens, Kensington, was the daughter of the late General David Thomson, RE, and his wife Emily; she was the widow of the Reverend Douglas Harry Grose Sargent, MA (1879–1935).

David Thomson (1833–1911) married Emily Lydia Birdwood (1845–1947) on 26 January 1867 at St Marylebone; he was a widower and a captain in the

Royal Engineers. Both their fathers were generals in the Indian Army; David and Emily were both born in India. In the 1891 census, David was a retired major general, living in Gloucester with his wife, her mother and seven children. He died in 1911; his wife lived to be 101 and died in 1947. One of their children, Christopher Birdwood Thomson (1875–1930) was an army officer who became a Labour politician and peer; he was killed in the R101 disaster.

Mary was born on 3 May 1879 in Chipping Sodbury, Gloucestershire; she had a twin sister, Alice May Lydia Thomson (1879–1965). They were the youngest daughters in the family. Mary married the Reverend Douglas Harry Grose Sargent on 16 May 1905 in Cheltenham. In the 1911 census, Mary's twin sister Alice was living in Hereford with Mary and Douglas and their three children. The following year Alice travelled to the United States to work as a governess in Santa Barbara. She later became a missionary and travelled to Egypt and India. She returned to England from India in early 1935.

Douglas was born in 1878 and attended Clifton College and St John's, Cambridge. He was ordained in 1901, and became the vicar of Holy Trinity, Hereford, 1910–1915. He was the assistant secretary of the Church Pastoral Aid Society 1915–1919. He then joined the Church of England Zenana Missionary Society, an organisation which focussed on supporting the welfare of women and girls overseas. He was the Society's clerical secretary from 1919 to 1928. He then became Vicar of St Luke's, Redcliffe Square, Kensington, from 1928 to 1935. He died on 19 July 1935 at the Nelson Hospital, Merton; he was taken ill after the service on 14 July, and died as a result of an operation for appendicitis. His wife was on a visit to Canada at the time of his death, and two of his sons were also abroad. His younger brother was the Reverend E.H. Gladstone Sargent, vicar of Christ Church, Virginia Water.

His elder brother was Sir Percy W.G. Sargent, born in the June quarter of 1873. He was in the RAMC during the First World War, and became a surgeon at St Thomas' Hospital. He married May Louise Ashman, who died in 1932. Percy died of pneumonia on 22 January 1933, Marylebone, aged 59. He was considered the greatest neurosurgeon of his time in England, and was a consulting surgeon to the Ministry of Pensions. He obtained the DSO and CMG and was knighted in 1928.

Mary attended the service on 18 June 1944. The alarm was raised when she did not go to the Earls Court YWCA for lunch, as she usually did. She used to sit just inside the Chapel by a pillar. Her death notice in *The Times* said:

> MARY J. widow of the REV. D. H. G. SARGENT, and beloved mother of the late Christopher Sargent, Bishop of Fukien, and of Gordon and Eric Sargent. No mourning please. Cremation at Golders Green tomorrow (Thursday 21st June) at 10.30.

The Reverend Christopher Sargent was a schoolmaster, missionary and bishop of the Anglican church. He taught at Wellington College until 1932, and then was invited to become headmaster of the Diocesan Boys' School in Hong Kong, a post he held from 1932 to 1938; he was ordained as a deacon in 1934 and became Bishop of Fukien in 1940. He died of pneumonic plague on 8 August 1943.

Miss Olive Gertrude Annie SMITH, aged 50, of 108 Belgrave Road, was the daughter of Sidney Edward and Anna Catherine Smith, of Derryvale, Roscrea, County Tipperary, Irish Republic. Sidney Edward Smith married Anna Catherine Birch (1858–?) in 1884 in Roscrea. Olive was born in County Tipperary on 7 September 1893, the youngest of four children. In the 1901 census, she was aged 7 and living at Derryvale with her parents, three older siblings, her aunt, a governess and two servants; by 1911 her father had died and Olive had left home. Her father (1859–1911) was a Lay Assistant Commissioner in the Irish Land Commission. In 1911 she was 17 and at school in Dublin. The 1939 Register shows her as a stenographer, living at 108 Belgrave Road. Her funeral was held on 29 June at Streatham Park Cemetery.

Amy Louisa WELLER, aged 30, of 145 Kilburn Lane, Willesden, Middlesex, was the daughter of the late William Weller. William (1878–1920) was a carman from Handborough, Oxfordshire, born in 1878 in Witney; he married Rose Mabel Doel (1883–1961) on 21 November 1903 at Kensington Register Office. Her father Benjamin was also a carman. In the 1911 census they were living at 243 Lancaster Road, Notting Hill; Rose had previously lived there with her parents in the 1891 census. Amy, their fourth and youngest child, was born on 31 March 1914. William served in France in the First World War in the Royal Field Artillery as a gunner; he joined up in 1915. He died on 27 August 1920 from aortic valvular disease and his widow was awarded an army pension. In the 1939 Register, Amy was living in Ladbroke Grove with her older brother William; she was a house matron and he was a gas stoker. In 1944 she was living in Chamberlayne Road, NW10. She was buried on 28 June in Kensal Green Cemetery. (Grave reference 51439.)

Chapter 6

'Recently, on Active Service'

Biographies of the Military Victims

There were sixty-five military victims of the Guards' Chapel incident; sixty-four died at the scene or later that day in hospital, while one died later the following year. Many of them were Guardsmen, but the toll included an American Army colonel, an Australian padre attached to the RAAF, two Canadian servicemen and two serving in the Free French forces.

This chapter gives the biographies of the military victims, with the exception of some who are listed in the previous chapter which deals with the civilian casualties:

Section Officer Cornelia Despard THORN, WAAF and **Major Terence Conrad THORN**, MC, Devonshire Regiment, attached Royal Engineers, are listed with Major Thorn's mother.

Second Subaltern Dorothy Rosemary Marian GIDLEY-KITCHIN, ATS, is listed with her mother Dorothy.

Captain George KEMP-WELCH, Grenadier Guards, is grouped with Colonel Gustav Guenther rather than with the Guards.

Lieutenant Michael Bradstock Alexander MITCHELL, Coldstream Guards, is listed with his mother and sister.

Captain Leslie Edwin Gordon WALL, Grenadier Guards, is listed with his wife Diana.

Wrens: two inseparable friends

Joan Duncan and Edith Farmer were both born in 1925, and became friends when they worked together at a London business house. They decided to join the WRNS together (as can be seen from their near-consecutive service numbers), and had volunteered for service abroad. Both were serving in HMS *Copra* at the time of their deaths. This was a Royal Navy shore base for personnel records and pay for staff attached to Combined Operations. The acronym stands for Combined Operations Personnel Records and Accounts. The London section, a shore establishment, was based at Shelley House in Chelsea, not far from the Chapel. That Sunday Joan and Ruth attended the Guards' Chapel service in uniform. A newspaper article described them as inseparable; they were buried in the same grave in Romford Cemetery and a large number of their service colleagues attended their funeral.

Wren Joan Ruth DUNCAN, aged 19, service number 72461, HMS *Copra*, Women's Royal Naval Service, was the daughter of Thomas P. Duncan (1889–1954) and Beatrice M. Carr (1886–1949), of Romford; they married in the March quarter of 1919 in West Ham. Joan was born in the March quarter of 1925 in West Ham and was the youngest of four children. She was a close friend of Edith Farmer (who died in the same incident).They were buried together in Romford Cemetery on Friday 23 June. (Grave reference: Sec. K.K. Joint grave 2011.) They are also remembered on the Combined Operations Roll of Honour. Their parents received letters of condolence from the King and the Bishop of Chelmsford.

Wren Edith Anne FARMER, aged 18, service number 72463, HMS *Copra*, Women's Royal Naval Service, was the daughter of George William Farmer and Lilian May East; they married in 1925 in Southwark. Edith was born in Southwark later that year, and was named after her mother's younger sister.

Her younger brother William wrote a poignant account for the BBC WW2 Peoples' War archive. His parents received a telegram on Monday 19 June from the War Office, telling them what had happened. That evening they went to William's mother's parents, Emily and John Eustace East, in Southwark, to tell them the news. 'We had things to do, so left them. Apparently they needed a stiff drink so went round to the pub. They too were killed by a flying bomb, so my mother lost her daughter and parents in two days.' [The pub was the King Harry's Head in Union Street, formerly known as the King Henry VIII. Forty-nine people were killed in and around Union Street that night.]

Canadian servicemen

Major Clarence Alvin BAKER, aged 35, was serving in the Royal Canadian Artillery at the time of his death; he was tall and fair and in battledress that day. He was the son of Frank Hamilton Baker (1881–1963) and Ella Jean Brown (1883–1965); they married in 1908. Frank was an engineer, and his father was originally from England. Clarence was born later that year; he had two younger brothers, one of whom died in infancy. In the 1935 census he was living with his parents and his brother in Vancouver and working as a clerk. He was the husband of Georgia (Georgie) Carney Myers (1910–?), of Vancouver, British Columbia, Canada. He was awarded the Canadian Efficiency Decoration. He was buried in the Canadian section of Brookwood Military Cemetery on 23 June. (Grave reference: 54. G. 3.) The gravestone is inscribed: 'He heard the call of his country and answered brave and true'. He is commemorated on page 241 of the Canadian Second World War Book of Remembrance.

Captain John Douglas GALL, service number 2351, aged 25, was a captain in the 22nd Armoured Regiment, Canadian Grenadier Guards, RCAC. He was the eldest son of Douglas Meikle and Mabel Gall, of Montreal. Douglas Meikle Gall married Mabel Perrigo on 10 January 1918 at St James the Apostle in Montreal. He was an electrical engineer and his father Hugh was born in Scotland. Mabel was born in 1892 in Quebec and was the daughter of the physician James Perrigo; she died in 1922. John was born on 18 March 1919. He married Marion Edna Wilmott Beer, of Montreal, on 15 February 1941. There is a photograph of him in the *Montreal Gazette* of 17 February 1941, with the description: 'Lieutenant John Douglas Gall, Canadian Grenadier Guards, A.C.A., Camp Borden, and Mrs Gall photographed leaving Trinity Memorial Church following their wedding Saturday afternoon.'

He was employed by Jenkins Bros Ltd before the war and joined the Officer Training Corps the day after war was declared; he helped recruit men for overseas and then went overseas himself in April 1942. He had just completed a course at the Staff College, Camberley.

He was buried in the Canadian section of Brookwood Military Cemetery on 23 June. (Grave reference: 54.G.2, next to Major Baker.) There is a plaque to him in the Guards Chapel, on the north wall:

IN MEMORY OF / CAPTAIN / JOHN DOUGLAS GALL / CANADIAN GRENADIER GUARDS / 22ND CANADIAN ARMOURED / REGIMENT / 1939–1944 / BORN 18TH MARCH 1919 / KILLED IN THE GUARDS CHAPEL / 18TH JUNE 1944

He is also remembered on page 311 of the Canadian Second World War Book of Remembrance.

Free French Forces

Little is known about why these men attended, or indeed whether they attended together; they may well have wished to celebrate the start of the liberation of France following the Normandy landings.

Caporal Martin BACCHIOLELLI, corporal, Free French Forces (Forces Françaises Libres), aged 25, was based at Dolphin Square with the FFL at the time of the incident. His parents were Jérome Bacchiolelli and Marianne Torre from Corsica; they married in 1918 and had six children. Martin was the oldest; he was born in Cuttoli Corticchiato in southern Corsica on 6 May 1919. He did his military service on the island and then joined the Algerian *bureau des impôts*. When Free French forces were being raised, he joined the

19th Regiment, along with his friends from the Hussein Dey district of Algiers. A convoy left for England and he was part of it. At the time of his death, he was part of 31st Company. He was severely injured at the Guards' Chapel and taken to St George's Hospital, where he died later the same day. He was buried at Brookwood Military Cemetery in the French section. He is also remembered on the war memorial in his home village, and his niece Martine is named for him.

Pierre Maurice Menrie GRAS, Free French Forces, aged 19, was living at 70 Inverness Terrace, London W2, at the time of the incident. He was born on 18 September 1924 in Angoulême, Charente. He was in the Forces Aériennes Françaises Libres (Free French Air Force) and was serving in the Air Command in London. Unlike his compatriot Martin Bacchiolelli, he is not buried in the French military section of Brookwood Military Cemetery, and he is not listed on the CWGC site. He was in uniform when he attended morning service in the Chapel. He was severely injured and taken to St George's Hospital, along with Martin Bacchiolelli; both died later that day.

Auxiliary Territorial Service

There were four women killed in total. Rosemary Gidley-Kitchin, 2nd sub-altern, had attended the service with her mother Dorothy. A number of others were injured, including Elisabeth Sheppard-Jones and Kath Hunt. Casualties could have been much higher if the ATS section due to attend the service had not been excused duties at the last minute.

Private Kathleen JACKSON, service number W/188917, Auxiliary Territorial Service, aged 27, was the daughter of Elizabeth Jackson, of 35 Percival Crescent, Sutton-in-Ashfield. Her father, Norman Albert E. Jackson (1888–1930), married Elizabeth Kelly (1892–?) in Derby in the December quarter of 1910. Norman was an engineer in the 1911 census. Kathleen was born in Sheffield on 25 June 1916, one of seven children. She joined the ATS in 1942. She was attending the service with her friend, Valerian Peacock; both were killed instantly. They were working in A Section, No. 1 War Office Signals ATS, 26 Catherine Place. She is listed on the Scottish Roll of Honour. She was buried in Sutton-in-Ashfield Cemetery, Nottinghamshire, on 22 June 1944. (Grave reference: A ext 9590.) Her name is listed on the Second World War section of Sutton's main war memorial, located in the cemetery.

Private Valerian PEACOCK, service number W/210690, Auxiliary Territorial Service, aged 19, was the daughter of Joseph and Mary Jane Peacock, of Billingham; Joseph Peacock married Mary Jane Stephenson in the December quarter of 1923 in Auckland. Valerian was born in the June quarter of 1925, in Auckland. She attended the service with Kathleen Jackson; both were in uniform. She was buried in Billingham (St Cuthbert) Churchyard. (Grave reference: Section X, grave 21.) She is listed on the Scottish Roll of Honour, and is remembered on the St Cuthbert War memorial and in its book of remembrance.

Margaret Harford wrote, in her memories of the ATS:

> One Sunday morning there was a church parade to the Guards Chapel nearby and the Chapel had a direct hit. One of our girls was killed and another injured.* I was friendly with her. It was a very upsetting time. Long after the war I went to Edinburgh Castle and somewhere there was a large room with rolls of honour** for every war casualty – her name was there. It was an emotional moment.

* Christabel Whitfield is believed to be the one injured; see Chapter 7, The Guards' Chapel and the survivors. Margaret Harford served with them in A Section, No. 1 War Office Signals.
** The Scottish Roll of Honour includes those who have Scottish ancestry, as well as those who served in the Scots Guards, and a number of those who died at the Guards Chapel are listed.

Private Phyllis Mary POTTER, service number W/237282, Auxiliary Territorial Service, aged 23, of Melford Road, London E6, was the daughter of Frederick and Edith Potter, of East Ham, Essex. Frederick Nathan Potter (1885–1956) and Edith Catherine Philpot (1884–1962) married on 17 August 1914 at Whitton, St Phillip and St James Church; Frederick was a carpenter. In the 1939 Register he was a foreman and building worker for East Ham Council, and was also an ARP rescue worker. Phyllis, their only child, was born in the December quarter of 1920 in West Ham. She is believed to have attended the service with her boyfriend, a police constable. She was badly injured and taken to St George's Hospital, where she died the same day of her injuries. She was buried in Brookwood Military Cemetery on 23 June. (Grave reference: 33A.B.14.) She is listed on the Scottish Roll of Honour.

Special operations: two men of mystery

Colonel Guenther was working in the US Army's psychological branch and was of German descent, while Captain Kemp-Welch had joined the Special Operations Executive and was the son-in-law of Stanley Baldwin. They led contrasting lives, but both appear to have chosen careers that involved espionage. Army records exist for both men; however, it is unlikely that the material found tells the entire story.

Colonel Gustav Bismark GUENTHER, US Army, aged 48, was the son of Gustav Guenther and Emma Franke; they married in 1892. Gustav senior was born in 1865 in Peterwitz, Silesia; he emigrated to the US in 1891, became a naturalised US citizen in 1896, was working as a grain buyer in 1910 and later became mayor of Chilton, Wisconsin. He died in 1925. His son Gustav was born on 21 April 1896, the third of five children, in Chilton, Calumet, Wisconsin. Gustav junior's mother tongue was German. In later life he rejected the use of Bismark as his middle name, choosing instead to reduce it to the more anodyne 'B'.

Gustav graduated from St John's Military Academy in 1914 and was nominated for a cadetship at West Point Military Academy in 1916. His 1917 draft registration card describes him as 6ft tall, with blue eyes and brown hair. He married Helena T. Kott (1899–1980) on 4 March 1919, and they had two children.

In 1925 he was an instructor in the Cavalry Branch at Fort Riley, Kansas. In 1928 he travelled from France to New York on the *Leviathan* with his wife and children; they were heading to Camp Holabird, Maryland. By 1935 he was a major and was the military attaché to the War Department; in 1938 he was the US military attaché to Estonia, where he received the Order of the Cross of the Eagle 3rd Class for his services. He spent five years in the Baltic States and at one stage was the military attaché in Riga. In 1939 he travelled from Southampton to New York; he was accompanied by his wife and children and was working for the War Department.

During the early part of the war he worked for the War Department in Washington and made several flights across the Atlantic on military business before coming to London as a senior officer in the US Army's psychological warfare branch. He became a lieutenant colonel in 1940 and a colonel in 1941. That year he was working in Military Intelligence Division, Washington, Intelligence Branch, in charge of the Eastern European section. After the declaration of war on the Axis, he became the first head of OSS (Office of Strategic Services) operations in Cairo; he directed secret intelligence, mainly against German-occupied Greece and the Greek islands. Part of OSS was devoted to special operations and was rather like the British SOE; the two liaised at times, not always successfully. In 1942 he became chief of Special Operations Branch, London; he held this post until early 1943, when he returned to Cairo for a time. By 1944 he was a senior officer in the US Army's psychological warfare branch, based in London. His obituary in *Stars and Stripes* describes him as Public Relations chief of the Psychological Warfare Branch of the ETO (European Theatre of Operations). It is interesting to contrast the open source material available about his duties with that provided for Captain Kemp-Welch's work for SOE.

Guenther was a friend of Eisenhower. He worked with Ivan Cobbold (who also died in this incident) during his time in London; he probably accompanied him to the service, in the absence of General Bedell Smith, who was too busy to attend. He was originally buried at Brookwood Military Cemetery; in July 1948 his body was returned to Arlington National

Cemetery, Virginia. The inscription on his headstone states he was 'Colonel, Army Ground Forces, World War 1 & 2'. (Grave reference: Section 12, site 713.)

Captain George Durant KEMP-WELCH, service number 131986, Grenadier Guards, aged 36, was one of the twin sons of Brian Charles Durant and Verena Georgina Kemp-Welch, and the husband of Diana Kemp-Welch, of Astley Hall, home to the Baldwin family. Brian Kemp-Welch (1878–1950) married Verena Georgina Venour (1881–1968) on 3 September 1904 at St Giles in the Fields, London. They had three children. George was born on 4 August 1907 in Chelsea, and was educated at Charterhouse (1921–25) and Sidney Sussex College, Cambridge (1928–31), where he studied history and economics but did not take a degree; he was the twin brother of Peter Wellsbourne Kemp-Welch, another well-known cricketer, who served in the Coldstream Guards and gained an OBE in October 1944. Their sister Elizabeth (1906–2001) was better known as Betty Kenward, who wrote 'Jennifer's Diary' for the *Tatler*.

George captained Cambridge at cricket and association football and played cricket for Warwickshire. He also toured abroad, playing cricket in Holland, Egypt and Jamaica, and football in Switzerland and Madeira. He played fifty-seven matches between 1927 and 1935, scoring more than 4,000 runs. He was a formidable opening batsman, and in 1932 he was part of the team taken by Lord Tennyson to the West Indies. George joined his father's company, Schweppes, in 1925, and was appointed to its board in 1935; he also held a number of other directorships before joining the Grenadier Guards. On 24 February 1934, at Kensington Register Office, he married Diana Lucy (1895–1982), the eldest daughter of Stanley Baldwin, the Conservative statesman, and cousin of Rudyard Kipling; she was formerly married to Richard Gordon Munro and had a son by him. The wedding was a quiet one, and attended by only a handful of friends; his twin brother acted as a witness. Diana's divorce had been very recent, hence the low-key ceremony. In the 1939 register, George was a company director, living at 69 Eaton Square, along with his sister-in-law, Betty Baldwin (who would be injured at the Café de Paris bombing eighteen months later); he is also listed as living at East-ridge, Cowfold, Horsham, with his wife.

He joined the Grenadier Guards on 29 May 1940. He was described as being about 5ft 10in tall, with dark brown hair and eyes, and weighing about 10st 12lb. He was in the 4th Battalion until 9 June 1941. He became ADC commanding 56 Division, then ADC to colonel in chief, Eastern Command, and finally PA to DCGS Home Forces at GHQ from 8 April 1942. In early 1943, Captain C.E.A. Villiers recommended he apply for work with SOE; Captain Villiers was a former Grenadier Guardsman and presumably aware of

Kemp-Welch's aptitude for classified work. Major-General Gubbins, then Deputy Director of SOE, carried out the recruitment interview.

George Kemp-Welch's SOE file suggests a man of rather endearing modesty. He admits his knowledge of French is poor, and states he cannot ride, sail, fly a plane, mountaineer, box, swim, ski, sail or sketch. He can, however, shoot, drive a car ('not well'), run and bicycle. He has a knowledge of map reading. He is very familiar with the north of Scotland, Caithness, Galloway, Worcestershire, London and Warwickshire. He feels he would be best suited for 'any work in which my experience could be used', and mentions his work on the Schweppes advertising committee.

Perhaps unsurprisingly, SOE felt his talents might be better employed in London, rather than in occupied France. The Director of Plans decided he was to be employed as GSO3 (equivalent of captain) in the directorate attached to London HQ; he was appointed to the Plans section from 2 June 1943. His work was described as 'general office duties, chiefly preparation of progress reports, reviews of activities, and normal routine matters'. Anyone with knowledge of the intelligence community will appreciate that the somewhat bland job description is designed as a smokescreen; in the regimental history he is described as being attached to the Ministry of Information (SP), presumably Special Projects. No doubt the experience of administrative work both with Schweppes and as an aide de camp would have made him a useful addition to SOE, as would his military and social background. However, his true responsibilities will never be known.

His body was one of the last to be found, three days after the incident. Lieutenant Colonel J.D. Kennedy broke the news to his wife on 21 June; her family arranged for the cremation at Golders Green the following day. Afterwards his ashes were buried in Astley (St Peter) Churchyard, in the south-east corner of the second extension; this is near Astley Hall, the Baldwin family home. He is also listed on the Charterhouse Roll of Honour. There was a memorial service for him on 30 June 1944 at St Michael's, Cornhill. He and his twin brother are commemorated by an inscription on the font in the Guards Chapel.

> On top of base: IN MEMORY OF / LIEUTENANT COLONEL P.W. KEMP-WELCH, O.B.E. / COLDSTREAM GUARDS / 1939–45 / AND HIS TWIN BROTHER / CAPTAIN G.D. KEMP-WELCH / GRENADIER GUARDS / GUARDS CHAPEL 18TH JUNE 1944

> On sides of base: GIVEN BY HIS MOTHER IN MEMORY OF ALBERT SYLVAIN BATES VAN DE WEYER, LIEUTENANT AND CAPTAIN GRENADIER GUARDS FROM 21ST NOVEMBER, 1865, TO 28TH DECEMBER 1874

Major Windram and the Coldstream Guards Band

Major Windram died along with five of his musicians when the chapel was destroyed; four of the musicians are buried together at Brookwood Military Cemetery. A further twelve musicians were badly injured and one died later of his injuries. They had been playing in the gallery above the main body of the Chapel. All the instruments were damaged beyond repair.

Many of the musicians had gone to play at the New York World Fair together, back in the summer of 1939, a tour that was cut short by the increasing probability of war with Germany. For some, their service went back much further; Major Windram and George Carr had served together for twenty-seven years.

Major (Director of Music) James Causley WINDRAM, service number 47956, Coldstream Guards, aged 57, of 21 Sloane Court, Chelsea, was the son of William Charles and Catherine Windram, and the husband of Olive Atkinson Windram, of Annalong, County Down, Northern Ireland. William Charles Windram married Catherine Causley in 1885 in Honiton. He was bandmaster of the Highland Light Infantry and later became commissioned bandmaster with the Royal Marines. James was born on 9 August 1886 in Chorlton, Manchester. He attended various Army garrison schools. He then enlisted in the Gordon Highlanders in 1900; his father had been bandmaster with them from 1891 to 1898. In the 1911 census James was resident at the Royal Military School of Music, Kneller Hall, as a lance sergeant in the Gordon Highlanders; he gained the special baton for the best conductor of the year. Gustav Holst dedicated his Second Suite in F (Op.28 No.2) to James Causley Windram; it was written in 1911 and first published in 1922.

James married Ida Earl on 29 December 1913 at St Mark's Church, Portsmouth, and they had two children; she died in 1937. He served with the Northumberland Fusiliers as bandmaster for 16 years and became Director of Music of the Coldstream Guards on 23 November 1930. He was very popular and led an active musical life. He was promoted to captain (Director of Music) on 1 August 1938. On 30 March 1939, he married Olive Atkinson Carruthers, of Mullartown House, Annalong. They travelled to New York for the World Fair on the *Aquitania* in April 1939 with a large number of other band members; he was described as making the trip his honeymoon. They moved to Sloane Court in June 1940.

Windram had experienced health problems from 1934 onwards, including appendicitis, a sprained ankle and difficulties with his other foot. In August 1941 he had quinsy and had to be admitted to hospital; he was unfit for duty until early 1942, and the illness left him with cardiac problems. By 1943 he was suffering from angina and auricular fibrillation of the heart. At that time, Colonel Trew, in a confidential report, described him as: 'A very competent

Director of Music. He is keen, has initiative and gets the best out of the Band, which he handles well'.

On 16 June 1944, Colonel Trew wrote: 'his future is at present under consideration owing to his heart, which I fear may not stand up indefinitely to the very strenuous duties imposed nowadays on a Director of Music'. This might involve taking the regimental band abroad, a physically challenging role. (The next Director of Music, Captain Douglas Alexander Pope, followed the Allied Forces to France later that year.) Major Windram had been excused marching for seven days on 14 June 1944 because of rheumatoid arthritis. A confidential medical report had been requested on 7 June, and he was due to have a medical interview on 19 June; there was also the possibility of alternative employment with the BBC. There is a strong suggestion that the service on 18 June would have been his last day of active service – as it proved to be in reality. Major Windram was severely injured at the Guards' Chapel that day, as was his wife. They were taken to St George's Hospital, Hyde Park Corner. He died of a heart attack later that day, while awaiting the amputation of his leg. He was buried at St Pancras Cemetery, East Finchley, on 26 June, in the family grave; his coffin was carried by six musicians in red tunics. All the Directors of Music of the Brigade of Guards and Household Cavalry who were not prevented by other duties attended the funeral, and the BBC sent the head of their military band section, Harry Mortimer. (Grave reference: Screen wall Sec 7.P. Grave 15.)

As a memorial to Major Windram and those musicians killed, their fellow musicians presented a beautiful conductor's stand, which can be found in the Guards' Chapel, while a plaque was laid in the Chapel at Kneller Hall. R.V. Jones described Windram as 'one of the most human of military band conductors, who used to delight us in St James's Park by telling us about every piece of music that he was about to play'. His Guards record noted: 'He was always so willing to help in any way and so cheerful under difficulties'. A further tribute to him and his musicians was presented in the Chapel on the 70th anniversary commemoration in 2014.

Musician George Edward CARR, service number 4256661, Coldstream Guards, aged 41, was the elder son of George William Henry Carr (1879–1918) and Alice Leah ('Lally') Fry (1883–?); they married in 1901 and had two sons. His father enlisted in 1898 (service number CH/10471) and re-enlisted in 1910; he served with the Royal Marine Light Infantry and rose to the rank of colour sergeant. He was killed in action on 7 April 1918 on the Somme, and is buried in Mesnil Communal Cemetery Extension. (Grave reference I.A.4.) George Edward Carr was born in the September quarter of 1902. He joined the Royal Northumberland Fusiliers at an early age, and served with Major James Causley Windram before joining the Coldstream Guards, where he played third clarinet. In April 1939, George Carr was one of more than fifty musicians who accompanied Major Windram to New York to play at the World Fair. He married Mary Russell Hunter (1910–91) the day before war was declared, on 2 September 1939 in Tynemouth; they had a son, named after his father and grandfather, in 1941. The notice in *The Times* announcing Major Windram's death states: 'also in grateful memory of 27 years' devoted service, Guardsman George Carr who was killed in the same action'. He was buried in Brookwood Military Cemetery on 23 June. (Grave reference: 33 A.B.7.)

Lance Serjeant Arthur Victor HEWLETT, service number 390198, Coldstream Guards, aged 43, of the Cottage, Strawberry Vale, East Finchley, was the son of William Joseph Hewlett and Minnie Emma Wells (1875–1923). They married in Brighton in 1896, and Arthur, their third child, was born there on 27 April 1901. William was a carriage painter; he died at Brighton in the December quarter of 1906, aged 33. In the 1911 census, Minnie was a widow, living with her widowed mother and siblings; Arthur and his elder brother William Henry were attending school in Rottingdean. Arthur served in the Sussex Yeomanry Cadets, then signed up for the Queen's Bays (2nd Dragoon Guards) on 1 November 1916 at the age of 15; he was formerly a kitchen porter. He served with the Egyptian Expeditionary Force and British Expeditionary Force from 1919, then served in Palestine for eighteen months before going to India from 1920–25. He joined the Coldstream Guards on 17 February 1926; he was 5ft 10in tall, with blue-grey eyes and brown hair, and was a musician. He went on tour with the band in Canada from June to September 1926; he also accompanied the band to New York to play at the World Fair in spring 1939, and is recorded as having played a cornet solo with Major Windram the previous year. His military conduct was described as 'exemplary' on his transfer to the Army Reserve. He was playing first cornet at the time of the Guards' Chapel incident. He was buried in Brookwood Military Cemetery. (Grave reference: 33A.B.6.) He left everything to his elder brother, William Henry Hewlett, who was also a musician and played the cornet; they had shared a house in Finchley for many years and had served in the Dragoon Guards and Coldstream Guards together.

Musician Frederick Dowdney KENT, service number 2653113, Coldstream Guards, aged 36, was the son of Charles Clifton Kent (1868–1942) and Sarah Cook (1869–1941); they married in 1890 in Beverley, Yorkshire. Frederick was born in Croydon on 23 May 1908, and was their youngest child. In the 1911 census they were living in Tulse Hill with their six children; Charles was described as a professional musician in the music halls. He died in 1942 at the Musicians' Convalescent Home, Beare Green, Surrey. Lance

Corporal Charles Clifton Kent (1893–1916), Frederick's eldest brother, was killed in action in France on 1 July 1916; he was serving with the 2nd Battalion of the Royal Fusiliers and is remembered on the Thiepval Memorial. Frederick was originally from the Corps of Drums; in the 1939 Register, he was described as a regular army musician with the band of the Coldstream Guards. He was playing percussion in the Guards' Chapel on 18 June 1944. He was buried in Brookwood Military Cemetery on 23 June. (Grave reference: 33A.B.8.)

Lance Corporal Edwin Lloyd SELLERS, service number 2655807, Coldstream Guards, aged 28, was the son of Edwin Bygate and Mabel Sellers, of Barnsley; Edwin (1891–1954) married Mabel Bennett (1892–1949) in Barnsley in 1912. Edwin Bygate Sellers was a colliery bywork man at Rob Royd colliery, Barnsley; his father Ellis had been a colliery deputy overman at the same colliery. Edwin (known as 'Ted') was born on 4 April 1916 in Barnsley. He was educated at Longcar Central School. He enlisted on 9 November 1932 in Sheffield and had previously been a miner; he was 5ft 9½in tall, with hazel eyes and brown hair, and was a Methodist. He became a musician in 1934. He went to New York with Major Windram to play at the World Fair in April 1939. On 14 October 1939 he married Florence Ivy Isobel Hipkins (1915–2010) at the Methodist Church, Fentiman Road, Lambeth; she was usually known as Ivy. His younger brother Ellis served with the Royal Corps of Signals, and was in the evacuation from Dunkirk. Ted and Ivy had one daughter, Elizabeth, who was born in January 1944. He played first horn in the Coldstream Guards Band. He had the reputation of being a musician of outstanding ability; he had played with the band in all parts of Great Britain and abroad as solo horn and had figured in many of the famous London orchestras and with BBC broadcasting combinations. Only the day before his death he had taken part in a broadcast. He was the winner of a London Trinity College Scholarship and had been awarded the King's Coronation Medal for his musical attainments. He had been promised work in one of the BBC orchestras at the time of his death. His funeral was at St Edward's, Barnsley, and he was buried in Barnsley Cemetery. (Grave reference: Section E, grave 56.) He is remembered on the St Edward's Second World War Memorial plaque, Barnsley.

Musician Ralph Herbert ('Ray') SHORTEN, service number 3649008, Coldstream Guards, aged 40, of Anhalt Road, Battersea, was the son of Alice Louise Shorten (formerly Hancock, née Birbeck) and the late William Henry Hancock, and the husband of Eleonore Shorten, of Battersea, London. Alice Louisa Birbeck married William Henry Hancock in 1900 in Brighton; by the 1911 census they were estranged, and she was living with William Shorten and had taken his surname. They married in 1917 in Lambeth after William Hancock's death.

Ralph was born on 15 April 1904 at St Pancras. He was the second of three Hancock children and in 1911 was attending Holborn Union School. He joined the Prince of Wales Volunteers on 12 May 1924; he was previously a clerk. He was a musician, and attended the Royal Military School of Music from July 1926 to November 1927. He served in the British Army of the Rhine from November 1928 to October 1929, and joined the Coldstream Guards as a musician on 11 December 1933. He was 5ft 7in tall with blue-grey eyes and brown hair. He married Eleonore Maria Van Helvoirt Pel, who is believed to be originally from Amsterdam, on 11 June 1934 in Battersea Parish Church. In April 1939 he was one of the musicians who travelled to New York to attend the World Fair for six weeks. In late 1941 he wrote to request to serve in the UK rather than abroad; he had relations in Amsterdam and Nice and 'did not wish to further jeopardise their position by serving abroad against the enemy nations under whose domination they now live'; this request was refused in July 1942. He played second cornet in the Coldstream Guards' Band. He was buried in Brookwood Military Cemetery; the funeral was at 2.30 on Friday, 23 June. (Grave reference: 33.A.B.9.)

Musician Charles (Jock) HART, service number 537872, 1st Battalion, Coldstream Guards, aged 44, died on 13 April 1945. He was the husband of Margaret Hart, of Westminster. In 1937 and 1939 he and May Margaret Hart were living at 131 Queen Mary Buildings, Stillington Street. Like many of the other musicians, he attended the World Fair in 1939. It has been hard to establish further details, but he is believed to be Charles Alfred Hart, who was born in the June quarter of 1900; he married May M.B. Gallagher in 1929 in Camberwell and they had two children. He was injured at the Guards' Chapel and died of his injuries the following year. He was buried in Brompton Cemetery in an area dedicated to the Guards. (Grave reference: Plot N (Guards Plot), Grave 193534.) His headstone refers to him as Jock in the dedication.

Coldstream Guards (twenty-four died)

The total includes Major Windram and the bandsmen.

Guardsman William George Frederick ANNALS, aged 35, Coldstream Guards, service number 2652730, of 63 Loftus Road, Hammersmith, was the son of William George Annals (1880–1945) and Ethel Andrews (1889–?); they married in 1908 in Farnham and had two children. William was born in the June quarter of 1909 in Farnham; he was baptised on 16 May 1909 at Holy Trinity, Aldershot. He married Lily Louise West (1900–67), a pastry cook, in the March quarter of 1940 in Islington. He is commemorated on Panel 1 in Mortlake Crematorium.

Guardsman Leonard CONGREVE, service number 2663561, Coldstream Guards, aged 36, was the son of William Henry Congreve (1875–?) and Ellen Furniss (1878–1965) of Sheffield; they married in 1899 in Sheffield. William was a rolling mill labourer. Leonard was born there on 3 September 1907, the fifth of nine children and the only son to survive infancy. He married Nellie Walker (1908–?) in the June quarter of 1932 in Sheffield; they had two children, one of whom, Trevor, died in infancy in 1937. Leonard was buried in Sheffield (City Road) Cemetery on 24 June 1944, in the same grave as his infant son. (Grave reference: Section N N, grave 15055.)

Drummer James Frank COPEMAN, service number 2658383, Coldstream Guards, aged 22, was the son of Archibald Frederick Copeman (1887–1950) and Bertha Mould (1889–?) of Tacolneston, and the husband of Margaret Copeman, of Regents Park, London. His parents married in the June quarter of 1917 in Sleaford. His father served as a private in the Coldstream Guards in the First World War, service number 111777; he enlisted in September 1914 and served in France. He was discharged on 26 July 1916 because of a gunshot wound to his right leg, which had resulted in an amputation mid-thigh.

James was the second of a large family; he was born on 30 May 1922 at Depwade in Norfolk. He enlisted in the Coldstream Guards at Norwich at the age of 15, on 13 May 1938, shortly before his 16th birthday. He was just under 6ft tall, with grey eyes and fair hair; he had previously been a gardener. He trained as a drummer and was in the Corps of Drums. He married Margaret Downing on 2 June 1942 at All Saints, Tacolneston; their son was 15 months old when James was killed and their daughter was born three months after his death. James was buried in Tacolneston (All Saints) Churchyard, and is one of the five Second World War dead listed on the Tacolneston war memorial. A note on the Tacolneston Roll of Honour states:

> On 18 June 1944 a section of the Band conducted by Major Windram was playing for the service in the Guards' Chapel, Wellington Barracks, when a German rocket crashed through the roof and exploded, wrecking the Chapel. Amongst those killed were Major Windram and five of the musicians; a further twelve members of the Band were injured, and all the instruments destroyed beyond repair. As a memorial to Major Windram and those killed, fellow musicians presented a beautiful conductor's stand, which can be found in the Guards' Chapel, whilst a plaque was laid in the Chapel at Kneller Hall.

Guardsman George Morris DALTON, service number 2660806, Coldstream Guards, aged 38, was the elder son of Eli and Mary Matilda Dalton, of Headingley, Leeds. Eli, who was an engineer and iron founder, was born in December 1877 in Leeds; Mary Matilda ('Tillie') Wallace was born in the

December quarter of 1880. They married in 1902 in Leeds. George was born on 20 June 1905 (his Army record says 1906) in Leeds and was baptised on 29 September 1905 at Wrangthorn, St Augustine; he was named after his paternal grandfather, and was one of three children. Eli died in the December quarter of 1910 at Knaresborough. In the 1911 census Mary was living in Leeds with her three children, four servants and her mother. Later that year she married Henry Ingham; she died in 1935. George signed up on 3 April 1940; in the 1939 Register he was living in Leeds as a motor salesman, and he had previously worked as a motor engineer. He served in the 5th Battalion from January 1941, and joined the Westminster Garrison Battalion in November 1943. He was 5ft 10in tall, with blue eyes and brown hair. He was buried in Leeds (Lawns Wood) Cemetery. (Grave reference: Section 3, grave 54.) His parents are also buried there.

Guardsman George DAVIDSON, service number 2656863, Coldstream Guards, aged 28, of Hamilton Road, Longsight, Manchester, was the son of Alexander and Jane Davidson, and stepson of Samuel Clegg, of New Herrington in Sunderland. Alexander Davidson (1882–1935) married Jane Westmoreland (1895–?) in Houghton le Spring in 1907. They had five children; he was a miner, according to the 1911 census, and died in the September quarter of 1935. Jane married Samuel Clegg in the September quarter of 1940 in Durham Northern. George was born on 23 January 1916. He was in the 1st Herrington Scouts in his teens. He joined the Army in 1940; before that, he was a greyhound trainer at Belle Vue Stadium, Manchester. He married Henrietta Bessie Wheeler (1913–1943) in Manchester in 1940, and they had a daughter, followed by a son in the summer of 1943 in Manchester. Henrietta died soon afterwards of puerperal fever. George was buried in Herrington (St Cuthbert) churchyard. (Grave reference: Row 12, grave 25.)

Lance Corporal (James) Edward DUNN, service number 2656165, Coldstream Guards, aged 28, was the son of James and Lucy Dunn. James Dunn married Lucy Mansell in 1903 in Wellington, Shropshire. Their son James was born there on 7 July 1915; he was normally known as Edward. He signed up on 17 October 1933; he was previously a labourer. He was over 6ft 1in tall, with blue eyes and dark brown hair. His commanding officer rated his military conduct as 'very good', describing him as 'a sober and honest man who can do very good work. He possesses character and intelligence and is smart and reliable. He should do well in civil life'. He served in Palestine for a two-month period in 1936, but was otherwise on home service. Before being recalled to the army he worked at Burtons Factory on the East Lancashire Road, Swinton. He married May Phillips at Barton Register Office on 10 June 1939; they had a son in 1940 who later served in the Grenadier Guards. One of James's younger brothers was serving with the army in Sicily at the time of

James's death; he had been wounded and was in hospital. James was buried in Swinton Cemetery. (Grave reference: Sec. B grave 2623.) The inscription on the grave reads 'I can only tend his grave and leave a token to the best husband God ever made'.

Lance Serjeant John HALL, service number 2661797, Coldstream Guards, aged 29, was born on 29 June 1914 in Blackpool. He married Vera Sylvia Summers (1916–?) in Croydon on 25 February 1935; they had two sons in 1942 and 1943, but the elder one died in infancy. John was a fish and poultry dealer for the Co-op before he enlisted on 11 June 1940. He was just over 5ft 10in tall, with hazel eyes and fair hair. He served with Westminster Garrison Battalion, based at Regents Park Barracks. He had just completed a month-long weapons training course on 13 June 1944. He was buried in Marton (St Paul) Church Burial Ground, near Blackpool. (Grave reference: Plot 9, grave 1.) This was the family grave; his parents and baby son are also buried there.

Lance Corporal Edwin Lloyd HOLMES, service number 2661081, Coldstream Guards, aged 30, was the son of William Stevens Holmes (1869–1963) and Emma Jane Chapman (1874–1962); they married on 13 November 1892 in Newton Abbot. William served with the Royal Engineers in the First World War until 1919; prior to that he was a labourer. Edwin was born on 14 November 1913 in Totnes and was the tenth child of twelve. In the 1939 Register he was a marble worker (fancy), living with his retired father at Barton, Torquay. Edwin married Alice May Hewett (1905–1971) on 1 April 1940 at St Marychurch; she was living in Watcombe at the time of his death. He joined the Guards three weeks later and was posted to the Guards depot, Caterham. He was just over 5ft 9in tall, with hazel eyes and brown hair. He joined the Westminster Garrison Battalion in November 1943. He was buried in Torquay Cemetery. (Grave reference: Sec. MX. Grave 15672.) He is listed on the Torquay Roll of Honour for the Second World War, as is Cornelia Despard Thorn.

Guardsman Alexander HOOPER, service number 853787, Coldstream Guards, aged 26, was the son of Alexander and Lily Hooper of Castleford. Alexander Hooper (1884–1960) and Lily Lunn (1889–?) married in the December quarter of 1909 in Pontefract; he was a miner, but in 1939 was working at a glass works. They had two daughters and two sons; both sons died on active service in the Second World War. Alexander was born on 26 December 1918. He was originally a glass blower, then joined the Royal Artillery in April 1936. He joined the Coldstream Guards on 14 February 1939; he was just over 5ft 10in tall, with blue eyes and fair hair. He served with the Middle East Force from September 1939 to March 1940, and was with the British Expeditionary Force from 14 March to 2 June 1940, when it is believed he was evacuated from Dunkirk. He married Winifred Farrar (1919–1994) just under two weeks later, on 15 June 1940 in Pontefract. He served in North Africa from November 1942 to February 1944. He returned to the UK on 22 February 1944. He was buried in Castleford (Whitwood) Cemetery on 23 June 1944. (Grave reference: Section C. Grave 115.)

Alexander's younger brother, Sergeant Albert Hooper (1920–42), RAF (VR), service number 984904, died on 6 August 1942 and is commemorated on Panel 86 of the Runnymede memorial. He died flying a Whitley bomber from Wick on an anti-submarine patrol; it was lost over the North Sea on 6 August.

Guardsman Ronald Charles MITCHELL, service number 2659836, Coldstream Guards, aged 19, was the son of Elizabeth Mitchell (née Finch), of Dagenham. Elizabeth Emily Finch (1896–1962) married Thomas Charles Mitchell, a fitter, on 20 April 1919 at St James, Hatcham, Lewisham; he died in Romford in the June quarter of 1943, aged 48. (In 1939 he was a general labourer, living in Gale Street, Dagenham.) Ronald was born on 27 December 1924 in Greenwich. He was the middle child of five. He enlisted in the Coldstream Guards in December 1939 when he was just under 15 years old; he was 5ft 7½in tall, with brown eyes and brown hair. He started training at Pirbright in 1939, and continued to study as part of his Army training; he obtained a man's pay and privileges when he was 17½. He was buried at Barking (Rippleside) Cemetery. (Grave reference: Sec O M grave 41.) His gravestone bears the inscription: 'A sudden change, at God's command he fell; he had no chance to bid his friends farewell.'

Lance Corporal Frederick Dowdney MORLEY, service number 2652792, Coldstream Guards, aged 37, was the son of Frederick and Florence Morley, of Barnsley. Frederick Morley married Florence Pickles on 21 August 1904 at Barnsley St Peter; he was a labourer, and Florence was born in Pennsylvania, America. (Her father Joseph was a miner and may have gone there to work.) Their eldest son, Frederick, was born on 23 August 1906 in Barnsley, and is listed as Frederick Morley in both the birth and the Army records. In the 1911 census the Morleys were living at Railway Terrace, Carlton, Barnsley; they had three surviving children. Frederick (known as Fred) joined up on 22 April 1926; he formerly worked at New Monkston No. 1 pit. He was 5ft 10½in tall, with blue eyes and dark brown hair. He later trained as a saddler. He served in the Sudan in 1932 and in Egypt in 1933 and 1935; he was in France with the British Expeditionary Force from September 1939 to January 1940. He married Ann Sophia Horton (1911–?) in Tetbury on 1 January 1938; they had two sons, one in 1938 and one in 1940. Frederick was buried in Brookwood Military Cemetery on 23 June. (Grave reference: 33 A.B.10.)

Lance Serjeant Sidney Walter NEWBOULD, service number 2657482, Coldstream Guards, aged 25, was the son of Henry (1889–1961) and Mary Jane Newbould, of Walsall; Henry (Harry) married Mary Jane Jackson (1892–1979) in Walsall in 1910. Henry was a brick presser. Sidney (known as Sid) was born in July 1918 in Walsall. He attended Aldridge School; he left school at the age of 14 and went to work in a factory near Birmingham. In 1936 he joined the Coldstream Guards; he served in the 3rd Battalion in Palestine that year, at the time of the Arab revolt. In July 1939 he was in Egypt, at Mustapha Barracks, Alexandria. In 1941 he became friends with Betty Balegian, an Armenian who was looking after British officers' children and living in Ismailia, Egypt; they wanted to marry but the Army would not give permission. He was with the 3rd Battalion at Tobruk in June 1942, but managed to escape to Egypt, along with about 200 other men, after the battle of Gazala, when the rest of his brigade was captured. In 1943 they saw action at Medenine and Mareth in March (where Lieutenant Mike Mitchell, another Coldstream Guardsman and Guards' Chapel casualty, was badly injured), Wadi Akarit and Enfidaville in April, and Tunis in May; they then took part in the Allied invasion of Italy, including the battle of Salerno and the capture of Naples in September 1943, Volturno Crossing in October, Monte Camino in December and Garigliano Crossing in January 1944. Sid was wounded while in Italy and transferred back to London. In April 1944, the battalion returned to London and became a Training Brigade, possibly training troops for D-Day. He was based at Pirbright Camp in May 1944, where he won the sergeants' mess prize shoot. He was apparently trying to transfer to the mobile section of the Palestine Police shortly before his death, so that he would be able to marry Betty Balegian. He was buried in Aldridge (St Mary) Churchyard Extension. (Grave reference: Row Q, grave 23.) His parents are buried in the same grave.

Drummer Albert Charles RICHMOND, service number 2662384, Coldstream Guards, aged 31, was the son of Thomas George and Rachel Richmond, of Droylsden, and the husband of Elsie Richmond, also of Droylsden. Thomas George Richmond (1873–1949) and Rachel Halliwell (1874–1947) married in 1897 in Manchester; they were next-door neighbours. They had six children; Albert, the youngest, was born on 24 August 1912 in Droylsden. He married Elsie Finch on 8 April 1938 in Droylsden Parish Church and they had a daughter in May 1940. He enlisted in the Coldstream Guards on 3 July 1940; he had formerly been a back tenter. He was almost 6ft 3in tall, with blue eyes and brown hair; he became a drummer in the Corps of Drums and served with the 2nd Battalion, and later with the Westminster Garrison Battalion. He was buried in Droylsden Cemetery. (Grave reference: Section R. Grave 450.) He is listed on the Droylsden War Memorial Roll of Honour.

Guardsman William Henry SHAW, service number 4614268, Coldstream Guards, aged 23, was the son of Richard and Winifred Shaw, and the husband of Olwen Elizabeth Shaw, of Frome, Somerset. Richard Shaw and Winifred Heywood married in 1919 in Oldham. William was born on 31 October 1920 in Oldham and was originally a carpenter's labourer. He enlisted in the Guards at Huddersfield on 10 July 1939, after being in the Territorial Army since 1937; he was 6ft 1½in tall, with blue eyes and brown hair. He was posted abroad with the British Expeditionary Force in February 1940 and wounded by shrapnel on 17 May; he was evacuated to England on 25 May, presumably from Dunkirk. He later trained as a driver operator and became a specialist driver. He married Olwen Elizabeth Evans on 16 May 1942 at Sun Street Methodist Chapel, Frome. They had a son, David, in May 1943 who died aged 19 months in December 1944. William was buried in Oldham (Greenacres) Cemetery, as was his son. (Grave reference: Section L Row 13 Grave 17.)

Guardsman Anthony Sidney George TITCOMBE, service number 2661159, Coldstream Guards, aged 37, was the son of George and Ellen Rosa Titcombe, and the husband of Gertrude Maud Titcombe, of West Brompton, London. George (1878–1954) and Ellen (formerly Dunn, née Bellworthy, 1870–1937) married in 1898 in Faringdon; George was a brewer's drayman. Their youngest child was born on 30 March 1907 in Reading and named Sydney George. In 1927 he was travelling to Shanghai as a bookseller, aged 20, and intending to work in China. In 1928 he returned from Shanghai. He married Gertrude Maud Weiss (née Castle, 1911–94) on 20 June 1938 in Fulham (he was listed as Sidney G. Titcombe in the records at that point); she was born in Hong Kong and came from a military family. She had a daughter by her previous marriage, and they had a son in June 1939. In the 1939 Register Gertrude and her children were staying with her parents in Gosforth.

Anthony joined up on 29 April 1940, and was formerly a salesman and bookseller; he and a friend had owned a bookshop before the war. He was 6ft 2½in tall, with blue eyes and dark brown hair.

His son described him: 'I understand he had the odd beer with Dylan Thomas, and obviously wrote poetry himself, he was a great fan of the music of Taylor Coleridge, and I believe he played the piano, but to what standard I do not know.'

Anthony went overseas in January 1941 and served with the 3rd Battalion throughout the Libyan Campaign until reported missing in action at Tobruk on 20 June 1942. He had been taken prisoner. By 21 September 1942 he was in prisoner of war camp PG 65 (Gravina Altamura) near Bari in Italy; it was a transit camp for other ranks. On 25 May 1943 he was transferred to Camp PG or CC 145 PM 3300 (Campotosto/Montorio al Vomano (Teramo)) in Italy.

As of 8 September 1943 there were about 350 men in the camp. On 16 September 1943 he managed to escape to southern Italy, which was by then in Allied hands. He described his escape as follows:

> After the signing of the Armistice with Italy the guards over the camp were not very meticulous over their duties and PW [Prisoners of War] could walk out to the village. On the afternoon of 16 September, five of us including CSM Tubb walked out of the camp. The Italian Commandant, a captain, remonstrated with us but we took no notice and made our way SE through CATTANNO, BA[RI]SCIANO to MANOPELLO where we stayed owing to sickness for 15 days. I then went SE to MONTECHELLI near MONTENARO.

He rejoined the lines after a thirty-day walk to freedom; he returned to the UK on 24 December 1943. He had applied for leave to celebrate his wedding anniversary on 20 June 1944, together with the birthday of his son, but this could not be granted. He was buried in Brookwood Military Cemetery on 23 June. (Grave reference: 33.A.B.11.)

Lance Serjeant Edgar WATSON, service number 2651598, Coldstream Guards, aged 39, of Elm Cottage, Church Lane, Forthampton, was the son of George and Emily Watson (née Garton), of Ruston Parva, and the husband of Marie Watson, of Forthampton, Gloucestershire. His parents married in Driffield in 1903. He was born on 19 August 1904 in Driffield; he married Marie Albertine ('Mariette') Lemarchand (1894–1946) at Tewkesbury on 6 July 1936. He was a farm labourer until he enlisted with the Coldstream Guards on 20 February 1924. He was a transport driver in March 1925, and then served with them as part of the Shanghai Defence Force from 1927 (the year it was first formed in London) until 1939, when he returned to serve in the UK. He was just over 5ft 10in tall with brown eyes and brown hair. He was buried in Ruston Parva (St Nicholas) Churchyard. He is also commemorated on the 1939–45 memorial plaque in Lowthorpe church, in the church porch at Forthampton and on the roadside war memorial there.

Grenadier Guards (fifteen died)

Lance Corporal Alfred Reginald BOWYER, service number 2617261, Grenadier Guards, aged 24, was the son of James Bowyer (1872–1937) and Susan Elizabeth Pritchard (1880–1953) of Peterchurch; they married in Hereford in 1901. James was a jobbing builder in the 1911 census. Alfred, always known to his family as Fred, was born on 10 September 1919 in Peterchurch, Hereford, and was one of the youngest of twelve children; all his brothers but one went to war, with one serving in Italy and another in Egypt. He enlisted on 7 November 1939 in Hereford, and joined the Grenadier

Guards. He was 6ft tall, with hazel eyes and dark brown hair. He was not due to attend the service on 18 June 1944 (he was meant to be home on leave), but had swapped duties with a colleague; he was engaged to be married at the time of his death. He was buried in Peterchurch (St Peter) Churchyard, to the north-east of the church. He was much missed by his family, and his sister cherished the brass plate that used to hang on his bed in the barracks, his chest that contained his belongings at Wellington Barracks and the flag that covered his coffin for the rest of her long life.

Guardsman Sidney George BROUGHTON, service number 2620462, Grenadier Guards, aged 32, was the elder son of Annie Louisa Mulley (1870–?) and Noah Broughton (1865–1938), of Appleford, Oxfordshire; they married in 1910 in Abingdon. Noah was a woodman in 1881, a quarryman in 1901 and an agricultural labourer in the 1911 census. Sidney was born on 31 October 1911 in Abingdon, Berkshire. He left school at 14 and was a lorry driver for a haulage contractor for six years, with a clean driving record. He was a Baptist. In the 1939 Register he was working as a coal lorry driver and was living with his widowed mother and brother in Abingdon. He enlisted in Reading on 16 July 1940 and joined the Grenadier Guards. He was 5ft 11½in tall, with brown eyes and dark hair. He wanted to be a driver in the Army, but as of 1943 was a cyclist orderly, delivering despatches. His brother Arthur (1915–98) was also in the Grenadiers. Sidney was buried in Appleford (SS Peter and Paul) Churchyard, north of the chancel. His name is also listed on the memorial plaque inside the church; he was Appleford's only military casualty for 1939–1945.

Guardsman John Tatton Trevor CAVE, service number 2624469, Grenadier Guards, aged 18, was the son of John Henry Cave (1892–?) and Enid Sykes (1902–1991), of Armley, Leeds; they married on 24 April 1922 at Upper Armley, Christ Church. John Henry was a joiner at the time of the marriage. Their son John was born on 18 February 1926 in Bramley; he was called Tatton after his maternal grandfather and was usually known as Trevor. He had two sisters, Ruby and Rita. He joined the Grenadier Guards on 20 September 1943; he had previously been a clerk and had been a member of the Leeds Army Cadets for a year. He was 5ft 10½in tall, with blue-grey eyes and auburn hair. He was buried in Leeds (Armley) Cemetery. (Grave reference: Section G, grave 1248.)

Guardsman Alexander Only CROFTS, service number 14498932, Grenadier Guards, aged 18, was the son of Henry Only Crofts (1882–1955); Henry's first wife was Emily Maud Corke, but she died in 1918 after only three years of marriage. He married again in Rotherhithe in August 1920; his second wife was a widow, Margaret Leman or Lemon, née Monachan. Henry was a wood floor layer at the time of the marriage. Alexander was born in the March quarter of 1926 in Greenwich. He was given his father and paternal grandfather's unusual middle name. He was buried in Lewisham (Hither Green) Cemetery. (Grave reference: Sec. U. Grave 612 and Screen Wall. Panel 2 (the Hither Green Memorial)).

Guardsman Eric James CURRY, service number 14499452, Grenadier Guards, aged 18, was the son of Herbert and Mary Curry of Watford. His father, Herbert William Curry (1888–1964) married Mary Ann Sarah Clark (1886–?) on 3 April 1915 at St Stephen Walworth. In the 1911 census Herbert was a copperplate printer. In 1939 he was a printer's warehouseman. Eric was born in Watford on 1 January 1926; he had three older sisters. He worked as a printer's assistant. He was 6ft tall, with grey-blue eyes and dark brown hair. He was in the Home Guard from February 1942; he then enlisted in the General Service Corps on 10 March 1943, but deferred his entry until he could join the Grenadier Guards on 14 July 1943 at the age of 17½. He was buried in Brookwood Military Cemetery. (Grave reference: 33.A.B.2.)

The Lord Lt Col Edward Douglas John HAY (known to his friends as Eddie), service number 24133, Grenadier Guards, aged 55, was the son of William Montagu Hay, 10th Marquess of Tweeddale and the Marchioness Tweeddale, and the husband of Lady Audrey Hay (née Latham), of Theydon Mount and Quoitings, Marlow. He was the brother and heir presumptive of the 11th Marquess of Tweeddale.

Lieutenant Colonel Lord Edward Douglas John Hay was born on 2 November 1888 at Gifford, Scotland. He was a Presbyterian. He was the fifth child (and third son) of William Montagu Hay, 10th Marquis of Tweeddale and his wife Candida Louisa Bartolucci. His elder brother, Lord Arthur Hay, a captain in the Irish Guards, was killed in action, aged 25, in the Battle of the Aisne on 14 September 1914. He was educated at Eton and Magdalen College, Oxford, and joined the Grenadier Guards on 7 August 1916 from the Lothian and Border Horse Yeomanry. He served in France, Gallipoli, and Egypt until 1918. He was at the Peace Conference in Paris in 1918–19 and also undertook special missions to Austria, Hungary and Bulgaria; he served as staff captain to General Sir Edmund Ironside on a special mission to Hungary and Romania in 1921, and from 1921–23 acted as military secretary to Sir Herbert Samuel when the latter was High Commissioner in Palestine. He retired in May 1930 with the rank of major to look after a family property, but was re-employed in 1940. At that point he was working for the Auxiliary Fire Service. He was a captain from 8 November 1940, and was then posted to the Holding Garrison to be officer commanding on 18 November 1941. A year later, he was posted to Westminster Garrison. On 2 November

1943, he was appointed commanding officer, Westminster Garrison Battalion, with the rank of lieutenant colonel.

David Gurney wrote:

> [He] was ... very greatly loved. He commanded the Holding Battalion of Grenadiers and then commanded the Westminster Garrison Battalion when it was formed in November [1943]. Only a man like him could keep a mixed Battalion like this in order. He was enormously tactful at all times and would never tolerate any discrimination between the different Regiments in his Battalion.

Hay and Gurney were related by marriage; David's mother was the daughter of a Barclay on her mother's side.

Another tribute in the Household Brigade magazine described Hay as: 'universally beloved' and spoke of 'his unfailing kindness and patience'. He had an excellent sense of humour, and loved plants and gardening; David Gurney remembered a recent trip to Kew Gardens they had taken together.

He was married twice, firstly to (Bridget) Violet Florence Catherine Barclay (1895–1926) on 18 October 1917; they had a son (David George Montagu Hay, 1921–79) and a daughter (Marioth Christina Hay, 1918–2006). Bridget died on 17 March 1926. He married Audrey Clara Lilian Latham (1899–1985) on 5 July 1928; they had a daughter (Caroline Susan Elizabeth Hay, 1930–?) as well as two daughters from her first marriage. His leave was generally spent at Quoitings, Marlow. For a number of years his main residence was Hill Hall, Essex, where he was a JP and Deputy Lieutenant for Essex. In the 1939 Register, he and his wife were living at Coombe Cottage, Kingsbridge, with their three young children and a cook.

He died on 18 June 1944 in the Guards' Chapel. At that time he was commanding officer of the Grenadier Guards; he was walking back to his seat after reading the lesson, when the bomb hit and he was killed instantly by the blast, just before the Chapel collapsed. His regiment was about to deploy to France with the Guards Armoured Division. The funeral service was at Theydon Mount Church on 23 June, and brother officers of the Grenadier Guards were present; Major Arthur Penn (brother of Olive, who also died in the Chapel) represented the lieutenant colonel commanding the Grenadier Guards. He was buried in Theydon Mount (St Michael) Churchyard, to the east of the church. He is also listed on the House of Lords Roll of Honour (as the son of a peer), the Magdalen College Roll of Honour, the Scottish Roll of Honour, and with his brother Arthur on the Yester War Memorial in East Lothian.

Guardsman Denis Walter George HOOPER, service number 2613846, Grenadier Guards, aged 33, was the son of Bertie and Louisa Hooper and the husband of Olive Kathleen Hooper (née Coles, 1911–59), of West Kensington, London. Bertie Walter Hooper (1879–1962) was born in Barton Regis. He married Frances Louisa Yendole (1876–1950) in 1905 at Long Ashton. She was born in Nailsea and was working as a shop assistant there in the 1901 census. In the 1911 census Bertie was in the navy, serving in Malta on the *Cornwallis* as an engineer artificer second class; his wife, daughter and five-month-old son were staying with her parents in Nailsea.

Denis was born on 28 November 1910. He worked as a carpenter and handyman before enlisting on 7 November 1933 in Bristol. He joined the Grenadier Guards on 8 November 1933. He was 5ft 11in tall, with blue eyes and brown hair, and was posted to the 1st Battalion on 13 April 1934. He married Olive Coles on 16 November 1935 at Windsor Register Office; she was working as a cook. He was a recognised carpenter by profession, passing his Class 3 test in 1937 and his Class 1 in 1943. He was transferred to the reserve on 6 November 1937. His Guards file spoke of his exemplary character: 'a good clean honest hard working man. Has worked hard. Has been employed as a pioneer'.

He then went to work for a firm of drapers; he was mobilised on 1 September 1939 and posted to the 2nd Battalion. He was sent to France with the British Expeditionary Force on 29 September 1939; he served with the BEF until 28 December 1939, when he returned to the UK on leave until 7 January 1940. He served again with the BEF from 8 January 1940 until he was wounded at Dunkirk; one of his most upsetting memories was that of having to bury his rifle in the sand before being taken off the beach. He returned home on 23 May 1940; he was sent to an orthopaedic hospital to recover from his injuries. Allegedly he did not have to attend the Guards' Chapel service, but did so because a friend had to go and they were going greyhound racing afterwards, possibly at White City Stadium. He was buried in Brookwood Military Cemetery on 23 June 1944. (Grave reference: 33A.B.5.)

Guardsman William Henry NORTON, service number 2620397, Grenadier Guards, aged 27, of 22 Horace Street, Boston, was the son of Walter William and Elizabeth Norton, of Leicester, and the husband of Joan Norton of Leeds, Yorkshire. Walter William Norton (1874–1931) and Elizabeth Crowdell (1879–1956) married in 1905 in Leicester; he was a plumber and glazier. William was their youngest child, born on 6 April 1917 in Leicester. He was 5ft 9in tall, with grey eyes and black hair. He worked as a plumber, like his father before him, until he joined the Grenadier Guards on 12 July 1940, and continued to specialise in that trade; in 1943 he passed his Class 1 test. He married Joan Flockton on 27 June 1942 at St Aidan's Parish Church, Leeds. He was buried in Leicester (Welford Road) Cemetery. (Grave reference: Section O. Cons. Grave 208.)

Guardsman Jack SMITH, service number 14499377, Grenadier Guards, aged 18, was the son of Leonard and Martha Ann Smith, of Harehills, Leeds. Leonard Smith married Martha Ann Taylor in Leeds in 1920; he was a hairdresser. Jack was born in Bramley on 24 January 1926; he left school at 14 and worked for three and a half years at Messrs A. Kershaw (Engineers), Harehills, as a scientific instrument maker. He joined the General Service Corps on 3 March 1943, and transferred to the Grenadier Guards on 5 August that year once he turned 17½. He was 5ft 11¾in tall, with blue eyes and brown hair. His Guards file says: 'A fairly good man with a vigorous personality. May be a bit offhand at times.' He had two brothers; one served with the Royal Navy, the other with the 1st Derbyshire Yeomanry. He was buried in Leeds (Harehills) Cemetery. (Grave reference: Section U.2.Grave 19.)

Major Dick Henry Brewster THORNTON, service number 100546, Grenadier Guards, aged 36, of Bryanston Court, Mayfair, was the elder son of Gwendoline Thornton and the late Thornton B. Thornton, and husband of Rosemary Thornton of Marylebone, London. Thornton Benjamin Thornton was a very wealthy jute merchant, with an estate at Glendoll, Clova, Angus. The family home was at 31 Norfolk Street. Gwendoline and Thornton had two sons. The elder, Dick, was born on 21 July 1907 and was formerly a barrister; the younger son, Kenneth, was a stockbroker and married the daughter of the actress, Zena Dare.

Thornton Benjamin Thornton died in London on 21 October 1933 as a result of a car accident. He and his younger son were involved in an accident on the Great North Road while on their way back from Clova, where they had spent the shooting season; their car and a lorry collided head on. Thornton's funeral was at Golders Green Crematorium three days later. He left the sum of £335,431.

Dick was called to the Bar (Inner Temple) in 1933, and remained in practice until 1940. According to his Guards record, he spoke French and had visited the USA, France, Switzerland and the West Indies. He was a barrister-at-law, an MA and a member of the Medico-Legal Society.

He became engaged to Rosemary, only daughter of the late Arthur Cohen, on 25 October 1937. Her father had been a stockbroker and had served in the Grenadier Guards; he died in the south of France in 1927, leaving a considerable fortune. Rosemary was tall, dark-haired and blue-eyed, and very good-looking, according to her friend Peggy Graves. When Dick and Rosemary married on 16 December 1937, she walked up the aisle alone at St Margaret's Westminster, where her mother met her and gave her away, as she had no close male relatives. Two days later the couple sailed for New York on the *Normandie* on their honeymoon. They had a son in December 1938; at that point they were living at 8 Montagu Square, and were neighbours of Gwen

Horton at no. 23. In the 1939 Register they were staying at Tibbs Farm, Sevenoaks, with the Mosenthals; Harold Mosenthal was a merchant banker and his wife was a dress designer, Idare. The Thorntons had a house nearby: Woodend, Crockham Hill, Edenbridge, Kent.

Dick joined the Grenadier Guards on 4 September 1940 as a second lieutenant; he was 5ft 8in tall, with brown hair and hazel eyes. He became ADC in the Combined Airborne Division on 13 November 1941, where he worked with Major-General Sir Frederick Arthur Montague 'Boy' Browning, husband of Daphne du Maurier. Because of an old knee injury, Dick suffered some pain and had limited movement in his left knee and foot; he walked with a limp. After a medical board, it was decided he should be employed in a sedentary capacity. He was transferred to the London District Legal Aid Section on 15 July 1942. The Army Legal Aid scheme had been set up jointly with the Army and the RAF to help servicemen obtain help and advice, previously very much the preserve of the rich. He became a temporary captain in October 1942.

By this time Dick and Rosemary were living in London; they had a flat in Bryanston Court and, as Dick's battalion was quartered at Wellington Barracks, he could live at home. They were close friends of the writers Charles and Peggy Graves, who lived nearby; Rosemary had been one of Peggy's bridesmaids, and they met several times a week to socialise and play bridge. Peggy's book *Married to Charles* gives a vivid account of their friendship; she wrote that Dick had 'a most amusing sense of humour and was good company'. He had been promoted to major shortly before the Guards' Chapel incident.

In the afternoon of 18 June, Rosemary rang Peggy to say that Dick had been at the service that morning; could Charles make enquiries? Charles went to the Chapel and spoke to an orderly, who assured him he knew exactly where Dick would have been sitting, as he always chose the same place; it would be some hours before they could hope to rescue him. All the following day Peggy kept hearing of more people she knew that had been killed, including Gwen Horton and the Gordon Walls. On the Tuesday morning, Rosemary called her to say she could no longer believe there was any hope. Dick's body was finally found late on the Tuesday night. He is commemorated on Panel 3 at Golders Green Crematorium, and is listed on the Lord's Marylebone Cricket Club Roll of Honour for World War Two.

Guardsman Henry Alfred George THORNTON, service number 2620282, Grenadier Guards, aged 30, of 76 Clifton Rise, Deptford, was the son of Henry James and Florence Charlotte Thornton, of Bermondsey, London. Henry James Thornton (1881–1952) and Florence Charlotte Allinson (1885–1974) married in 1907 at St Olave, Bermondsey; Henry James was a carman. They had five children. Their son Henry was born on 17 July 1913 in Bermondsey. He worked for nine years as a foreman fur sorter at C.W. Martin & Son, fur dressers and dyers; he had previously been a restaurant clerk in Holborn. In the 1939 Register, Henry senior was a lorry driver, while his son was a dyed fur sorter. Henry joined the Grenadier Guards on 18 July 1940; he wanted to be considered for the trades of photography and maintaining engines. (He drove a motorbike). He was 5ft 11¾in tall, with grey eyes and brown hair. He married Kathleen Jean Mary Arthur in Deptford on 18 October 1941. They had a daughter in April 1944. He was buried in Brookwood Military Cemetery on 23 June. (Grave reference: 33.A.B.4.)

Warrant Officer Class II (Drill Sergeant) Nathaniel TURTON, service number 2606370, Grenadier Guards, aged 44, of Chelsea Barracks, was the son of Nathaniel and Letitia (or Esther) Turton of Liverpool. His father was a labourer, but had become a gas plumber by the time of the 1911 census. They had four children. Nathaniel was born in September 1899. He joined up on 26 February 1917; he was formerly a motor driver. He served in France and Egypt. He joined the Guards on 4 November 1919. By 29 July 1922 he had become a drummer. He was promoted to corporal on 17 February 1927 and to sergeant on 23 August 1927. However, in the spring of the following year, he was tried and convicted for 'striking a soldier'; in reality he had lost his temper and upended a bowl of porridge over him. He was sentenced to be 'reduced to the ranks' after a court martial, so then had to work his way up again; he eventually rose to the rank of drill sergeant. The Household Brigade magazine described him as someone 'who lived for his job and whose long experience and unflagging keenness brought so many credits to the Battalion'.

He married Emily Dwyer (1895–1931) in Kensington Register Office on 10 November 1923; their son (Nathaniel, after his father) was born in 1927 and Emily died at the end of 1931. Nathaniel later married Marjorie Geraldine Hill on 15 December 1936 at St Paul's Church, Knightsbridge, and they had a son in 1938. In 1938 the electoral roll shows them living at Regents Park Barracks (along with James Causley Windram and others). The marriage broke down. In 1944 he was engaged to someone else, and planned to marry later that year once his divorce came through; he asked his fiancée to come to the chapel that day, but she was Church of Scotland and declined. He was buried in Brookwood Military Cemetery on 23 June. (Grave reference: 33A.B.1.)

Guardsman Derek James WEAVER, service number 2624193, Grenadier Guards, aged 19. He was the son of Albert James Weaver and Millicent Weaver, of Oaklands Grove, Shepherd's Bush, London. Albert was a fishmonger in the 1911 census. Albert James Weaver (1887–1970) and Millicent Eldred (1893–1971) married in 1920 in Epsom. Derek was born on 28 April

1925 in Shepherds Bush and was their third child and elder son in a family of seven. He was closest to his elder sister, Clarice, and to his brother, Alec. He passed the 11-plus, but was unable to attend grammar school for financial reasons. He left school at 14; he was a star pupil and excelled in English. He was also a talented athlete. He worked for Johnson & Mathey, then moved to Chas. Phillips Chemical Co., Acton, as a warehouseman; he was 6ft tall, with brown hair and hazel eyes. He had been a private in the Home Guard for twelve months before he enlisted; he was serving on an anti-aircraft battery at Wormwood Scrubs. He enlisted at Caterham and joined the Grenadier Guards on 3 June 1943, soon after his 18th birthday. His test results were described as 'surprisingly good'. After training, he was posted to Westminster Garrison Battalion on 14 December 1943; their main duty was to guard important buildings in Westminster, like Downing Street, St James's Palace and neighbouring Buckingham Palace. He had decided that after the war he would join the Palestine Police Force. On Sundays he would normally return home to his family; he was not meant to be on church parade on Sunday, 18 June and his family were expecting him for lunch. Apparently he had volunteered for church parade in place of an ATS contingent which had been excused duties; he loved the services and had described them to his parents as 'absolutely marvellous'. His family later heard that Derek would have survived the bombing if he had stayed in his original pew. An officer had wanted to fill an empty pew separating the officers at the front of the Chapel from the men behind them. As Derek was at the end of his row he was told to move forward. Those he left behind survived, including James Dunn. He was buried in Brookwood Military Cemetery on 23 June. (Grave reference: 33A.B.3.)

Irish Guards (four died)

Guardsman Dennis George GIBSON, service number 2719737, aged 24, was serving in the 2nd Battalion, Irish Guards in 1944. He was the only son of Ernest and Florence Gibson (née Burtenshaw) of Wandsworth, and the husband of Lena Gibson of East Croydon, Surrey. He was born on 21 September 1919 in Wandsworth. He joined the Irish Guards at Caterham on 22 December 1939; he had formerly been working as a furniture sales clerk. His service record says he was 5ft 11in tall, with blue eyes and brown hair; he was described as 'a very useful shot' and 'above the average of his squad all round'. He served in Holland and France during 1940; he took part in the evacuation of the Hague in mid-May (the Irish Guards were there to cover the evacuation of the Dutch Royal Family and government), and in the Battle of Boulogne a week later. (The latter was an attempt to buy time for the BEF's evacuation from Calais and Dunkirk.) He married Lena Joan Avery at St Michael's Church, Tilehurst, on 1 March 1941. Their first son, Brian, was born in March 1943, but died in infancy; their second son, Barry, born in May

1944 in Croydon, was less than three weeks old at the time of his father's death. Dennis was buried in Wandsworth Cemetery. (Grave reference: Block 28, grave 41.)

Major John GILLIAT, service number 63033, was serving as a major in 1944 in the 1st Battalion, Irish Guards, aged 30. He was the second son of John and Lilian Gilliat, of Sunningdale, Berkshire. John Francis Grey Gilliat (1883–1948) was the director of the bank of Australasia, British West Africa and South Africa; he married Lilian Florence Maud Chetwynd (1876–1962) in 1909 in Westminster. She was formerly the wife of Henry Paget, 5th Marquess of Anglesey, her cousin, otherwise known as 'the dancing Marquess'. John served as a lieutenant in the Life Guards in France in the First World War. His younger son, also John, was born on 4 January 1914 in Paddington. He attended Eton, and his service record notes that he had travelled in Canada and Europe before joining the Guards in 1934 at the age of 20. He served in Egypt from 1936 to 1938, and was stationed at Cairo; the 1st Battalion was also posted to Palestine for three months to assist with internal security duties, but returned to England for Christmas 1938. He later saw service in Norway from April to June 1940. He was buried in Brookwood Cemetery, in the family plot, near his elder brother Simon, who had died in an air accident on 7 August 1936, aged 23. (Grave reference: St Chad's Avenue, grave 209123.) John is also named on the Windlesham Roll of Honour.

The true horror of the air accident was that both brothers were involved. At about 6.00pm on 7 August, John came by car from Pirbright to Farnborough to wait for his brother, who was to fly him to Lympne aerodrome for an officers' guest night; Simon was a pilot officer in 601 Squadron, Auxiliary Air Force. They took off. When the plane was about 100ft above the officers' mess, it turned down wind, stalled at about 100ft and crashed on the roof of the RAF cookhouse; shortly afterwards it caught fire. John survived because he was sitting in the back seat and was thrown onto the roof, although he sustained facial injuries. Crying 'My God. It's my brother. It's all my fault', he made frantic efforts to save the pilot, but the RAF and Farnborough fire brigades could not damp down the flames. The post mortem suggested the accident was due to pilot error.

Lance Serjeant Percy Leonard LIVERMORE, service number 2720194, Irish Guards, aged 31, was the second son of John and Alice Louisa Livermore, of Harold Wood. John Livermore (1874–1958) and Alice Louisa Young (1880–1962) married in 1905. Percy was born on 8 November 1912 in Romford, and was the middle child of seven. He was working as a builder's labourer when he joined the Irish Guards at Whipps Cross on 26 February 1940. His service record states he was almost 5ft 10in tall, with blue eyes and brown hair. He married Dorothy (or Doreen) Kelly, née Downes (1914–1985) on 11 August 1938 in Romford. They had four children: a daughter who died in infancy, and three sons. Their youngest son was born only six weeks before his father died in the Guards' Chapel. Percy was buried in Hornchurch Cemetery on Saturday 24 June 1944. The coffin, which was draped with the Union Jack, was carried by eight Guardsmen. (Grave reference: Sec. A, grave 1359.)

Guardsman Leslie Charles PHILLIPS, service number 2722011, Irish Guards, aged 24, was the son of Harold Charles and Lucy Phillips, and the husband of Ellen Phillips, of East Putney, London. Harold Phillips (1885–1955) married Lucy Ann Free (1893–1964) in August 1915 in Cambridge. They had six children. Harold was a cattle drover in 1915. Later that year he enlisted in the 3rd Battalion Norfolk Regiment, and served in France and Egypt. The 1939 Register describes him as a cattle drover and casual labourer. Leslie was born in Chesterton on 10 June 1920, and worked as a van driver's assistant for Matthew & Son, Cambridge, until he joined the Irish Guards on 8 August 1940 at Caterham. His service record describes him as just over 6ft tall, with brown eyes and black hair. He married Ellen Elkins in Wandsworth on 19 November 1943. He was buried in Brookwood Military Cemetery on 23 June. (Grave reference: 33A.B.12.)

Scots Guards (five died)

Lieutenant Colonel John Murray (Ivan) COBBOLD, service number 110300, Scots Guards, DL, JP, aged 47, was the son of John Dupuis Cobbold, DL (1861–1929) and Evelyn Murray (1867–1963), and the husband of Lady Blanche Cobbold (née Cavendish), of Glemham Hall, Suffolk. His parents married in Cairo in April 1891. Lady Evelyn Cobbold was an early convert to Islam; she had spent much of her childhood in Algiers and Cairo, spoke Arabic and was the first Englishwoman to make the pilgrimage to Mecca in 1933. She was a sister of the Earl of Dunmore, VC, who was lord-in-waiting to the king; she inherited her love of travel from her father, Lord Dunmore. John Dupuis Cobbold was in turn deputy lieutenant and sheriff of Suffolk and mayor of Ipswich; he was an excellent tennis player and travelled extensively, notably in Kashmir, the Caucasus, Russia and Asia Minor.

John was born at Holy Wells, Ipswich, on 28 January 1897. His nurse nicknamed him 'Ivan the terrible', and the name stuck; he was known as Ivan for the rest of his life. He was educated at Eton. He met his future wife in Canada while her father was Viceroy there; Lady Blanche Katherine Cavendish (1898–1987) was the second daughter of the 9th Duke of Devonshire, and she and Ivan married in the Guards' Chapel on 30 April 1919. They had four children. They had celebrated their silver wedding anniversary six weeks before the Guards' Chapel incident. One of Blanche's younger sisters, Lady Dorothy (1900–66), married Harold Macmillan (1894–1986, who later became Prime Minister, 1957–1963, and who served with the Grenadier Guards in the war), in 1920.

Ivan joined the Scots Guards on 3 September 1915 and served in France, where he was injured in 1917; he received a gunshot wound to the face. The injury flared up the following year and he was invalided out just before the end of the war. Later he joined the family brewing business, Cobbold & Co., and became chairman after his father's death in 1929. He was a keen sportsman and one of the best shots in the country. He became president of Ipswich Town FC in 1935; they turned professional in 1936 with his support.

He rejoined the Scots Guards on 18 October 1939. He undertook a range of roles and was clearly anxious to be of service. He was ADC to GOC, London area, followed by DAPM London District from June 1942. Two months later, he became liaison officer with the HQ of the European Theatre of Operations of the US Army (ETOUSA). At the time of his death he was the commanding officer of the Scots Guards; he was acting as liaison officer with SHAEF (Supreme Headquarters Allied Expeditionary Force, commanded by Eisenhower) and was working closely with General Bedell Smith, Eisenhower's chief of staff. (In 1942, the Long Room at Purdey's, the gun makers, was used by Bedell Smith and Eisenhower for battle planning, and it was later used for planning the D-Day landings. It is highly likely that Ivan's links with Tom Purdey made this possible.) The General had been invited to accompany Ivan to the Guards' Chapel service on 18 June, but had been too busy to leave his office. It is possible that Colonel Gustav B. Guenther (who died in the same incident), another friend of Eisenhower, accompanied him instead. Tom Purdey made enquiries about Ivan Cobbold later that day; Ivan was both a long-time customer of Purdey's and a personal friend, as well as a major shareholder in the firm. Ivan is commemorated on Panel 1 at Golders Green Crematorium, and on the Rannoch War Memorial on the east bank of Loch Rannoch. There was a memorial service for him on 30 June at St Mark's, North Audley Street.

Lord Cranworth penned a personal tribute to Ivan, published in *The Times* on 27 June 1944:

Ivan Cobbold was a man of many talents, great abilities, and infinite charm. Moreover, he was a patriot with every fibre of his being ... There was no one on his estate or in his business with whom he was not fully acquainted and with whose welfare he was not concerned.

As a sportsman Ivan was most distinguished. A good cricketer in the Eton XI and a fine player of all ball games, he will be best remembered as a great shot – indeed he had good claims to rank as the best of his contemporaries. When a well-known paper called for the names of the 12 best shots, his name was included in every list and usually at the top. He was an almost equally good fisherman. Moreover, he was equally interested in the sport of others. Thus, he spent much time, money and an infinity of pains in launching the Ipswich football team on what bade fair to be a most prosperous career.

In his busy life he never neglected public work in his country and when he undertook a job one knew that it would be done and well done. Leaving school while young he joined the Scots Guards and saw service in France, where he was wounded. He rejoined his old regiment at the outbreak of the present war and when killed was employed with the American forces in a post of supreme importance for which he was ideally qualified. In that position, he will be hard indeed to replace.

As a host he was at his very best. His aim was the happiness of each of his many guests. His home life was perfect. He was adored by his family. Their happiness was his happiness and their sorrows and disappointments his.

Such was the life Ivan Cobbold lived, and his manner of living it brought him much esteem and hosts of friends. But there was another Ivan of which the world knew less. This was the man who went about quietly doing kindnesses to those in trouble, whether monetary or otherwise. His heart, his hand, and his pocket were ever ready with the one proviso, 'No one is to know'. He was a man of true generosity and intense loyalty and these characteristics will stand in the memory of his friends as a monument more enduring than brass.

Lieutenant Harold William DODS, service number 200108, Scots Guards, aged 35, was the only son of Harold and Florence Louisa Dods, of Highfield House, Donington. Harold Dods (1867–1948) married Florence Louisa Holman (1885–1965) on 3 April 1908 at Holy Trinity, Paddington; he was a farmer and landowner. They had four children, three of whom survived to adulthood. The eldest, Harold William, was born on 25 March 1909 in Gosberton and was educated at Tonbridge School, where he was in the OTC from 1923–27; he had two sisters. He played cricket for Lincolnshire 1927–39; he and his father were both well-known cricketers. In the winter of 1937 he travelled to Uruguay as part of Captain T.E.W. Brinckman's cricket team, complete with umpire, all travelling first class. He became captain of Lincolnshire County Cricket Club and was appointed a JP in 1939, the youngest magistrate in the county. He served with the Scots Guards from 1941, training with the Officers' Squad at Caterham and then spending four months at Sandhurst before joining the Guards in August; he was formerly an agricultural merchant. He served as assistant to Captain Pearson, and found the work congenial and interesting. He married Marigold Bird (1922–92) on 17 February 1944 at St Lucia's Church, Dembleby; she was serving in the Women's Land Army and was the niece of a Grantham magistrate. He was given two weeks' privilege leave after the wedding. On 18 June 1944, his married sister, Mrs Lilian Crampton, had arranged to attend the service with him, but her train from Donington was half an hour late.

His funeral was at Donington on Friday, 23 June, at 2.00pm. He was buried in Donington Old Cemetery. (Grave reference: 380.) There is also a plaque to him in the memorial cloister of the Guards Chapel:

> Internal plaque: THE THREE MAPLE TREES / IN THE GARDEN / WERE GIVEN / IN MEMORY OF / LIEUTENANT / HAROLD WILLIAM DODS / SCOTS GUARDS / WHO WAS KILLED / IN THE OLD CHAPEL / 18TH JUNE 1944.

David Gurney, a fellow lieutenant in the Scots Guards, wrote:

> Harold will be missed very much by everyone here, especially by the Scots Guard Officers. He was stationed at the Tower and then at Chelsea, where he functioned as PAD officer and later as Assistant Adjutant. He came to Wellington Barracks with the Battalion in November of last year and became Assistant Adjutant early this year. One of his unofficial nick-names was 'Boodles' because of his fondness for that Club; he used to play Bridge there almost every evening ... Last year Harold became engaged to a charming land-girl called Marigold Bird. We were all delighted with his choice when he brought his fiancée to Chapel at Chelsea and they came for drinks with me on Guard. As Harold said at the time 'I have known Marigold since she was a child. She has carried my guns; we have danced at the 400 [Club, Leicester Square] together, I've taught her how to drink port. She will make a good wife'. They were married in February and Harold used to visit his wife in Kent where she worked on some sort of herb farm. Harold's views on most things were downright and Tory, but he had scores of very funny sporting stories.

Second Lieutenant James Arthur Grey DUBERLY, service number 320937, Scots Guards, aged 18, was the only child of Major Montagu Richard William Duberly OBE (1887–1976), and of Lady Eileen Duberly (née Stopford, 1887–1978), of Buckden; they married on 3 March 1924 at St Paul's, Knightsbridge. Montagu was an officer in the 3rd Sikh Pioneers and was awarded the OBE for special services. James was born on 3 September 1925 in Simla, India; he was named Arthur Grey after his paternal grandfather and James after his maternal grandfather, James Walter Milles Stopford, 6th Earl of Courtown, County Wexford. His name had been put down for the Scots

Guards as far back as January 1935. He was educated at Winchester College, 1938–1943; he was a prefect and the platoon commander of his house. He enlisted on 9 August 1943 and served in the ranks until 25 May 1944; he was described as 'a keen agile man who … should do well as he has the right manner to take charge of others.' He was 5ft 10in tall, with light brown hair and blue eyes. 'His one idea was soldiering and to make it his career'. He was posted to the Training Battalion of the Scots Guards on 26 May 1944, three weeks before he was killed in the Guards' Chapel. His body was one of the last to be identified; Captain Pearson rang Lady Eileen at 12 o'clock on Tuesday, 20 June and said that her son was missing. He could offer no hope of his being found alive. James was buried in Great Staughton (St Andrew) Churchyard; his funeral was at 2.30pm on 23 June, and there was a service of remembrance for him on 5 July. He is also commemorated in the Ferns Cathedral (County Wexford) 1939–1945 Roll of Honour, and the Buckden War Memorial, and in the War Cloister at Winchester College. In his memory, his parents endowed the college with the Duberly Prize for the best soldier in the Junior Training Corps; it is still awarded each term.

Lance Corporal Horace HYDE, service number 2698573, Scots Guards, aged 30, was the son of James and Fanny Hewitt Hyde, of Denton, and the husband of Edna Hyde of North Reddish, Stockport, Cheshire. James Hewitt Hyde (1883–1957) was a printer and married Fanny Brant (1881–1946) in Leicester in 1911. They had two children; Horace was the elder. He was born on 24 December 1913 in Chorlton; the 1939 Register describes him as a pattern card maker, and his father was a newspaper printer. They were living with Horace's mother and younger sister. Horace joined up on 27 June 1940. He was 5ft 10½in tall, with grey eyes and black hair. He married Edna Walton on 27 October 1940 in Stockport; he joined Westminster Garrison Battalion on 2 November 1943. He was buried in Manchester (Gorton) Cemetery. (Grave reference: Section G Grave 404.)

Guardsman George TRANTER, service number 2695860, Scots Guards, aged 28, was the son of Jabez and Alice Jane Tranter, of Glass Houghton, Castleford; Jabez Tranter (1885–1961) and Alice Jane Llewellyn (1890–1965), married in 1913 in Pontefract. George was the eldest of four children and was born on 21 August 1915 in Pontefract. He enlisted on 27 January 1938, and served at home until 18 November that year; he had previously worked as a dyer. He was 5ft 11in tall, with blue eyes and brown hair. He then served in Egypt from 19 November 1938 until 25 May 1940, after which he returned home. He was buried in Castleford New Cemetery. (Grave reference: Section U. Grave 199.) His father was later buried in the same grave. George was described as 'in every way a fine soldier and was respected by all his colleagues.'

Welsh Guards (two died)

Guardsmen Male and Stamp were the only Welsh Guards who died at the service, and two of the youngest victims.

Guardsman Ahmand [or Ahmond] MALE, aged 18, service number 2739032, (listed as Ahmond Male in the Guards records), was the stepson of Sydney Perkins and son of Florence Perkins (née Davies), of Glyn Neath. He was born on 10 July 1925 in Neath to Richard and Florence Male (née Davies); he was working as a labourer before he enlisted in Swansea on 3 May 1943 at the age of 17. He was buried in Neath Higher (Glyn Neath) Cemetery. (Grave reference: Block D. Grave 707.)

Guardsman Ernest Keith STAMP, aged 17, service number 2739031, Welsh Guards, was the younger son of Sidney Howard and Jessie Stamp, of Reading. Sidney Howard Stamp was a private in the 1st Battalion of the Royal Berkshire Regiment in the First World War and received the DCM for conspicuous gallantry and devotion to duty on 6 February 1918. His son Ernest was born on 11 January in either 1926 or 1927 in Reading; the official birth records state 1927 but his Welsh Guards record says 1926. He enlisted in Reading on 4 August 1943; before then he was working as a labourer. By alleging he was born in 1926, this would make him 17½ at the time he enlisted; in reality he was only 16. He was almost 6ft 3in tall, fair-haired and blue-eyed. He was the youngest Guards' Chapel victim. He was buried in Brookwood Military Cemetery on 23 June. (Grave reference: 33.A.B.13.)

Chaplains: Guards and Australian

Two chaplains died in the incident; one had recently become chaplain to the Brigade of Guards, while the other was due to return to Australia from his tour of duty overseas.

Chaplain 2nd Class the Reverend Ralph Henry WHITROW, TD CF, service number 40452, Royal Army Chaplains' Department, aged 47, of Weeke Rectory, was the younger son of Benjamin and Mary Whitrow, and the husband of Brenda Muriel Whitrow (1908–91), of Winchester. He was a Minor Canon of Winchester Cathedral and chaplain to the Brigade of Guards.

Benjamin Whitrow (1851–1912) married Mary Davey (1857–1928) in 1888 in Kent. He was a well-known chemist in Tunbridge Wells, and his wife was the first headmistress of Vale Towers Middle Grade School; although she left this post on her marriage, she continued to be involved as a governor of the High School. Ralph, their younger son, was born on 20 December 1896 in Tonbridge. He enlisted in the Royal Field Artillery on 28 August 1916. On 13 January 1917 he was gazetted second lieutenant, Special Reserve and crossed over to France. On 5 March 1917 he was posted to D Battery, 62 Brigade, 12th Division. He was made Mess president and 'discovered a talent for administration'. In October 1917 he was moved to D Battery, 148 Brigade, 30th Division. At this stage he was recommended for the MC: 'the recommendation didn't go through, but at least it shows he was well thought of by his superiors.' He took part in the final offensive on 18 August 1918 and took part in the final advance through Wulverghem, Messines, Houthem and Menin. After the Armistice he was at Aisne, a village in Belgium, and made an acting captain and adjutant of his brigade. He was demobbed on 20 June 1919.

He studied Modern History at Worcester College, Oxford, and then underwent theological training at Cuddesdon College, Oxford. He was ordained in 1923. He was a curate at St Luke's Battersea 1924–1930. He married Brenda Muriel Bent on 6 July 1932 at St Luke's; they had three children, one of whom died when only a few days old.

Ralph wrote to his elder brother Philip every Sunday for more than six years, from 1938 to 1944. The last letter was posted on his way to the Guards' Chapel service on 18 June. They give a vivid and detailed account of his life.

Ralph was called up on 5 September 1939, and on the following day, he marched with the men to Southampton. Later that month he was promoted to substantive third class and posted as Senior Chaplain to the 45th Division HQ. He took up his appointment in Exeter on 27 September, twenty-three years after his Army career had begun there in 1916. He did not enjoy life at HQ: 'too much pen pushing'. Of necessity he did a lot of travelling. In May 1940 he was posted to 45th Division HQ in Kent; six months later he was posted to the north of England.

In October 1941 he was diagnosed with spondylitis ossificans ligamentosa, which rendered him unfit for overseas service. Had he lived longer, his spine would eventually have fused rigidly together.

He much preferred life in a battalion with the men, or better still back in his Winchester parish. Throughout the war he was responsible for finding and paying his locums in Winchester, and for the maintenance of the Rectory. The Bishop of Winchester was helpful, but only after matters came to a head in 1943. In August 1943 Ralph was posted to London, where he found himself doing two jobs: working at the War Office, which was the real reason for the move to London, and 'the job at Chelsea Barracks'. The latter included responsibility for hundreds of men, garrison services, as well as all the Chaplaincy services for one quarter of the whole of London to supervise. As he remarked ruefully: 'I am really earning my pay'.

Two months later he was posted to HQ Midland District in Nottingham, where he was responsible for Nottinghamshire, Derbyshire and Leicestershire. He remained there until his move to the Guards' Chapel.

In a letter dated 11 May 1944 he wrote to his brother that 'I have been fetched up here to be DACG [Deputy Assistant Chaplain General] London District. I do not actually report until tomorrow'. He 'assumed duty' on 17 May 1944. He continued: 'I am not very pleased at having to live in London again. But of course it is a very great promotion really as no one but a regular has ever been DACG before. It is the most important 2nd Class job there is ... Not my line at all as you know, but of course I'm flattered'. He had replaced the Reverend Hugh Norton, who had been there for six years.

The last few weeks of his life were not his happiest. He could not afford to live in the mess, even if there had been room for him, so was expected to find his own accommodation. This was impossible in London at that time, so he stayed with his elderly widowed mother-in-law in Streatham. He used to have supper alone at his club, sit for a while and then travel to Streatham. His daughter summed him up:

> He was a caring man who obviously enjoyed (and was good at) the pastoral aspect of being a clergyman, who, like many men in wartime, hated being away from his wife and family and with limited opportunities to use his pastoral skills. He enjoyed the simple things of life like walking, cycling and a good book to read in front of a fire with his pipe.

In his final letter to Philip, he wrote 'I must write today as we have a Bishop preaching tomorrow and I have to give him lunch, and if he sits a bit I might well get behind with my correspondence.' This was the Bishop of Maidstone, who survived the service because he was sheltered by the apse.

There was a requiem for him in Winchester Cathedral on 23 June 1944, followed by a funeral service at St Paul's Church, Weeke. He was buried in Winchester (West Hill) Old Cemetery. (Grave reference: Square 27, grave 3693; his wife was later buried in the same grave.)

Chaplain Squadron Leader the Reverend Gordon Gladstone WOOD, aged 42, was the son of Alfred and Janet Wood, and the husband of Gwendoline Enid Wood, of Beverley Hills, New South Wales, Australia. Alfred Wood (1867–1941) and Janet Wemyss (1866–1959) married in 1895 in Melbourne. They had three children; Gordon was the youngest. He was born on 24 June 1901 in Moonta Mines, South Australia, and married Gwendolen (Gwen) Enid Staples (1907–83) on 30 June 1928 in Bexley, New South Wales; they had two children, Grahame and Narelle. The *Canberra Times* of the period described him as 'an Australian Air Force padre, Squadron Leader Woods' [*sic*]. He held a licentiate of theology and was ordained in 1927; he was a Methodist. He enlisted on 27 November 1940 in Wellington, NSW, and became an RAAF chaplain. His first posting was at the RAAF Bomber Training squadron at Evans Head, NSW, where he served for two years.

His RAAF record has been digitised. It includes two reports from senior officers in 1942:

G.G. Wood did a good job at this unit. As well as his church duties he was president of the recreation club. He was keen on recreation and did much towards the wellbeing and amusement of the troops. He displayed organising ability as well as keenness with regard to recreation and sport.

This officer showed initiative in making the services as attractive as possible by the use of films and choral presentation. In this way he increased his attendances; he furnished a chapel within the Chaplains' block and a rest room which was popular among the troops.

He then served as a squadron leader attached to RAAF Overseas HQ at Kodak House, Kingsway, London, where he formed the RAAF choir there, the 'Glee Club', and served as their conductor. During his service in the UK, his specific task was to look after the welfare of Australian airmen, and he travelled extensively to the airfields scattered throughout the UK. He was a counsellor, providing moral and spiritual support to airmen, and in case of loss, to their families back home. He had completed his term of duty and was due to return to Australia in early June; however, his transport home was delayed because of D-Day. As a consequence of the delay, he continued his service in London, and was then due to fly home on 19 June. On Sunday 18th, his last day in the UK, he chose to attend the Guards' Chapel ceremony as he was so impressed by his previous visit there. His death was advised by telegram to his family in Australia, but his letters home continued to arrive by aerogram for weeks after his death.

He was buried in the Australian section of Brookwood Military Cemetery on 23 June 1944. (Grave reference: 4.N.16.) His name is on the Australian War memorial in Canberra, panel 97, and a memorial chapel was dedicated to him in the Uniting Church, Arthur Street, Wellington, New South Wales, where he had been superintendent minister, 1937–40. There is also a memorial to him and his wife in Woronora Cemetery, Sutherland, New South Wales.

Chapter 7

The Guards' Chapel and the Survivors

The Guards' Chapel incident cast a long shadow. Many of the injured were in hospital for months; one of the musicians died early the following year from his injuries. Some casualties suffered life-changing injuries, while others were haunted by what had happened and the loss of their friends and colleagues. For all those involved, either directly or indirectly, 18 June 1944 could never be forgotten.

It is hard to quantify the human cost of the Guards' Chapel tragedy; 124 people died, many of them had families. Some left behind young children. Back in 1944 there was no formal support system in place; for example, there was no NHS, no system of benefits for single parents and, once the war ended, no workplace nurseries. Brothers, sisters, aunts, uncles, parents and grandparents: any or all of these might be called upon to help keep a family together. The Guards were generous in supporting those widowed or in poverty, but life for those who had lost a loved one must have been very hard, both emotionally and financially.

What of the survivors? We know that 141 people were seriously injured in the incident. The swift response of the rescue effort undoubtedly saved many lives, rescuing people from the rubble and giving them immediate first aid. However, it is often hard to establish what happened to those who escaped alive. Ironically, the Commonwealth War Graves Commission records of the military and civilian war dead make it comparatively easy to establish at least some basic facts about most of the dead. In contrast, there is little published or publicly available about the survivors. They are not often mentioned in newspapers and reports because of the embargo on giving details about V1 attacks that might assist the enemy; there were also concerns for morale. For the researcher, it is often difficult to identify the survivors with any certainty, still less trace their lives after the incident. Some individuals stand out, such as Max Dolmatin, who was born near Minsk, and went halfway across the world to make a new life in America with his family, but who ended up in the US Army in London on 18 June 1944. Others remain anonymous, because of the lack of concrete facts.

Let us begin by tracing the lives of two of the survivors, whose struggle to escape from the Chapel was described in Chapter 4.

Keith Lewis, an 18-year-old Grenadier Guardsman, had been trapped in the wreckage for some hours; he was minutes from death when rescued, and had suffered broken bones and a badly lacerated scalp. He was taken to St Thomas' Hospital; he remained in hospital and convalescing for three months to recover from his injuries. When he returned to the Guards, he was told to report to Sergeant Major Francis Joy, who had a reputation for discipline. To Keith's surprise, he was asked to sit down and offered a cup of tea, a most unexpected welcome. (He had already been told that the sergeant major had been seen in tears a couple of days after the incident because of the loss of 'his boys'). Keith suffered from PTSD, but was not initially aware of it. He was on guard when the V2s were coming over later in 1944. He joined the 1st Battalion Grenadier Guards in 1945; he fought with the Guards Armoured Division in Germany during the closing months of the war. He later transferred to the Royal Army Dental Corps, and retired in 1960 for health reasons.

He subsequently had a very successful career, running a language teaching business, largely in Germany and Switzerland, with his German-born wife. For many years he divided his time between Oxford and Dusseldorf. In April 2000 he returned to the Guards' Chapel for the first time since the bombing; he wrote an account of the incident for the *Grenadier Gazette* in 2001.

Later in 2010, he was interviewed for *Blitz Street* with Tony Robinson. This dealt with what it was like to live through the Blitz and subsequent Second World War events; Keith gave a vivid account of his experiences on 18 June 1944 in episode three of the series.

In 2014, he played a key role in the 70th anniversary service at the Guards' Chapel, as 'the survivor'. All who were there were moved by the dignity with which he spoke.

Elisabeth Sheppard-Jones, a young ATS officer, had also been trapped in the rubble. Elisabeth survived, but would never walk again; her spine had been fractured and her spinal cord severed. However, she lived on until 2004, when she died aged 83. Her doctor claimed she was the longest-living paraplegic of all time.

She was born in May 1920 in Penarth, and was the daughter of a local doctor. At the age of 18 she left home and came to London. She joined the ATS and started as a plotter in a searchlight battery; she was rapidly promoted and by 1944 was an officer at the Clerks' Training Centre, Golders Green. She and Pauline Gye, her childhood friend from Penarth, attended the Guards' Chapel service together; Pauline was killed outright, probably by the same block of masonry that broke Elisabeth's spine.

Elisabeth remained in hospital in the Lindo Wing at St Mary's, Paddington, for a long time; she was still there at Christmas 1944, and well into 1945. In October 1945 she was transferred to Stoke Mandeville, a Ministry of Pensions hospital expanded in the Second World War; this specialised in service casualties with spinal injuries. She was there until 1948. Then she returned home and was able to be mobile and independent by using an electrically-powered tricycle. She had a specially-adapted bungalow built, not far from her family, and moved there in 1952. She became a manager at Headlands School, which was an independent school for children with special needs; she was also a successful author, and wrote books on Welsh history and children's books.

Others at the ceremony

The Bishop of Maidstone, Leslie Owen (1886–1947), then bishop to the Armed Forces, was to have been the guest speaker at the morning service; he was one of the very few left apparently uninjured. He was very shaken by the explosion and suffered a slight scratch, but was able to make his way out, unaided, over the debris to the vestry. Bravely, he volunteered to help with the rescue effort, but once reinforcements arrived, he was advised to go home. He suffered from delayed shock and was confined to bed for several days afterwards.

Although at the time he appeared almost unscathed, he died less than three years later; this may well have been caused by his inhalation of dust after the explosion. (Several others at the scene referred to the 'choking dust'.) He became Bishop of Lincoln in September 1946, but the following month he had to undergo a course of treatment (thought to be for lung cancer). He was diagnosed as terminally ill at that point. He then contracted pneumonia; although he made a partial recovery, by late February 1947 he was gravely ill and he died on 2 March.

Olive Atkinson Windram (née Carruthers) was the wife of the Director of Music, Major Windram. She shared his love of music and had studied at the LRAM. She was severely injured at the service, and taken to St George's Hospital in the early afternoon. Her husband died later that day. Olive had a serious head injury, and over a week later was still too ill to be able to attend his funeral on 26 June. At some point she was moved to South Audley Street Hospital. From there she went to the Emergency Hospital, Old Windsor as part of the wartime Emergency Medical Scheme; this was part of the St George's group of hospitals and was felt to be a safer place to convalesce than central London. She remained there for some months. She had been bombed out of their former home, 21 Sloane Court; they had been living there since June 1940. As soon as she had the opportunity, she returned to her family home at Mullartown House, Annalong, County Down and remained there until her death in the 1970s. For many years, she would place an 'In memoriam' notice in *The Times* on the anniversary of her husband's death, referring to him as 'my beloved Jay'.

The musicians

Thirteen of the Coldstream Guards Band were taken to hospital after the Guards' Chapel incident. Charles ('Jock') Hart died of his injuries the following year and his biography is in Chapter 6 (military). Some bandsmen were able to resume their careers and several lived on into the next century; others were damaged physically or mentally by their experiences in the Chapel and had their lives shortened as a result. Biographies of the twelve survivors follow.

Jack Ellory (Alfred John Ellory, 1920–2009) played the flute in the Coldstream Guards Band. Ironically, 18 June was his birthday. He was buried in the debris for several hours, but was eventually dug out, still holding his flute, and taken to Westminster Hospital. He recalled the members of the brass section, who had been sitting just behind him, appearing dusty but outwardly untouched. In reality, they had all been killed outright by the blast.

He joined the Guards band at 15, and won scholarships to Trinity College and the Royal College of Music. He played with the Philharmonia Orchestra from 1945. Later he turned freelance, and played first flute in many orchestras and bands. He provided music for a number of radio and television series, including *The Avengers* and *The Professionals*. He worked with a wide range of people, from Sir Thomas Beecham to Frank Sinatra, and was a leading flautist and session musician. He played on some of the James Bond film scores in the 1960s. He is perhaps best known nowadays for his contribution to the Beatles' song 'The Fool on the Hill', although his contribution to the *Pink Panther* soundtracks is also noteworthy. He was so well-known that when he died in 2009 he received obituaries in both *The Times* and the *Telegraph*. He had a sharp sense of humour and was an excellent raconteur.

Eric Denzil Hoare played the oboe. He was born in 1915 in Tavistock. He was one of the many musicians who went with the band to the World Fair in New York in 1939. He later became a sergeant. He married Alice Proctor in Wandsworth in 1941, and was living in Battersea in 1945. He died in 1999 in Cambridgeshire.

Harry F. Lockwood played solo clarinet. His father Arthur (1868–1941) served in the Army in India; he married Florence Parr (1883–1911). Harry was born in Parel, Bombay, on 27 July 1906, the eldest surviving son; his full name was Henry Frederick Edward, but he was known as Harry. The family returned to England in 1910; Florence died a few months after the birth of her fourth son. Arthur remarried in 1912.

Harry joined the Coldstream Guards' Band, and travelled to the World Fair with them in 1939. After the Guards' Chapel incident, he was removed from St George's to Slough Emergency Hospital to be away from the V1 threat in London. He married Ada Woodall (1913–1967) in Manchester in the December quarter of 1944. He died in November 1951 in Atkinson Morley Hospital of a brain tumour.

Harry's younger brother, Eric Norman Lockwood (1908–1943), died 23 October 1943 on active service when HMS *Charybdis* was torpedoed and sank off the coast of France.

Ernest R. Dalwood also played solo clarinet. He was born on 30 October 1921, one of six children. He had no formal training on the clarinet until he joined the Coldstream Guards band at the age of 15. He won a scholarship to study at the Royal College of Music under the renowned British clarinettist Frederick Thurston, and travelled with the other musicians to the World Fair in 1939 when he was only 17. He married Joan Fairfield in 1947; the following year he won a spot in the BBC Symphony Orchestra.

In 1953 he came to Edmonton with his wife Joan and served with the RCAF Tactical Air Command Band until 1958. There were few musicians in Edmonton at the time, so members of the service band also performed for the Edmonton Symphony Orchestra (ESO). He was their principal clarinettist for twenty-three years. He then taught woodwind at the University of Alberta's department of music. He died in 2012, aged 91. A colleague praised him for 'always mak[ing] a point of giving young musicians a go', while a friend said he was 'one of the kindest, funniest and most supportive persons I ever met'.

Dougie Drake played rep clarinet. Albert Henry Douglas Drake (usually known as Dougie) was born in March 1918 in West Derby. He was the son of Raleigh Frobisher Douglas Drake and Gertrude Mahon; they married in 1917. Raleigh was a cavalryman in the Royal Dragoon Guards in the First World War, and some of Dougie's ancestors served in earlier historic battles, such as Sebastopol, Balaclava, Inkerman and Alma. Joseph Drake was a troop sergeant major in the 4th Dragoon Guards and was awarded the DCM in 1854 for the Heavy Brigade Charge at Balaclava. When Dougie was 17 he tried to join the Dragoon Guards, but was turned down because of his eyesight; he therefore joined the Coldstream Guards' Band.

Dougie was the first band sergeant major and enlisted on 2 December 1935, aged 17. He was awarded the MSM and the 1937 Coronation medal. He went to the World Fair in New York with many of his colleagues, a number of whom were later killed at the Guards' Chapel in 1944. He himself was badly injured. He suffered a fractured skull, a broken shoulder, a leg broken in two places and concussion. He spent six months in hospital.

After the war he married Margaret Thomas in Neath, in 1948. He continued to serve with the Guards until his retirement in January 1975; most of his service was in the band. He died on 7 November 2010, one of the last survivors of the incident.

Pat (Edward) Neal played second clarinet. He was born in about 1902, and attended the World Fair with his colleagues. However, I have been unable to find any more information about him.

Harry Davis played alto saxophone. Herbert Henry Davis was born in Newcastle-under-Lyme on 27 December 1903; he was the son of Herbert Ethcote and Florence Davis. He enlisted with the Cameronians on 22 July 1918, and attended a year's course at Kneller Hall School of Music 1921–22. He was discharged as a bandsman in 1928, and enlisted as a musician in the Coldstream Guards the following day. He attended the World Fair in 1939. He was badly wounded at the Guards' Chapel service in 1944; he sustained head injuries, lacerations to the face, hands and left elbow, and a contused lumbar spine and ribs. He recovered sufficiently to serve in northwest Europe with the band from December 1944 to January 1945. He was awarded the MSM in 1951, but was discharged as permanently unfit due to tuberculosis in February 1954. It is believed he died in 1956.

Lionel M. Goring played the bassoon. Lionel Morton Philip Goring was born on 24 October 1912 at Steyning in Sussex. He married Daisy Barber in 1938, and the following year he went to New York with the Coldstream Guards Band. He later joined first the BBC Scottish Orchestra and then the BBC Symphony Orchestra; he was playing bassoon for the BBC in 1964 and later acted as an instrumental coach for the Schools Prom performances at the Royal Albert Hall in the 1970s. He died in December 1987 in Worthing.

Edward 'Dick' Gay played second horn. He was baptised Albert James Gay on 25 June 1905 at St Jude's Church, East Brixton, to Leandro (or Leander) Angelo Gay (1877–1952) and his wife Ethel (née Woodall). Leandro was a professional musician, like his father, Angelo Giovanni Zerbini Gay (1851–1915). Contemporary news reports talk of Angelo conducting a brass band in the late 1870s, while later he played the cornet. In 1856, Leander was a member of the Grenadier Guards' band. Later, he was the bandmaster of the 5th Essex Rifles band; they presented him with a silver watch in 1864 as a token of thanks. In 1875 he was the bandmaster of the Victoria Park Sunday band, which he ran in his spare time.

Albert was usually known as Edward or Dick. He joined the Coldstream Guards Band before 1939 and accompanied them to New York that spring.

I have no further information about him after the Guards' Chapel incident, but it is believed that he never recovered from the shock of the bombing.

John 'Jo' Hiam played the euphonium. John Albert Hiam was born on 1 June 1895 in Marylebone; he was named after his father, John Albert Hiam (1865–1902). He was known as Jo. He appears in the 1939 passenger list for New York as John A. Hiam, aged 43. After the bombing he was removed from St George's to the Emergency Hospital at Slough. He never fully recovered from his injuries and died in service on 20 January 1949.

Leonard Davies played E-flat bass (the tuba). He was born in about 1905; the 1939 passenger list describes him as Leonard J. Davis, aged 34. After the Guards' Chapel explosion, he allegedly climbed out of the rubble covered in dust and asking 'What happened?' He was taken to St George's Hospital. He never fully recovered and left the band on a pension; he died in his early sixties.

Don Stutely played string bass. Arthur Gordon Stutely (or Stuteley) was born on 4 March 1906 in Liverpool; he was normally known as Don. His parents were Gordon Edwin Stutely (1876–1940) and Mildred Daisy Barlow (1881–1941); they married in 1904 in Liverpool. Don was their only child. The son of a bandmaster, Gordon was a member of the Hallé Orchestra and played many instruments, including the clarinet and violin. The 1911 census lists him as a professional musician, conductor, teacher and instrumentalist. He wrote a suite for strings called *Salt o' the Sea*, which was often performed in the 1930s. He conducted the BBC Radio (Liverpool) String Orchestra and the Merseyside Military Band. In 1930 he was the musical director in charge of the Liverpool Manchester Railway Pageant.

His son Don also had a distinguished musical career. He was playing at the Café de Paris in June 1930, and went on to play with a succession of highly acclaimed dance bands in London. He played with the Roy Fox band in 1931 and 1932 when singer Al Bowlly was on guitar and vocals; Al became one of the best singers in the country, but was killed during the Blitz in April 1941. Don also played the ocarina, a sign of his versatility. Later he played string bass with Bert Ambrose and his orchestra at the May Fair Hotel. Once war broke out, it is believed he joined the Coldstream Guards Band. He married Marjorie Lillian Jarvis (1915–2003) in 1940. He was injured at the Guards' Chapel in 1944, and taken first to St George's Hospital and then to the Emergency Hospital in Slough.

In the 1940s he played with the bandleader Geraldo at the Savoy Hotel. Most of the UK's top musicians played with Geraldo's orchestra at some point. There appears to be no further information available about his later career. Don died on 20 January in 1991 in Doddington, Kent.

ATS survivors

Jane Knight Sandy. Joan Constance Sandy, usually known as Jane, was born in the December quarter of 1921 in Woolwich. Her father was a soldier and, as an army child, she became accustomed to moving around. When the ATS was set up in September 1938 she cycled to Aldershot to volunteer at the age of 16; she lied about her age to ensure they thought she was over 18. She was a qualified shorthand typist and initially used her shorthand in signals companies. She gained a commission as a subaltern in October 1942 and was moved to 10 Signal Regiment in London District. On 18 June 1944 she attended morning service at the Guards' Chapel and was trapped in the rubble. She was posted as missing, but was eventually dug out by a guardsman and taken to St Thomas' Hospital, along with Kath Hunt, another ATS subaltern.

She recovered and, a few months later, served in Naples, where she became one of the first female signalmasters. In 1946 she joined the United Nations Relief and Rehabilitation Administration in Germany. Three years later she joined P&O and worked for them for twelve years, ending as assistant purser. She then married and ran a small accommodation agency in Maidenhead and then Kingston. She became a supporter of the Royal Signals Association and remained an avid traveller. She died on 30 December 2009, aged 88.

Christabel Whitfield was another ATS survivor. She was a private in No. 1 Company, No.1 War Office Signals, 26 Catherine Place, SW1. Their headquarters was the Buckingham Court Hotel, just opposite the side entrance to Buckingham Palace. Their dining room, kitchens and billets were at Catherine Place. She was taken to St George's Hospital suffering from concussion. I have been unable to discover any further information about her subsequent life.

Kath Hunt, a subaltern (ATS), had attended Chapel with Mrs and Miss Gidley-Kitchin. She was described as P.K. Hunt in the casualty list; the K stood for Kathleen, usually abbreviated to Kath. She had been serving at the Clerks School in Spaniards Lane, Hampstead, along with Elisabeth Sheppard-Jones. Chief Commander Ferguson made enquiries about her and her companions. She was initially believed to have died, as they had, but was later discovered to be in hospital with shock. Again, no further information has been found about her life after she left hospital.

Injured Guardsmen

Peter Stevenson was in the Grenadier Guards. He was born in 1926 and enlisted in 1943. He was wounded at the Chapel; he had incised wounds, a damaged scalp and a fractured patella, and was initially thought to have died. He was taken to St George's Hospital, and returned to duties on 9 July 1944.

He was posted to Europe and suffered shrapnel wounds to his face and jaw from a mortar bomb in October; he was sent to hospital and evacuated to the UK the following month. He continued to serve in the Guards until 1947.

Louis James Price was another Grenadier Guardsman who was severely injured in the Chapel and taken to St George's Hospital. He was born in August 1925 and enlisted on 8 March 1943. The incident left him with multiple injuries, including a cut ear and a chipped bone in his ankle. He was discharged in 1947; he was described as 'a hardworking and dependable man with a pleasant personality. He has always carried out his military duties well and cheerfully'.

James Dunn was another Grenadier Guardsman. He was usually known as Jim, and came from Coventry. He was a friend of Derek Weaver, who died in the incident. He sustained a chest wound in the bombing. While in hospital, he spoke openly to Derek's mother about the incident; he was very bitter about what had happened and said he would never go to church again. He told her that Derek would have survived the bombing if he had remained in the pew where he first sat with the other Guardsmen. Instead he was forced to move forward to fill an empty pew. Presumably the injured Grenadiers were those who had remained in the previous pew.

Injured American servicemen

These were taken to St George's Hospital.

Max Dolmatin was a private serving in HQ Coy, PICMIS, APO 887. This was the ETOUSA Planning staff in London (European Theater of Operations, United States Army in London, normally referred to by its PO address, APO 887). Maxim Frank Dolmatin was born in Listopadovichi, near Minsk, Russia (now Belarus), in about 1911, and arrived in New York in 1927 with his mother and younger sister. He was in the US Army from 13 November 1942 to 13 November 1945; he was serving in London in June 1944 but presumably was well enough to move to Paris with his unit in September that year. He married twice and died in 1996. He is buried with his parents in Hamburg, New York.

James Kenny was serving with the 851st Ordnance Heavy Auto Maintenance Company, APO 587. This was a US bomb squadron that left the Mountain Home Air Force base in Idaho to move to Eye, East Anglia, in April 1944. They crossed to France about a month after the initial invasion of Europe. I am unable to make a more specific identification of James Kenny.

Vincent Pascalini (or Pasqualino) of the 94th RAM 1st battery is believed to have been born in New York in 1917 as Vincent C. Pasqualino; he enlisted on 30 March 1943 and was released on 29 January 1946. He died in 1996.

Injured civilians

Mrs Phyllis Attenborough, of 28 Buckingham Palace Mansions, was found semi-conscious in the Chapel soon after 3.00pm; her handbag was found elsewhere in the debris. She was taken to St George's Hospital. She was born Phyllis Layton in June 1895 and married Lieutenant Colonel James Attenborough in 1915; he was awarded the CMG that same year while serving with the Royal Fusiliers. In 1939 she and her husband James and his brother were living in Kensington; James was described as a 'solicitor, now at war'. In 1944, her husband knew Phyllis had gone to the Guards' Chapel service and made enquiries. Despite her injuries, she survived for more than forty-five years, dying at the age of 95 in 1990.

Albert Victor Charles Buteux, of 18 Gambetta Street, Battersea, was born in 1926, so would have been about 18 at the time. He was taken to St George's Hospital. In 1947 he was living at the same address as in 1944; in 1952 he married. He died in 1993, almost fifty years after the incident.

Mary Hayward was a nurse at St George's Hospital; she attended the service with two friends, also nurses. One, Beryl Clark, was killed; another, Anne, escaped with minor injuries. Mary was rescued from the Chapel at about 12.15pm, an hour after the explosion, and taken to St George's. She was badly cut about the head and very confused, as well as suffering from shock.

Mary gradually recovered, but she did not come back to St George's to nurse. She lived in Hertford with her aunt and uncle. Her nerves were badly shaken and it took her a long time to regain her health. Eventually she joined Princess Mary's RAF Nursing Service.

Barbara Howard, from Cambridge, lived at the YWCA with my mother's friends Beatrice, Ellen and Marjorie; she suffered head injuries. I have been unable to trace any further information about her.

Jessie Souter, younger sister of Marjorie. Both had left Monymusk, near Aberdeen, to do war work in London. Jessie went to the Chapel with her sister's friends from the YWCA Earl's Court, and was seriously injured, with a cut leg and face; she was taken to St Thomas's Hospital along with Barbara Howard. A newspaper report said she was still in hospital a month later. I believe she may have moved to the Schiff Home of Recovery in Cobham; this was a convalescent home linked to six London hospitals, including St Thomas's. A Jessie E. Souter is on their electoral register in May 1945.

Survivors mentioned in David Gurney's account

Tommy Coke (1908–1976) had taken Ivan Cobbold to the Chapel, but had decided not to attend as he had experienced a bad night. At that point he was a major in the Scots Guards. He was invariably known as Tommy to distinguish him from his father, Tom. Tommy survived and went on to become 5th Earl of Leicester in 1949; his friend Ivan died in the Chapel that day.

Robin Arthur Barnes-Gorell, captain of the guard that day, was born in 1899 and married Iris Mary Baillie (1900–1967) in 1937. He died in 1966.

Nigel Mitchison was the subaltern of the guard that day. Nigel Wansborough Sturges Mitchison was born in 1922 and educated at Radley. He left school in 1940 and joined the Coldstream Guards; in 1942 he became a second lieutenant, and eventually a captain. He married in 1948 and died in 1985.

Peter Daubeny was the ensign dismissing the men on the square. His full title was Sir Peter Lauderdale Daubeny; he was born on 16 April 1921 in Wiesbaden, into a military family with no theatrical connections. He began training as an actor in 1938, and in 1939 he was taken on as a student at the Liverpool Repertory Theatre. He became a lieutenant in the Coldstream Guards and fought with the Eighth Army in North Africa until he lost his left arm. He was invalided back to Britain. He abandoned plans to act, and decided instead to pursue a career in theatrical management. He was most successful, ran a series of World Theatre seasons and was knighted in 1973; he died in 1975.

David Gurney was a young Scots Guards lieutenant at the time of the incident. David Hugh Gurney was born in 1921, and came from the influential Quaker Gurney banking family. His father was Sir Hugh Gurney, MVO, KCMG (1878–1968), who was in the diplomatic service until retirement in 1940; his mother was Mariota Susan Carnegie (1892–1980). They married in 1911. David was educated at Eton before joining the Guards. His first-hand account of the incident is taken from a letter sent to the Dods family in 1944. He was a keen photographer and recorded the incident and its aftermath on camera. In 1949 he decided to make his career as a professional photographer. Sadly, he was killed in a car accident near Newmarket on 10 October 1951, and is buried at St Mary's, Earlham.

Others who changed their plans to attend the service

Walter Bedell Smith (1895–1961) was due to attend Chapel with Ivan Cobbold, but was too busy. He was a senior US Army general, reporting to General Eisenhower. In 1944 he was the chief of staff at SHAEF (Supreme headquarters Allied Expeditionary Force in Western Europe), again under Eisenhower. On 18 January 1944 he set out for Europe with 2½ tons of personal baggage loaded onto a pair of B-17s. He was based at Bushy Park, Teddington, in a hutted camp. After the war, among other roles, he became head of the CIA 1950–53. He is buried in section 7 of Arlington National Cemetery.

Another friend of Ivan Cobbold had also been invited to attend. This was **Stanley Rous** (1895–1986), the secretary of the Football Association (later FIFA president). Ivan had sent him an invitation to join him at the service, but Stanley had already accepted an invitation to talk to a Rotary Club in London about his work with the Red Cross (for which he was later knighted). He declined the invitation, saying he had a prior engagement. A mutual friend assured him Ivan Cobbold did not like being turned down. Stanley would have been sitting next to him at the service. Ever after, he said that whenever he was invited to speak at a Rotary function, he always tried to accept.

Mary Loveday Beazley (1925–2013) was the daughter of an admiral, Sir Henry Bernard Rawlings (1889–1962). She would have liked to join the WRNS, but did not wish to pull strings to join; instead she took a job in Heal's parachute factory in London. At the time of the Guards' Chapel bombing she had been kept awake all through the previous night by the noise of the anti-aircraft guns. As a result, she decided not to go to the service next day; it was the first time in almost a year that she had missed it. She and a friend chose to go to the country for the day instead, to Surrey; they were on a bus on Westminster Bridge, en route to Waterloo, when it stopped at a bus stop and 'there was the most almighty bang'. It was the V1, exploding in the Chapel.

Captain Harry Crookshank (1893–1961), the Postmaster General and a former Grenadier Guards officer, had been a regular worshipper at the Guards' Chapel for many years. He would have been at the service, but had an appointment which had taken him out of London the day before. When he appeared in the Commons a few days later he was given a warm welcome.

The **Scots Guards** and **Welsh Guards bands** were each originally due to perform at the service, but a double swap meant that the Coldstream Guards Band took their place.

Herbert John Barker was due on Church Parade that morning as duty sergeant. He arranged for his post to be covered by another sergeant, who was sadly killed in the bombing.

* * *

As stated earlier in the book, a number of relatives had come to the Chapel to pray for their sons and husbands who were serving abroad. It is not always possible to prove who survived the war, but with help from their relatives I can confirm that at least two of the Guards officers came home safely.

John Jameson (1919–1988) was in the 3rd Battalion, Grenadier Guards in Italy at the time of the incident; he lost his mother and his wife. He later remarried and had two sons; one of them attended the memorial service in 2014.

Greville Gidley-Kitchin lost his mother and his sister in the incident. They had gone to the Chapel to pray for him, as they knew him to be in Kent, preparing to go to France with the 4th Battalion of the Guards Armoured Division. He was camped at Charing with his battalion and all their Churchill tanks; he knew his mother was staying in London that Sunday but was unable to contact her.

Once he discovered what had happened, he went to London and helped his father with the various arrangements that had to be made. Two days after the funerals he rejoined his battalion and they left for France within weeks. On 28 July battle orders were received; on the second day of the battle at Caumont his tank was hit by a shell from a concealed Panzer tank. The driver and co-driver were killed; Greville jumped out but was badly burned by phosphorus as he did so. He spent the next year in a series of hospitals, recovering. He was still convalescing at the end of the war. He is one of only a handful of officers from the 4th Battalion left alive at the time of writing.

Chapter 8

Rebuilding the Chapel

The Guards' Chapel is the place of worship for the Household Division. This comprises the Guards Division, which is five regiments of Foot Guards (Grenadier, Coldstream, Scots, Irish and Welsh Guards) and the Household Cavalry's two regiments (Life Guards and the Blues and Royals). The Chapel has always been a place where Household Cavalrymen, Guardsmen and their families come for baptisms, weddings, funerals and memorial services, as well as for regular worship. It has been an integral part of their lives for generations.

Its history dates back to the 1830s. The building of Wellington Barracks, Birdcage Walk, was completed in 1834. At that point there was no chapel, although Dr William Dakins, principal chaplain to the Forces from 1830–44, was anxious for the troops to have a dedicated building so that they could worship regularly. The first service in the new garrison church, then known as the Royal Military Chapel, took place on 6 May 1838. At that stage it was quite an austere building, with a neo-classical design based on a Greek temple and a very plain interior. It cost approximately £5,500 to build and could accommodate a congregation of over 1,000 people.

In 1877, the War Office approved plans for a reconstruction of the interior, as by then it was felt to be inappropriately plain. They provided the land and the building, but passed over responsibility for the decoration to the Brigade of Guards. George Edmund Street, a distinguished architect of the day, prepared plans to add an apse and redesign the interior in the Lombardo-Byzantine style, a favourite style for military chapels of the period. The chapel, by now far more ornate, reopened on 25 May 1879. It included round-arched arcades and barrel-vaulted ceilings with alternate ribs of Bath stone and Roman red brick. There was an impressive mosaic, the gift of Queen Victoria, above the chancel arch; this can still be seen today. She also donated the communion plate; a pew was reserved for her in the centre of the west gallery.

Much of the money for the interior was raised by families in memory of soldiers and officers who had served in the Brigade. Memorials to officers of the Brigade of Guards became a key feature of the new scheme, and these continued to be added after the chapel reopened. Other memorials included those commemorating the Duke of Cambridge, King Edward VII, and the thousands of Guardsmen of all ranks who died in the war of 1914–18. The

King George V Memorial, a new mosaic altar and inlaid sanctuary step, was unveiled by King George VI in 1937. Alabaster, marble, mosaics, terracotta, stained glass and metal work were all used to embellish the chapel. It became famous for its beauty and the richness of its decoration; each element acted as a memorial to members of the Brigade. Colours were also deposited there: the first colours placed in the chapel had been borne by three Guards' battalions in the Crimean War. In 1880 and 1881 the first Waterloo colours were laid there.

Queen Victoria gave the first set of silver communion vessels in 1838. The silver cross used for normal services was presented in 1900. At the time of the centenary service in 1938, King George VI gave the six silver candlesticks. The cross and candlesticks are still in use today.

Once war broke out, all the colours and communion plate were photographed and removed to a place of safety; later the whole interior was photographed and records of all the inscriptions on the memorials were noted. This proved to be a wise precaution. The chapel was damaged on several occasions during the Second World War prior to 1944. The stained glass windows were blown out by a near miss in 1940; what could be saved was collected, placed in numbered bags and kept for eventual reconstruction. A week or so later the roof was badly burned by incendiary bombs, and the chapel had to be closed for a time while the roof was repaired and reinforced. The decision to use concrete rather than wood for this seemed logical, as the threat from incendiary bombs at that time was considerable.

On 18 June 1944, shortly after 11.10am and during morning service, a V1 hit the chapel. It entered at the western end and exploded, destroying the roof, the upper portions of the supporting walls and most of the pillars and the portico of the Chapel's western door. Only the apse, chancel and a couple of wall pillars remained. The six silver candlesticks and the cross remained intact, but most of the memorials were damaged beyond repair. Understandably, the priority at the time was to rescue the wounded; it was only the following Wednesday that the instruction to preserve all architectural stonework and inscribed marble from further damage was issued. (A single terracotta panel from the Chapel survives; it is now preserved at the Museum of Army Flying, Middle Wallop, near Andover.)

On Sunday, 25 June a drumhead service was held beside the ruins of the Chapel. It was attended by officers and men of the Brigade of Guards, as well as by relatives of many of those killed and members of the rescue services who had attended the incident a week before. The simple service of worship and rededication was conducted from a rostrum draped with the Union Jack by the Reverend H.R. Norton, now assistant chaplain-general, Eastern Command, but a month previously the chaplain to the Brigade of Guards; he had been recalled from Italy immediately after the incident, as his successor, the

Reverend Ralph Whitrow, had been killed on 18 June. Lieutenant-General Sir Charles Loyd, GOC, London District, read the lesson, and the sermon was preached by the Reverend Dr C.D. Symons, chaplain-general to the Forces. He reminded the congregation that the Chapel was not only a memorial to those who had gone before, but it was also the very symbol of the spirit of the Brigade and the source from which that spirit came.

In early September 1944, the campaign for funds to restore the Chapel began. Lieutenant-General A.E. Codrington, senior colonel of the Brigade of Guards, and Lieutenant-General Sir Charles Loyd, the major-general commanding the Brigade of Guards, issued an appeal for subscriptions. The intention was to redecorate the Guards' Chapel; while the rebuilding was the responsibility of the War Department, the 'interior decoration is the privilege and responsibility of the Brigade of Guards'. Cheques and donations were requested, to be made payable to the 'Guards' Chapel Restoration Fund'.

The money began to arrive. In December 1944, the 6th South African Armoured Division, fighting in Italy with the 24th Guards Brigade, sent a cheque for £5,125 as a contribution towards the restoration of the Guards' Chapel. The triple bronze doors at the main entrance to the Chapel are the result of their gift. By the time the Chapel was rebuilt the sum had grown significantly and was also used to pay for the renovation of the mosaics in the apse.

From November 1944, the Brigade was allowed to use St Peter's, Eaton Square, for their parade services, but the aim was always to have a replacement chapel near the Barracks. Restrictions on building after the war meant that a temporary chapel was needed; a Romney hut was erected inside the ruins of the old Chapel. The nave of the prefabricated hut was arranged so that it joined the undamaged east end of the Chapel, where the choir and the altar were placed. The hut could accommodate 450–700 people.

The hut was used for the first time on 25 December 1945, when there was a parade service and the Band of the Coldstream Guards played. Five of the musicians had been in the Chapel bombing the previous year; it must have been a very emotional experience for them. By then, the fund to restore the Chapel had reached almost £30,000. From then on, services were held in the Romney hut every Sunday, and it continued to be used until 1962.

Rebuilding finally began in the mid-1950s with H.S. Goodhart-Rendel's War Memorial Cloister, which was designed to house the Regimental Rolls of Honour of all those who died serving 1939–45; it consists of seven bays, each with a book of remembrance. One of the books is for all those who died in the Guards' Chapel on 18 June 1944. The Cloister was designed to provide an entrance from Birdcage Walk to the new Chapel; it was dedicated on 28 May 1956 in the presence of Queen Elizabeth II. Members of the Household Brigade and their friends were responsible for funding this.

Unfortunately Goodhart-Rendel, a former Grenadier Guards officer, died in 1959 before he could finish his post-war project for the rest of the Chapel.

The commission for a new Chapel was given to Bruce George (1915–2016), of the architectural practice George Trew and Dunn. The design was approved in 1961 and building work started in 1962. The brief set out to integrate the surviving apse and chancel, what remained of the stained-glass windows (removed in 1940) and Goodhart-Rendel's Cloister, with a new building, constructed on the existing foundations. The majority of the furnishings and fittings were provided as gifts or memorials.

Apart from the apse and the font, there was no attempt to reconstruct the old memorials and plaques from the old Chapel; instead, all the remaining fragments from the 2,000 memorials damaged beyond repair in 1944 were laid under the floor. In this way, the new Chapel would emerge from the foundations of the old, and its base would be formed of the old memorials. The names of all those who had memorials in the old Chapel have been inscribed on the stone tablets that are now inside and outside the west wall. The new west doors have the Brigade Star and the 'flash' of the South African Division on their push bars; the metal for these came from the bell of the old Chapel, which had been too badly damaged to be reinstated.

The Chapel was completed in November 1963 and was dedicated on 26 November by the Archbishop of Canterbury in the presence of Prince Philip, Duke of Edinburgh, representing the Queen, the Queen Mother, Princess Margaret, Princess Royal and Princess Alice, Countess of Athlone. It was awarded the Civic Trust Award in 1964.

It was rebuilt in a modern rectangular style, although it echoes the idea behind the original; it is an interpretation of a classical temple. It has a reinforced concrete frame construction, with brick infill panels; the external walls are covered with white marble chippings and mica, bound together with white Portland cement and lightly hammered to provide a rough textured finish. The internal walls are plain and white, with a rough plaster finish. There is a glazed west window that runs the width of the building and contains stained glass from the original Chapel. The south side is made of six equal bays which accommodate the Regimental Cloisters; each bay has a narrow south-west facing window. The north side has fifty-two plain vertical slit windows. The memorials are made of metal plaques attached to the walls. Some further stained glass has been added; Gordon Beningfield, perhaps better known as a wildlife artist, but also a skilled glass engraver, produced eight memorial windows for the Chapel between 1972 and 1994. John Hutton, Laurence Whistler and Rosemary Barnett also designed memorial windows for the new Chapel. The nave pews are made of afrormosia wood and can seat 500. The choir stalls are of the same wood, known for its beautiful coloration, and above them are the musicians' and organ galleries.

Because the rest of the Chapel is so stark and simple in design, it brings the altar and sanctuary into sharp relief. The apse's coloured marble and gold mosaics draw the eye down the nave to the main focus of the building. The altar, which also survived the bombing, is of marble and mosaic, while the silver cross and candlesticks are those left standing after the V1 explosion. If you stand in the choir and turn to look back up the nave to the west door, the vast majority of what you see, apart from the font, is from the new Chapel. However, if you face the altar, almost all the elements, richly detailed and vibrant with colour, are as they would have been before that fateful day in 1944.

Epilogue

The 70th Anniversary Commemorative Service

Some years ago I began my own annual commemoration of my mother's friends and all those who died with them at the Guards' Chapel. Every June I would give the Chapel my updated list of those who died, with brief biographies. I would normally take these to the Chapel as close to the anniversary of the incident as possible. It was a ritual that mattered to me; I took time to update what I had found out, and increasingly I came into contact with some of the relatives of those who had died.

In 2012 I broke with tradition and emailed my information. When I sent it, I asked if there would be a service of commemoration in 2014 for the seventieth anniversary. I was assured that there would be; Lesley Manchester, the senior chaplain's personal secretary, would contact me once the details were agreed. I mentioned this to the relatives and waited for further news.

The following year I was invited to come to the Chapel and meet Lesley and the Reverend Kevin Bell. I was very moved to be asked to play a small part in the planning of the ceremony; they wanted to use my material on those who had died, and to include some of it in the programme. We talked about the focus of the ceremony; Padre Kevin said that he felt the relatives should be at the heart of the ceremony. He hoped it would bring closure. From my contact with them, I knew that many of the relatives retained vivid impressions of what had happened and I thought it would be a very emotional day for many. I had experience of a similar seventieth anniversary ceremony in my home town where those invited had been political and military figures, rather than those who had lost loved ones; I could remember the distress of the relatives and was concerned that this should not happen again.

My fears were groundless; the senior chaplain, his secretary and the Chapel Committee did a superb job in organising a memorable and moving tribute to all those who died. I was given access to a range of material, which helped me update all my biographies so that a selection could form part of the programme; I even managed to trace the surviving Corsican niece of the Free French Corporal who was buried at Brookwood Military Cemetery. I ensured that Lesley had all the contact details that I had gathered for relatives.

There was a lot of work behind the scenes. I helped the publicity team, led by the Reverend Dr Bill Beaver, officiating chaplain to the Household Cavalry Mounted Regiment, as they compiled the order of service. We selected a cross-section of biographies and photographs to appear; I put together material on the background to the incident and the role of the rescue services. I was aware that the letter by Lieutenant David Gurney (quoted in chapters 2 and 4) was a significant source, but I had not appreciated that, thanks to Sergeant Fred Barrett of the Coldstream Guards, we also had a selection of Lieutenant Gurney's photographs taken at that time. A team of us carried out the proofreading, and I enjoyed noting any instances of Padre Bill's US usage, such as 'automobile accident'; originally from Colorado, he served as an intelligence officer during the Vietnam war.

Sunday, 22 June 2014, like 18 June 1944, was a fine day. My son and I made our way into London in good time and found our way to the Chapel, where we took our designated seats. I had helped with the content for the programme, but this was the first time I had seen the finished article. It was a beautiful document, lavishly illustrated; it contained all the details of the service itself in a central section. Other pages described what had happened that day, with information about the aftermath and the role of the rescue services. There was a list of all those who had lost their lives in the Chapel, along with more detailed biographies and photographs of seventeen of the victims. The portraits gave a snapshot of the variety of people involved, including Guardsmen, the Director of Music, a society figure who was the wife of a Scots Guards lieutenant colonel, a female journalist, a probable spy and six family members from two different families.

The service began promptly at 10.45am. Uniformed Guardsman took their places along the aisle. The Lord Bishop of London, the Right Reverend and Right Honourable Richard Chartres, KCVO, DD, FSA, CStJ, arrived at 10.50 and was received by the major general commanding the Household Division, the chairman of the Chapel Committee, the senior chaplain and the churchwarden.

The service that followed was thoughtful and very moving. It was designed to honour those who lost their lives or were wounded, and to give thanks to those who rushed to aid them on that day. Poignantly, it followed the exact order of service as begun on 18 June 1944; as on that day, the Band of the Coldstream Guards was playing. After a selection of music, including items by Vaughan Williams, Grainger and Purcell, the Chapel choir sang the introit and the service began. It followed the format of the 1944 service until it reached the end of the Lesson.

At that point the officiating chaplain to the Grenadier Guards said: 'It was during the *Te Deum* which follows that this peaceful house of God became a charnel house, and in a split second this place of light and life became a hell of death and destruction. The Choir will pause in the middle of the *Te Deum* recalling this awful occurrence and together we will observe an act of remembrance at its conclusion.'

The *Te Deum* began, then paused. The silence was palpable; everyone was remembering what had happened at that point in the service seventy years before. Once the *Te Deum* had ended, the act of remembrance began with the Last Post as a final farewell to those who had died. It was followed by Laurence Binyon's 'Ode of Remembrance' from *For the Fallen*, read by Garrison Sergeant Major William Mott. 'They shall grow not old as we that are left grow old, age shall not weary them, nor the years condemn. At the going down of the sun and in the morning we will remember them'.

Keith Lewis, the last known survivor of the incident, moved forward and repeated 'We will remember them'. The congregation then echoed his words. Finally, Reveille was sounded to mark the end of the act of remembrance.

The service then resumed with the Apostles' Creed and the Lord's Prayer. These were followed by three Collects, the Anthem and the State Prayers.

Once more, there was a minute of silence for personal prayer; we were invited to remember the departed who lost their lives in the Chapel. The entire congregation paused, remembering that day seventy years before when the Chapel was destroyed.

The hymn, 'All people that on earth do dwell', to the tune of the 'Old Hundredth', was followed by a sermon by the Right Reverend and Right Honourable Richard Chartres, Bishop of London. He preached wonderfully and inspired everyone with his spirit and his well-chosen words.

He talked of the 'tragic toll of dead and injured. Today we remember them in company with Mr Keith Lewis, last of the survivors, together with relatives of those who were here on that fateful day.' He pointed out that in the Second World War 'civilians were also in the front line'.

'Today we remember those who fell here that June Sunday morning and also salute the courage of the Heavy Rescue Service and the other agencies, uniformed and voluntary, who helped so many to safety.'

He talked about the modern world and how in future the Eastern civilisations will play a significant role, much as they have done for most of human history. It was a thought-provoking sermon and linked the incident in 1944 with the challenges of the present day.

A superb piece of music followed. The *Elegy to the Fallen Guards Musicians* was written by Dr Martin Ellerby during his tenure as composer-in-residence to the Regimental Band of the Coldstream Guards; it was a powerful tribute to the Director of Music and the musicians who died, and a fitting memorial. During the performance, Alan Cooper laid a memorial wreath on the conductor's rostrum on behalf of serving and former members of the band of the Coldstream Guards. The inscription read 'Presented by the Past and Present

Members of the Coldstream Guards Band in memory of their comrades killed in the Guards Chapel 18th June 1944'. Both the music and the wreath emphasised the heavy price paid that day by the band and their Director of Music.

After the next hymn, we sang the National Anthem. There was the Collect for the Household Division, followed by the recessional hymn, 'Now thank we all our God'. The final piece of music was the 'March' from Holst's *Second Suite in F*; the composer had dedicated the suite to James Causley Windram, Director of Music, so it provided an appropriate end to the ceremony.

Most of the congregation gathered outside for the reception that followed the service, but the relatives were asked to stay behind. The Bishop of London then entered the choir stalls by the altar; he was joined by the survivor, Keith Lewis, and over sixty members of the bereaved families. These included the daughter of the British chaplain (Lucy Whitrow) and the granddaughter of the Australian chaplain. No fewer than eleven members of the Sheridan family were present to remember Rose Sheridan, the wife of an Irish Guardsman who had been due to attend the service himself, but who was called away at the last minute. The Mitchell family had come to pay tribute to the three Mitchells who died. Warrant Officer Nathaniel Turton's granddaughter was there on behalf of her family, as was Agnes Moscrop's great-niece. Greville Gidley-Kitchin was there to commemorate his mother and sister. Barry Gibson was less than a month old when his Guardsman father was killed at the Chapel; this was his opportunity to mark the seventieth anniversary of his death. Seventy years on, children, grandchildren and great-grandchildren had come to remember their relatives and to celebrate their lives.

The Bishop spoke gently to the relatives and asked for their stories. People showed the jewellery they were wearing in memory of their loved ones: a brooch, a bracelet, a ring. They talked of the effect the incident had on them and on their extended family. I was asked how I had become involved, and was very moved to be given a round of applause to thank me for my research. Pastoral conversations led naturally to a time of quiet and prayer. The Bishop then blessed lapel badges for the Household Division and these were distributed to the families. Finally we came out of the Chapel into the sunshine, where a photograph was taken on the Chapel steps.

Further photographs were taken. Keith Lewis, the last known survivor, was photographed with the present choir. This was a special reunion of sorts, to mark the fact that he was singing with the choir on that dreadful day. The reception was held in the open air, in brilliant sunshine. It was an opportunity for relatives and friends of the Chapel to meet, and for people to share their memories. I was very grateful to be given the opportunity to meet at least some of the relatives I had grown to know via email. The time was all too short, and I can only wish I had been able to speak to more of them.

It was a fitting service to remember what had happened that terrible day and to pay tribute to all those who died, as well as to all those who tried to save them. I think everyone who attended was profoundly moved by the thoughtful order of service, while the music was superb and evocative. It was a memorable day as the Guards' Chapel and its congregation paid tribute to everyone connected with the tragic bombing on 18 June 1944, with dignity and with respect. They will not be forgotten.

Appendix

Those Who Died

	Age	Unit	Funeral/Burial
ALLFREY, Mrs Dorothy	65	–	Golders Green Crematorium
ANNALS, Guardsman William George Frederick	35	Coldstream Guards	Mortlake Crematorium
ARNOLD, Miss Peggy Louise May	24	Nurse, Westminster Hospital	Walthamstow Cemetery (Queens Road)
ATKINS, Miss Amy	73	–	Golders Green Crematorium
ATKINS, Mr Philip	70	–	Golders Green Crematorium
BACCHIOLELLI, Caporal Martin	25	Forces Françaises Libres (Free French)	Brookwood Military Cemetery
BAKER, Major Clarence Alvin	35	Royal Canadian Artillery	Brookwood Military Cemetery, Surrey
BERRY, Mr Arthur Ernest	38	–	Westminster City Cemetery
BOSTOCK, Mr John	74	–	Details not known
BOWYER, Lance Corporal Alfred Reginald	24	Grenadier Guards	Peterchurch (St. Peter) Churchyard
BROUGHTON, Guardsman Sidney George	32	Grenadier Guards	Appleford (SS Peter and Paul) Churchyard
CALDICOTT, Mr Herbert Vigers	70	–	Cremated privately; no details known
CARR, Musician George Edward	41	Coldstream Guards	Brookwood Military Cemetery
CATTARNS, Miss Ada Ellen	72	BRCS, WVS	Lewisham (Hither Green) Cemetery
CAVE, Guardsman John Tatton Trevor	18	Grenadier Guards	Leeds (Armley) Cemetery
CLARK, Miss Beryl Violet	22	SRN, St George's Hospital	Details not known
COBBOLD, Lieutenant Colonel John Murray (Ivan)	47	Scots Guards	Golders Green Crematorium
COLEMAN, Captain (retd) Alan Fraser	55	–	Westminster City Cemetery
COLEMAN, Mr Cyril Johnson	49	–	Bloxham (St Mary) Churchyard
COLEMAN, Mrs Edith	55	–	Westminster City Cemetery
CONGREVE, Guardsman Leonard	36	Coldstream Guards	Sheffield (City Road) Cemetery
COPEMAN, Drummer James Frank	22	Coldstream Guards	Tacolneston (All Saints) Churchyard

	Age	Unit	Funeral/Burial
COURTNEY, Mrs Sarah Louisa	72	–	Gap Road Cemetery (Merton)
CROFTS, Guardsman Alexander Only	18	Grenadier Guards	Lewisham (Hither Green) Cemetery
CROOKE, Miss Olive Louisa	73	–	Westminster City Cemetery
CURRY, Guardsman Eric James	18	Grenadier Guards	Brookwood Military Cemetery
DALTON, Guardsman George Morris	38	Coldstream Guards	Leeds (Lawns Wood) Cemetery
DAVIDSON, Guardsman George	28	Coldstream Guards	Herrington (St Cuthbert) Churchyard
DAVIES, Mr Bryn	35	–	St. Cynog's Churchyard, Ystradgynlais
DEADFIELD, Miss Clara Georgina	53	–	Details not known
DEWAR-DURIE, Mrs Isabelle Elisa	73	–	Farlington Churchyard, Hants
DODS, Lieutenant Harold William	35	Scots Guards	Donington Cemetery
DUBERLY, 2nd Lieutenant James Arthur Grey	18	Scots Guards	Great Staughton (St Andrew) Churchyard
DUNCAN, Wren Joan Ruth	19	HMS *Copra*	Romford Cemetery
DUNN, Lance Corporal James Edward	28	Coldstream Guards	Swinton Cemetery
FARMER, Wren Edith Anne	18	HMS *Copra*	Romford Cemetery
GALL, Captain John Douglas	25	Grenadier Guards of Canada	Brookwood Military Cemetery
GARDNER, Miss Beatrice Isabel	22	–	Alperton Cemetery
GARLAND, Miss (Edith Kathleen) Kay	37	–	Honor Oak Crematorium
GIBSON, Guardsman Dennis George	24	Irish Guards	Wandsworth (Earlsfield) Cemetery
GIDLEY-KITCHIN, Mrs Dorothy Helen	55	–	Ewshot (St Mary) Churchyard
GIDLEY-KITCHIN, 2nd Subaltern Dorothy Rosemary Marian	21	ATS	Ewshot (St Mary) Churchyard
GILLIAT, Major John	30	Irish Guards	Brookwood Cemetery
GORDON-LENNOX, Lady Evelyn	67	–	Boxgrove Priory
GRAS, Monsieur Pierre Maurice Menrie	19	Forces Aériennes Francaises Libres (FAFL – Free French)	Details not known
GUENTHER, Colonel Gustav Bismark	48	US Army	Arlington National Cemetery
GYE, Miss (Dorothy) Pauline	24	CSP, Air raid warden	Details not known
HALL, Mr Albert William (aka William Albert Garland BEER)	70	–	Westminster City Cemetery
HALL, Lance Serjeant John	29	Coldstream Guards	Marton (St Paul) Church burial ground

Name	Age	Unit	Funeral/Burial
HAY, Lieutenant Colonel The Lord Edward Douglas John	55	Grenadier Guards	Theydon (St Michael) Churchyard
HEWLETT, Lance Serjeant Arthur Victor	43	Coldstream Guards	Brookwood Military Cemetery
HOLMES, Lance Corporal Edwin Lloyd	30	Coldstream Guards	Torquay Cemetery
HOOPER, Guardsman Alexander Olmy	26	Coldstream Guards	Castleford (Whitwood) Cemetery
HOOPER, Guardsman Denis Walter George	33	Grenadier Guards	Brookwood Military Cemetery
HORTON, Mrs Gwendolen Anna Le Bas	43	–	Guilsborough Cemetery
HYDE, Lance Corporal Horace	30	Scots Guards	Manchester (Gorton) Cemetery
IRVING, Mrs Annie Ellen	54	–	Details not known
JACKSON, Private Kathleen	27	ATS	Sutton-in-Ashfield Cemetery
JAMESON, Mrs Mary	24	–	Putney Vale Cemetery
JAMESON, Mrs Phyllis	55	–	Putney Vale Cemetery
JONES, Miss Ethel Annie	54	–	Details not known
KEANE, Mrs Alice Gabriel Lumley	67	–	Details not known
KEMP-WELCH, Captain George Durant	36	Grenadier Guards	Astley (St Peter) Churchyard
KENT, Musician Frederick Dowdney	36	Coldstream Guards	Brookwood Military Cemetery
LANE, Captain (retd) Sampson Beamish	73	–	Details not known
LIVERMORE, Lance Serjeant Percy Leonard	31	Irish Guards	Hornchurch Cemetery
LUMLEY-SMITH, Lady Gwendolen Muriel Maud	57	–	Putney Vale Cemetery
LUMLEY-SMITH, Miss Moya	31	–	Putney Vale Cemetery
MALE, Guardsman Ahmand	18	Staff officer, SJAB	Neath Higher (Glyn Neath) Cemetery
MAULTBY, Miss Mabel Annie	41	Welsh Guards	Details not known
McDONALD, Miss Marian Daphne	40	BRCS	Details not known
MILLEN, Miss Elizabeth Amy	56	–	Details not known
MILLEN, Miss Millicent Marjorie	49	–	Details not known
MILTON-WILLMOTT, Mrs Diana	46	–	Westminster City Cemetery
MITCHELL, Miss Janet Lockett	20	BRCS	Golders Green Crematorium
MITCHELL, Lieutenant Michael Bradstock Alexander	22	Coldstream Guards	Golders Green Crematorium
MITCHELL, Guardsman Ronald Charles	19	Coldstream Guards	Barking (Rippleside) Cemetery

	Age	Unit	Funeral/Burial
MITCHELL, Mrs Vera Margaret	50	WVS	Golders Green Crematorium
MORLEY, Lance Corporal Frederick Dowdney	37	Coldstream Guards	Brookwood Military Cemetery
MOSCROP, Miss Agnes	19	–	Newcastle-upon-Tyne (West Road) Cemetery
NEILSON, Mrs Hettie Ruthin	63	–	St Marylebone Crematorium
NEWBOULD, Lance Serjeant Sidney Walter	25	Coldstream Guards	Aldridge (St Mary) Churchyard
NORRIS, Miss Margaret Ellen	22	–	Golders Green Crematorium
NORTHING, Miss Lilian	54	–	Golders Green Crematorium
NORTON, Guardsman William Henry	27	Grenadier Guards	Leicester (Welford Road) Cemetery
OGDEN, Miss Edith Winifred Cazenove	48	–	Westminster City Cemetery
PEACOCK, Private Valerian	19	ATS	Billingham (St Cuthbert) Churchyard
PENN, Miss Constance Olivia	64	–	Putney Vale Cemetery
PHILLIPS, Guardsman Leslie Charles	24	Irish Guards	Brookwood Military Cemetery
POTTER, Private Phyllis Mary	23	ATS	Brookwood Military Cemetery
RICHMOND, Drummer Albert Charles	31	Coldstream Guards	Droylsden Cemetery
ROPER, Mrs Phyllis Margaret	59	–	Believed to have been buried at St Michael's, Thorpe le Soken, Essex
SARGENT, Mrs Mary Josephine	65	–	Golders Green Crematorium
SELLERS, Lance Corporal Edwin Lloyd	28	Coldstream Guards	Barnsley Cemetery
SHAW, Guardsman William Henry	23	Coldstream Guards	Oldham (Greenacres) Cemetery
SHERIDAN, Mrs Rose May	39	–	Streatham Park Crematorium
SHOOTER, Miss Edna Mary	34	Nurse, King's Cross Hospital	Westminster City Cemetery
SHORTEN, Musician Ralph Herbert	40	Coldstream Guards	Brookwood Military Cemetery
SMITH, Guardsman Jack	18	Grenadier Guards	Leeds (Harehills) Cemetery
SMITH, Miss Olive Gertrude Annie	50	–	Streatham Park Cemetery
SOUTER, Miss Marjorie	31	Welsh Guards	Monymusk Churchyard (Aberdeenshire)
STAMP, Guardsman Ernest Keith	17	–	Brookwood Military Cemetery
THOMSON, Miss Ida	18	–	Details not known
THORN, Section Officer Cornelia Despard	33	WAAF	St Marks Churchyard, Torquay
THORN, Mrs Elizabeth Amy	84	WVS	Golders Green Crematorium

	Age	Unit	Funeral/Burial
THORN, Major Terence Conrad, MC	56	Devonshire Regt att RE	Golders Green Crematorium
THORNTON, Major Dick Henry Brewster	36	Grenadier Guards	Golders Green Crematorium
THORNTON, Guardsman Henry Alfred George	30	Grenadier Guards	Brookwood Military Cemetery
TITCOMBE, Guardsman Anthony Sidney George	37	Coldstream Guards	Brookwood Military Cemetery
TRANTER, Guardsman George	28	Scots Guards	Castleford New Cemetery
TURTON, WO2 Nathaniel (Drill Sargeant)	44	Grenadier Guards	Brookwood Military Cemetery
WALL, Captain Leslie Edwin Gordon	45	Grenadier Guards	Bobbing (St Bartholomew) Churchyard
WALL, Mrs Violet Maude (Diana)	52	WVS	Bobbing (St Bartholomew) Churchyard
WATSON, Lance Serjeant Edgar	39	Coldstream Guards	Ruston Parva (St Nicholas) Churchyard
WEAVER, Guardsman Derek James	19	Grenadier Guards	Brookwood Military Cemetery
WELLER, Miss Amy Louisa	30	–	Kensal Green Cemetery
WHITROW, Chaplain Ralph Henry	47	Royal Army Chaplains' Department	Winchester (West Hill) Old Cemetery
WILSON, Mrs Adelaide Louisa	71	WVS	Details not known
WILSON, Mrs Violet	74	WVS	Golders Green Cemetery
WINDRAM, Major James Causley (Director of Music)	57	Coldstream Guards	St Pancras Cemetery
WOOD, Chaplain Gordon Gladstone	42	RAAF	Brookwood Military Cemetery
WORRALL, Mrs Hilda Mary	49	WVS	Westminster City Cemetery

Also:

	Age	Unit	Funeral/Burial
HART, Musician Charles (Jock)	44	Coldstream Guards	Brompton Cemetery (died 13/4/1945 as a result of this incident)

There is an unknown woman, who was buried in Westminster City Cemetery.

Bibliography

Books

Bates, H.E., *Flying-Bombs over England* (Froglets Publications Ltd, 1994).

Brutton, Philip, *Ensign in Italy* (Leo Cooper, 1992).

Clewett, Pamela Mary, *Reminiscences of the Hospital at the Corner: St George's, 1939–45* (Original papers available to consult at Wellcome Library and Imperial War Museum. Issued as typed monograph, 1983).

Curtis, Michael, *A Pilgrimage of Remembrance: an anthology of the history of a Scots Guards Company in the Italian Campaign 1944/5* (Michael Curtis, 2004).

Douglas, Major A.G., MBE, *The Guards Chapel: the Royal Military Chapel, Wellington Barracks* (Pitkin Books, 1971).

Gardiner, Juliet, *Wartime: Britain 1939–1945.* (Headline Review, 2005).

Gordon, Jane, *Married to Charles* (Heinemann, 1950).

Jones, R.V., *Most Secret War: British Scientific Intelligence 1939–1945* (Hamish Hamilton, 1978).

Longmate, Norman, *How We Lived Then: a history of everyday life during the Second World War* (Hutchinson, 1971).

Longmate, Norman, *The Doodlebugs: the story of the flying bombs* (Hutchinson, 1981).

Nicholson, Virginia, *Millions Like Us: women's lives in the second world war* (Penguin, 2001).

Ogley, Bob, *Doodlebugs and Rockets: the battle of the flying bombs* (Froglets Publications Ltd, 1992).

Sansom, William, *The Blitz: Westminster at war* (Oxford University Press, 1990).

Sheppard-Jones, Elisabeth, *I Walked on Wheels* (Geoffrey Bles, 1958).

Waller, Maureen, *London 1945: life in the debris of war* (John Murray, 2004).

Ziegler, Philip, *London at War, 1939–1945* (Sinclair-Stevenson, 1995).

Articles

Lewis, Keith, 'Surviving the flying bomb: death and destruction in the Guards' Chapel', in *The Grenadier Gazette*, 2001, no. 24, pp. 42–3.

Household Brigade Magazine, Autumn 1944, pp. 71–3, 105–7, and Winter 1945, pp. 161–3.

Websites

BBC WW2 People's War – Childhood experience of the war in London (includes account by William Farmer of his sister Edith's death at the Guards' Chapel):
http://www.bbc.co.uk/history/ww2peopleswar/stories/54/a3139454.shtml

BBC WW2 People's War – the Guards' Chapel V1 Flying Bomb (first-hand account by George Laity): http://www.bbc.co.uk/history/ww2peopleswar/stories/66/a5098566.shtml

Flying Bombs and Rockets, http://www.flyingbombsandrockets.com

West End at War (Enid's friends: my mother's friends and the Guards' Chapel incident):
http://www.westendatwar.org.uk/page_id__213.aspx?path=0p3p

West End at War (Guards' Chapel, Wellington Barracks):
http://www.westendatwar.org.uk/page/guards_chapel_wellington_barracks?path=0p28p

West End at War (WO2 Nathaniel Turton):
http://www.westendatwar.org.uk/page_id__184.aspx?path=0p3p

Videotapes
British Pathé news (Guards' Chapel from about 3 mins in, shots 207–210 show the altar and candles undamaged after the explosion):
  http://www.britishpathe.com/video/front-line-london
British Pathé news (longer version, includes section on Guards' Chapel):
  http://www.britishpathe.com/video/bomb-damage-london-2

Sources for biographies
Ancestry http://home.ancestry.co.uk
Commonwealth War Graves Commission http://www.cwgc.org
Find My Past http://www.findmypast.co.uk

Unpublished sources
Correspondence from relatives of those killed in the Guards' Chapel.
Guards' Chapel Commemorative Programme, 22 June 2014.
Gurney, David: letter to the family of Harold Dods.
Royal Voluntary Services: unpublished material relating to the event.
Westminster Archives: documents relating to the Guards' Chapel incident and the rescue effort.

Indices

Index of Dead and Injured

General Index